ΜΑΛΛΟΝ ΧΡΗΣΑΙ: FIRST-CENTURY SLAVERY

AND

THE INTERPRETATION OF 1 CORINTHIANS 7:21

ΜΑΛΛΟΝ ΧΡΗΣΑΙ: FIRST-CENTURY SLAVERY
AND
THE INTERPRETATION OF 1 CORINTHIANS 7:21

by

S. Scott Bartchy

Published by

SOCIETY OF BIBLICAL LITERATURE

for

The Seminar on Paul

DISSERTATION SERIES, NUMBER ELEVEN

1973

ΜΑΛΛΟΝ ΧΡΗΣΑΙ: FIRST-CENTURY SLAVERY AND

THE INTERPRETATION OF 1 CORINTHIANS 7:21

by

S. Scott Bartchy
Institute for the Study of Christian Origins
Wilhelmstrasse 100
7400 Tübingen, West Germany

Ph.D. 1971
Harvard University

Advisors:
Helmut Koester
Krister Stendahl
John Strugnéll
Glen Bowersock

ISBN 0-88414-022-9

Library of Congress Catalog Card Number: 73-83723

Printed in the United States of America

Printing Department, University of Montana,
Missoula, Montana 59801

ACKNOWLEDGMENTS

My first words of deeply felt appreciation are for the professors at Harvard University who advised me during the preparation of this dissertation and who examined me upon its completion: to Krister Stendahl, who, knowing of my strong interests in the relation of religion to society and in the history of the interpretation of the New Testament, first suggested that I write a history of the exegesis of 1 Cor. 7:21, a very perplexing text which has played an exceedingly important role in many Christians' thinking about social change; to Helmut Koester, the gracious chairman of my dissertation committee, who contributed much to my thinking about the theology and ethics of the Corinthian Christians; to John Strugnell, who challenged me to go beyond the history of interpretation to find a new resolution of this text's ambiguities; and to Glen Bowersock of the Classics Department, who gave me confidence at a critical period in my research that my understanding of slavery in the first century A.D. did indeed form the basis for a breakthrough in the understanding of 1 Cor. 7:21.

Secondly, I wish to thank most warmly the supporters and board of the Institute for the Study of Christian Origins (Disciples Institut zur Erforschung des Urchristentums) in Tübingen, Germany, for accepting my dissertation topic as a research project of the institute. Within this new institute, the purpose of which is to understand more fully the early Christian congregations in their varied social, economic, political, legal, religious and cultural environments, I found much stimulation and encouragement to work on research which I believe is vital also for the solution of today's problems. Among those scholars who have worked in this institute, I am grateful to James Brashler, Werner Hausen, Warren Lewis and Fred Norris, who were especially helpful in sharpening my thinking and in proofreading the final text. I am very pleased that this book is also regarded as the first, published, major project of this institute.

My research and thinking were further enriched by the libraries and scholars of Eberhard-Karls-University in Tübingen. In particular I am obliged to Prof. Friedrich Lang and Prof. Ernst Käsemann for their personal kindness and interest in my work.

In addition, I wish to acknowledge with gratitude the assistance of Prof. K. H. Rengstorf, director of the Institutum Judaicum Delitzschianum in Münster, and of his assistant Mr. Krieg for making available to me more than five hundred references from the manuscript of the "Complete Concordance to Flavius Josephus" in advance of its publication.

Also I am indebted to Prof. Robert Kraft, former editor of the Monograph Series of the Society of Biblical Literature, who guided my dissertation through provisional acceptance into that series, as well as to Prof. Nils Alstrup Dahl, the chairman of the "Paul Seminar" of the S.B.L., who recommended this work for the Dissertation Series. Special thanks are due to Prof. Robert Funk, who has directed the publication of this dissertation and who is giving outstanding leadership to the task of providing inexpensive and rapid exchanges of information among scholars. My decision to have this work published in the S.B.L. Dissertation Series should be understood as an act in support of his efforts.

Finally, I am most grateful to the typists of this book: to Diane Walker Bartchy, my wife, who tirelessly encouraged me as I wrote and who prepared with great care the final text for submission to Harvard University; and to Joann River Armour, who exercised unusual skill in preparing the final text for publication.

Tübingen, Germany   S. Scott Bartchy
September 1973

A B B R E V I A T I O N S

AJA = American Journal of Archaeology

AJP = American Journal of Philology

AV = Authorized Version of the Old and New Testaments (A.D. 1611)

CAH = Cambridge Ancient History

CBQ = Catholic Biblical Quarterly

CIL = Corpus Inscriptionum Latinarum

CR = Classical Review

GDI = Sammlung der griechischen Dialektinschriften

HThR (HTR) = Harvard Theological Review

HZ = Historische Zeitschrift

IB = Interpreter's Bible

IDB = Interpreter's Dictionary of the Bible

JBL = Journal of Biblical Literature

JBR = Journal of Bible and Religion

JQR = Jewish Quarterly Review

JRS = Journal of Roman Studies

JTS = Journal of Theological Studies

NEB = New English Bible (A.D. 1970)

NTS = New Testament Studies

OCD = Oxford Classical Dictionary

RAC = Reallexicon für Antike und Christentum

RE = Real-Encyclopaedie der klassischen Altertumswissenschaft (Pauly-Wissowa)

RGG^3 = Die Religion in Geschichte und Gegenwart. 3. Auflage

RSV = Revised Standard Version of the Old and New Testaments (A.D. 1953)

TDNT = Theological Dictionary of the New Testament

ThLZ (TLZ) = Theologische Literaturzeitung

ThW = Theologisches Wörterbuch zum Neuen Testament (Kittel)

ZNW = Zeitschrift für die neutestamentliche Wissenschaft und die Kunde des Urchristentums

ZThK = Zeitschrift für Theologie und Kirche

CHAPTER I

INTRODUCTION TO THE TEXT AND ITS INTERPRETATION

A. *The Problems of Interpretation in 1 Cor. 0721.*[1]

1 Corinthians 0721 has been of special interest to Biblical
interpreters, ethicists and students of the relation of religion to society
because this verse seems to be one sentence in which Paul specifically re-
lates his Christian faith to what appears to them to be the most obvious social
problem of his time: slavery. In this verse, without having to deal with
the complicating factors of Paul's personal authority and interests which
play such important roles in his discussion of the slave Onesimus in his
letter to his friend Philemon, we are encouraged to find either:
1) Paul the "social conservative," whose determination to hold the *status
quo* led him so far as to urge slaves to remain in slavery, even if this
meant rejecting an opportunity to go free; or:
2) Paul the "social realist," who certainly would not have wanted his
seemingly conservative-sounding advice in chapter 7 to be taken by slaves
who were Christians to mean that they could not accept freedom if it
became available to them.

For example, in 1915 a Roman Catholic exegete, F. X. Kiefl, dean
of Regensburg Cathedral, published a book entitled, *Die Theorien des
modernen Sozialismus über den Ursprung des Christentums: Zugleich ein
Kommentar zu 1 Kor. 7, 21,* in which he speaks of this verse as "eine tödliche

---

[1]The current variety to be found in methods of citing Biblical references
(principally differences in punctuation and the use of supralinear figures)
encourages me to follow the suggestion of Ian A. Moir and others, that a
Biblical reference system be employed in which the first two figures are
understood to give the chapter and the second pair the verse number. For
example: Mt. 2104, Lk. 0316 or 1 Cor. 0721. He suggests also that a number
be used for each of the Biblical books (e.g., *1 Cor.* 0721 would be *7*20721
in his system), which seems to me a useful idea, especially where electronic
sorting and counting devices may be used. But since this last suggestion has
not received wide approval as yet, I do not employ it here. See Ian A.
Moir, "A Proposed 'Grid' System for Recording Biblical References" *NTS* 13
(1967) 292-293. Abbreviations for books of the Bible follow the usage of
the *Theological Dictionary of the New Testament* (1964) I.
   Other abbreviations employed in this book follow the usage suggested by *The MLA Style Sheet* (1951); and "Notes for Contributors and Abbreviations," *American Journal of Archaeology* 69 (1965) 199-206. Forms not
found there follow the usage of "Abbreviations" *TDNT* (1964) I, xvi-xl.
   Note also that 0721 is divided as follows:
   0721a = δοῦλος ἐκλήθης
   0721b = μή σοι μελέτω
   0721c = ἀλλ' εἰ καὶ δύνασαι ἐλεύθερος γενέσθαι
   0721d = μᾶλλον χρῆσαι

1

Waffe gegen die hegelianische und marxistische Auffassung vom Ursprunge des Christentums."[2] For he saw modern socialism as "der eigentliche Antichrist," and he read 0721 as the chief expression of Paul's conservative view of the relation of Christianity to its social environment: "even if you have the opportunity to become free, stay a slave."[3]

On the other hand, four years earlier, another Roman Catholic exegete, Prof. Dr. Alphons Steinmann, had written an extensive treatment of this verse, entitled, *Paulus und die Sklaven zu Korinth: 1 Kor. 7, 21 aufs neue untersucht* (1911), in which he argued for a "take freedom" interpretation on the grounds that Paul's Jewish origins, his understanding of the exclusive character of God's lordship and his conscience as a pastoral counselor would not allow advising a slave to reject the welcome opportunity to become free.[4]

In many ways Kiefl's book was a reaction to Steinmann's work, and both of them drew extensively on the history of the interpretation of this verse to support their warring conclusions.[5] The "Auseinandersetzung" between them continued throughout that decade,[6] and their writings serve to

---

[2]Kiefl, (cited hereafter as *Die Theorien*) p. 57.

[3]Kiefl speaks of the "sittlichen Heroismus des Pauluswortes." p. 72. His first topic in his chapter, "Das exegetische Problem 1 Kor. 7, 21" is: "Die exegetische Bedeutung der Stelle als Argument gegen den Sozialismus." Walter Bauer favorably reviewed this book, saying: "Er hat auch zweifellos in der Hauptsache Recht. Sein Verständnis von 1 Kor. 7, 21 ist zutreffend und die Darlegung wegen der reichlichen Berücksichtigung der alten Ausleger besonders dankenswert." *TLZ* 1916, cols. 511-512.

[4]In 1910, Steinmann had published his *Sklavenlos und alte Kirche: Eine historisch-exegetische Studie über die soziale Frage im Urchristentum* (M. Gladbach, 4. Auflage, 1922), in which he wrote seven pages on the topic of Paul and the slaves in Corinth. Stimulated by those who were then writing that the "take freedom" interpretation was a "post-Reformation error," Steinmann attempted in 1911 to justify his interpretation in greater detail, giving special attention to the history of interpretation and to the question: how did Paul treat the concrete problem in Corinth after having expressed himself *in abstracto* in Gal. 0328? This work will be cited as Steinmann, *Paulus und die Sklaven.*

[5]Kiefl argued that apart from the "odd persons, probably Gnostics" known to John Chrysostom, no theologian in the first 1500 years of Christianity interpreted 1 Cor. 0721 with "take freedom." *Die Theorien*, p. 70. Steinmann, on the other hand, stressed that no writer in the first two centuries mentions 0721 and that Origen, Jerome and Ephraem Syrus understood this verse in the sense of "take freedom," even when they misunderstood its context. "Zur Geschichte der Auslegung von 1 Kor. 7, 21," *Theologische Revue* 15/16 (1917) col. 346.

[6]See Steinmann's critical review of Kiefl's *Die Theorien* together with his "revised" history of interpretation: "Zur Geschichte der Auslegung von 1 Kor. 7, 21" *Theologische Revue* 15/16 (1917) cols. 340-348. The discussion continues (without adding any new arguments) in Kiefl's "Erklärung" and Steinmann's "Antwort," *Ibid.* cols. 469f.

indicate *both* the variety of difficulties involved in reaching a "correct" interpretation of 0721 *and* the fact that neither of them was able to make any significant advance toward solving this long-standing *crux interpretum.*[7]

What factors have made the understanding of 0721 so difficult, and how could the same words be open to two such contradictory interpretations? The major difficulty in 0721 is the absence of the words needed to complete the verse's final phrase, μᾶλλον χρῆσαι. Paul wrote the sentence as follows: δοῦλος ἐκλήθης; μή σοι μελέτω· ἀλλ' εἰ καὶ δύνασαι ἐλεύθερος γενέσθαι, μᾶλλον χρῆσαι.[8] And from these words themselves, his meaning is not at all clear. The object of χρῆσαι must somehow be supplied, either from 0721abc, from the context of 0717-24, from chapter 7, from the entire letter or from Paul's other letters.

In the Vulgate and the Authorized Version this unclarity is nicely preserved without resolution.[9] Translators in the twentieth century, however, have not hesitated to resolve the unclarity, although no concensus has

---

[7] Hans Windisch concludes his review of Steinmann's *Paulus und die Sklaven* as follows: "So wird der Vers trotz Steinmanns fleissigen Bemühungen auch weiterhin eine *crux interpretum* bleiben." *Deutsche Literaturzeitung,* 1912, cols. 1172-1173. Some part of 1 Cor. 7 is mentioned by Hermas (one reference), Irenaeus (5 references), Tertullian (94 references), and Clement of Alexandria (26 references). But the first direct comment on 0721 known to us comes from Origen. See pp. 6-7 for a chart of the history of interpretation of 0721.

[8] The Greek text presents no difficulties. The only variant reading, the dropping of καί from 0721c, appears first in Codex Boernerianus (G) from the 9th century. The late date of this Greek/Latin MS. makes this reading valuable chiefly for the history of the text's interpretation. See below the exegesis of 0721 on p. 178.

[9] *The Vulgate:* "Servus vocatus es? non sit tibi curae: sed et si potes fieri liber, magis utere." *The Authorized Version:* "Art thou called *being* a servant? care not for it: but if thou mayest be made free, use *it* rather."

been reached as to the correct interpretation.[10] And we may ask: was Paul's meaning clear to the *first* recipients of this letter? Did those first-century Corinthian Christians naturally supply either τῇ δουλείᾳ or τῇ ἐλευθερίᾳ, which are the opposing suggestions made by the translators and

---

[10]These translators have expressed their interpretations with varying degrees of certainty. For example, in the text of both the *Revised Standard Version* and the *New English Bible*, the slaves are advised to take freedom if they can, but each version also indicates in a footnote that precisely the opposite advice may be intended: RSV--"But if you can gain your freedom, avail yourself of the opportunity" (footnote: "make use of your present condition instead."); NEB--"But if a chance of liberty should come, take it" (footnote: "But even if a chance of liberty should come, choose rather to make good use of your servitude."). The German translation by H. Menge has "so bleibe nur um so lieber dabei" in the text, and the "take freedom" interpretation is given as an alternative in a footnote.

The translators of *La Bible de Jérusalem* appear to have been more certain of Paul's meaning when they wrote: "Et même si tu peux devenir libre, mets plutôt a profit ta condition d'esclave." For although this version has many footnotes, no alternative reading is suggested. Strikingly the same practice is followed in *The Jerusalem Bible* (which was translated from the ancient texts, yet with reference to *La Bible de Jérusalem*, but the *opposite* meaning is given: "But if you should have the chance of being free, accept it."

Some other modern translations completing the verse with "stay a slave" and not suggesting any ambiguity are the *Zürcher Bibel* ("sondern wenn du auch frei werden kannst, so bleibe um so lieber [in deinem Stand]"), the German version by Fr. Tillmann ("selbst wenn du frei werden kannst, bleibe lieber dabei"), and *The New Testament: an American Translation* by E. J. Goodspeed ("even if you can gain your freedom, make the most of your present condition instead").

Other recent translations unambiguously completing the verse with "take freedom" are *The New Testament in Modern Speech* by R. F. Weymouth ("and yet if you can get your freedom, you had better take it"), *The New Translation* by J. Moffatt ("of course, if you do find it possible to get free, you had better avail yourself of the opportunity"), *The N. T. in Modern English* by J. B. Phillips ("though if you find the opportunity to become free you had better take it"), *The Amplified N.T.* ("but if you are able to gain your freedom, avail yourself of the opportunity"), *Good News for Modern Man* by R. G. Bratcher ("but if you do have a chance to become a free man, use it"), and the *Luther Bibel* ("doch kannst du frei werden, so ergreife es viel lieber").

Commenting on the revision of the Russian N.T. begun in Paris in 1951, Bishop Cassian wrote: "I translate *mallon chrēsai* quite literally, 'rather use.' This translation is no more ambiguous than the Greek original ... and it will be for the Commission to decide which of the three (the neutral plus either 'use the opportunity of becoming free' or 'use the advantages of the conditions of a slave') should be adopted." "The Revision of the Russian Translation of the N.T.," *The Bible Translator* V (1954) 31.

found in the history of interpretation?[11] For those Corinthians was some *other* word or phrase the "natural" one to be understood, perhaps for reasons not considered by later intrepreters?[12] Or did Paul's abrupt style leave even the Corinthians wondering about what he meant?[13]

If Paul himself had completed 0721d, the grammatical relationships and peculiarities in the rest of the verse would have called for only brief comments. As it is, the meanings of the following words or phrases have been vigorously debated:

---

[11]It seems ironic that H. Schlier, writing on ἐλεύθερος in Kittel et al., *TDNT* II, supplies τη δουλείᾳ, while K. Rengstorf, writing on δοῦλος in the same volume adds τῇ ἐλευθερίᾳ. See the chart, "Table I," which sketches the history of 0721's interpretation, below on pages 6-7.

[12]A unique deviation in this history of exegesis has been suggested by two Dutch scholars, H. Bavinck and F. W. Grosheide. Writing in 1908, Bavinck agreed with those who prefer to add "take freedom" but he suggested that in this passage it is of little significance to Paul whether or not a man is a slave or free. Rather, the important thing is using the newly acquired freedom as a better opportunity for living according to the Christian calling. Bavinck wrote: "Maar indien gij--zoo zegt Paulus verder--indien gij ook (zelfs) vrij kunt worden, maak daar liever gebruik van, niet om maar vrij te zijn, doch om juist in dien staat van vrijheid te beter uw Christenzijn te openbaren en naar uwe Christelijke roeping te leven." "Chr. beginselen en maatsch. verhoudingen," *Chr. en Maatsch* I, 1 (1908), 36 (quoted by J. J. Koopmans, *De Servitute Antiqua et Religione Christiana: capita selecta* [diss. Groningen, 1920], p. 128.)

Then in 1924, Grosheide reflected further on this interpretation, suggesting that the "Christian calling" itself could be the object of "rather use" in 0721d. See his "Exegetica: 1 Kor. 7, 21," *Geref Theol. Tijdschr.* 24 (1924), 298-302. Almost thirty years later Grosheide wrote with greater certainty: "We must keep in mind that in this verse the vocation stands in the center. This prompts us to supply the word 'your vocation' after *use*. The phrase would thus mean: if you can be free, make a better use of your vocation." *Commentary on the First Epistle to the Corinthians*, in the *New International Commentary on the New Testament* (Erdmans, 1953), p. 170.

[13]Paul himself notes in R 0308 that his teaching about God's grace and man's freedom had been misunderstood. And the author of 2 Pt. 0314 later comments that Paul's letters contain "some things hard to understand." The liveliness and abruptness of Paul's style, as well as the density of his thought, must have called out for an 'interpreter,' even among the first readers of his letters. See G. Bornkamm's article, "Paulinische Anakoluthe im Römerbrief," in which he contends that the anakolutha which he exegetes are not stylistic failures to carry through the sentences as originally conceived, but rather are intentional constructions with apparent theological significance. *Das Ende des Gesetzes* (Munich, 1961), pp. 76-92.

TABLE I

A Synopsis of the Interpretation of 1 Cor. 0721

A.D.	Scholars favoring "take freedom"	Scholars favoring "use slavery"
200	Origen (go free from *marriage*)	
300	Ephraem Syrus (go free to preach) Jerome (from marriage)	
400	The unnamed exegetes with whom Chrysostom disagrees	Chrysostom Severian Ambrosiaster The Peshitta Cyril of Alex. Pelagius Theodoret
500		Oecumenius Pseudo-Primasius
700		John of Damascus Photius
800	Haimo of Auxerre (from marriage)	Photius
1100		Sedulius Scotus (stay in marriage) Hugh of St. Cher
1200		Theophylact Peter Lombard Hervaeus Thomas Aquinas
1500	Erasmus Luther Calvin	
1600	Th. Beza H. Grotius C. Lapide	D. Estius
1700		J.A. Bengel
1850	H.A.W. Meyer C. Hodge Neander	J.E. Osiander A.P. Stanley De Wette
1860	Hofmann	Kling H. Alford J.A. Monod
1870	Th. Zahn	E. Reuss
1880	T.S. Evans Bisping J.A. Beet Godet	Holsten Overbeck Edwards Heinrici Weizsäcker Ellicott Schedermann Schmiedel Clemen
1890	J.B. Lightfoot	

TABLE I (p. 2)

A.D.	Scholars favoring "take freedom"	Scholars favoring "use slavery" 20th Cen. N.T.	
		Feine Gutjahr	
1900	H. Goudge Orelli (*RE*³)	B. Weiss v. Harnack	
		J. Weiss W. Bousset	
1910	J. H. Moulton	Bachmann	
	v. Walter Robertson-Plummer	F.X. Kiefl	
		Junker	
1920	A. Souter C.H. Dodd	E. Goodspeed v. Dobschütz (*RE*³)	
	A. Steinmann	Koopmans J. Leipoldt	
	Weymouth's N.T.	Allo Rohr	
1930	Schlatter		
	Moffatt		
	Rengstorf (*ThW*)		
1940		Schlier (*ThW*) Greeven	
		D. Bonhoeffer	
	R.S.V.	Kümmel	
1950	P.R. Coleman-Norton Klausner		
	C.T. Craig (*IB*)		
	Orchard-Sutcliffe		
	W. Bienert	J. Lappas Zürcher Bibel	
1955	W.D. Davies W. L. Westermann	Cullmann E. Barker	
	W. Foerster Luther Bibel	W. Bauer E. Neuhäusler	
	D. Daube	E. A. Judge C. Williams (Peakes)	
1960	C.F.D. Moule J. B. Phillips	La Bible de Jérusalem	
		J. N. Sevenster Käsemann	
	New English Bible	W. Schrage	
		J. Héring	
	M. Thrall	Schnackenburg H. Bellen	
1965	N. Turner		
	The Jerusalem Bible	C. K. Barrett	
	Today's English Version	H. Gülzow Conzelmann Bornkamm	
		Kugelman (Jerome Comm.)	
1970	C. H. Hunzinger		

1. χρῆσαι: is this verb to be translated: "make use of" (its usual
meaning)? Or is the aorist imperative form sufficient ground
for translating it with "take" or "grasp" (implying a new situation)?

2. μᾶλλον: is this adverb an elative comparative, to be translated: "by
all means," or a contrasting comparative (expressing exclusion),
to be translated: "rather"? If "rather" is the correct translation, is the
contrast with being "able to become free" (0721c), with "not being concerned
about being a slave" (0721ab), with following the general principle which
Paul repeats in 0717, 0720 and 0724, or with "being concerned about becoming
a freedman" (in antithetical parallelism to 0721b, with the "concern" in
this case expressed perhaps in "boasting" that one was now free)?

3. εἰ καί: should these two words be construed together as introducing a
concessive clause: "although" or "even though" (of a condition
represented as immaterial even if fulfilled)? Or should they be read separately,
in which case εἰ would be construed with the "indicative of reality" and translated: "if indeed," and καί would be an emphatic particle which could either
stress the entire phrase "if indeed you are able to become free" (contrasting
it to "were you a slave when you were called" in 0721a) or emphasize only
"being able" (in which case the offer of freedom would be constrasted with
seeking freedom by one's own efforts, which could be implied in "don't worry
about being a slave" in 0721b).

4. ἀλλά: does this adversative particle introduce a *contrast* to "don't
worry about it" in 0721b: "but" or "yet," or express an *extension* of μή in 0721b: "rather (than being concerned about your slavery) ..."
Or does this particle introduce a restriction of the general principle expressed
in 0720 (and in 0717 and 0724)? And then how is the unusual combination, ἀλλ'
εἰ καί, to be construed in view of the variety of possibilities for each word?

5. δύνασαι ἐλεύθερος γενέσθαι: does this phrase refer to an action initiated
by the Christian slave (such an action perhaps being already
discouraged in 0721b), or to an action initiated by the owner of the slave
over which the slave would have no control (a case similar to the Christian
spouse whose unbelieving partner breaks up the marriage--0715)?

6. γάρ (in 0722): does this conjunction, which expresses cause, inference
or continuation, introduce a reason supporting 0721ab ("don't
worry about being a slave") or 0721cd (which would be read: "even though you
can become free, stay a slave")?

     In addition to the problems within 0721 itself, the disputed
exegesis of 0720 has had a decisive influence on the interpretation of

0721. The word κλῆσις, especially, has occasioned a longstanding debate.[14]

Does κλῆσις mean the "call from God in Christ," i.e., an *act* of calling (as in all other Pauline uses of the word)?[15] If so, it may be that Paul in 0721d was urging the Corinthians to "use" this "calling," as Bavinck and Grosheide have suggested.[16] Or does κλῆσις gain a new connotation in 0720: "status in society" or "earthly condition" (in reference to the discussion of circumcision/uncircumcision and slave/free as situations of life in the context of God's calling activity)? If so, consistency with "remain in your earthly position" in 0720 would require Paul to have said "use your position as a slave" in 0721d.[17]

Beyond the immediate context of 0720 and its parallels which open and close the pericope 0717-24, the whole of chapter 7 also presents difficulties for the interpretation of 0721. For Paul, on the one hand, seems to have a special interest in admonishing the Christians: "stay as you are"--he urges the unmarried to remain unmarried (0707a, 0708, 0726b, 0727cd, 0737d, 0738, 0740a) and the married to stay married (0710b, 0711c, 0712-13, 0727ab, 0739a). In addition, Jewish Christians are to retain the marks of their Jewishness and Gentile Christians, likewise, are not to become circumcized, i.e., Jews (0718-19). And freemen are not to sell themselves into slavery (0723). In this context it is easy to see Paul also urging Christian slaves to remain in slavery, even if the opportunity of freedom should present itself.

Yet, on the other hand, in almost every case which Paul considers in chapter 7, he makes an exception to the particular general principle he is recommending: It is better not to touch a woman, but because of immorality each person should be married (0702); it is good to remain unmarried, but it is better to marry than to burn with passion (0709); a wife is not to leave her husband, but if she does, Paul gives her two options (0711ab); a Christian is not to break up a mixed marriage, but if

---

[14]A brief summary of this debate is given by K. L. Schmidt in *TDNT* III, 491-492.

[15]Only 1 Cor. 0126 might be an exception to this "theological" use of κλῆσις by Paul; see below pp. 140-141 for a discussion of this text. The concept "calling" is certainly very important for the pericope 0717-24: the verb, καλέω, appears in 0717, 0718 (twice), 0720, 0721b, 0722 (twice), and 0724. The noun, κλῆσις, appears in 0720 and may be the antecedent of ἐν ᾧ in 0724.

[16]See above, p. 5, n. 12.

[17]Note also that the assumption that Paul in 0721 was urging the Corinthians to stay in a particular social status, namely slavery, has given decisive support to reading κλῆσις as "status in society" in 0720.

the unbelieving partner does so, the Christian should not resist (0715); a Christian does well if he keeps his "virgin" partner as she is, but if they marry, he is not sinning (0736-37). In the context of these many exceptions, 0721d can also be seen as an exception: "but if you are indeed able to become free, rather than staying a slave, take freedom."

The exegete of 0721, then, faces difficulties in grammar, in syntax and in the context. And as he mulls over these problems, his understanding of Paul's theology, of the theology of the Corinthians and of the social and legal circumstances of the first century A.D. will play significant roles in his thinking. A survey of the scholarship since the debate between Steinmann and Kiefl will illustrate the manner in which these factors have, or have not, been influential in recent attempts to explain the meaning of 0721. This survey will also prepare the way for clarifying the approach to these problems which is taken in this dissertation.

B. *Recent Attempts to Explain the Meaning of 1 Cor. 0721.*

Although numerous scholars after Steinmann and Kiefl commented on 0721 in a variety of contexts, no large scale treatment of its problems appears until 1954, in the work of Josef Lappas, *Paulus und die Sklavenfrage.*[18] At first glance this work appears promising because of the seventy pages which he devotes to the institutions of slavery in the Old Testament and in the Greco-Roman world, and the thirty pages he gives to 1 Cor. 0721. Unfortunately, his method and results are disappointing for at least two reasons: 1) He treats superficially the institution of slavery and he relies on scholarship which was already outdated in 1954. 2) He treats the Pauline texts in the same, superficial manner, namely by collecting the opinions of others without undertaking his own exegesis. He offers no new arguments, and with respect to 0721, he finally agrees with those who have said "use slavery."

The only recent article which deals specifically with 1 Cor. 0721 is H. Bellen's "Μᾶλλον χρῆσαι: Verzicht auf Freilassung als asketische Leistung?"[19] One aspect of his method is very good: he attempts to use the whole of chapter 7 in solving the riddle of 0721. This leads him to notice one important feature of Paul's manner of arguing, namely, that Paul often speaks of two courses of action, both of which he accepts, but one of which he definitely prefers. Bellen answers positively the question posed in his title, arguing that the conduct which Paul urges upon the slave is

---

[18]Diss. Vienna, 1954.

[19]*Jahrbuch für Antike und Christentum* 6 (1963) 177-180.

analagous to the asceticism which Paul obviously prefers: as a Christian
man or woman is to renounce marriage, so a Christian slave should renounce
manumission.

Bellen's interesting argument fails, however, for a number of
reasons, the most important of which are: 1) He overlooks Paul's words in
0707, that the asceticism which he prefers is the expression of a "gift,"
not the result of an achievement. 2) He does not inquire about the theology
and ethics of the Corinthians to whom Paul is writing, which means that he is
not aware of the asceticism already being practiced by the Corinthians.
3) He ignores 0723 and its implication that slavery was a state of existence
to be avoided. 4) He does not ask whether or not the slave had the option
of rejecting manumission. For these reasons, alone, his interpretation is
unsatisfactory.

In contrast, the dissertation by Darrell Doughty, *Heiligkeit und
Freiheit: Eine exegetische Untersuchung der Anwendung des paulinischen
Freiheitsgedankens in I Kor. 7*, seeks to clarify the theological-ethical
disagreement which lies at the basis of the discussion between Paul and the
Corinthians, as the necessary beginning point for understanding any part of
chapter 7.[20] Building on recent attempts to understand more exactly the
theology of the "opponents" of Paul in the various congregations to which he
writes, Doughty rightly insists that the *basic* difference between Paul and
the Corinthians was not in their respective views of marriage and celibacy,
but rather in their theologies, i.e., in their views of the eschatological
salvation-situation and of Christian existence in the world in general.[21]

Doughty has seen that even though chapter 7 may appear to be a
piece of early Christian mission casuistry in which different problems of
married life and celibacy are discussed one after the other, the entire
chapter is really an ad hoc response to burning questions and problems within
the Corinthian church itself. Paul develops his answers in chapter 7 in
direct response to a false ascetical understanding of sexual life in general.
And the two, more theoretical sections, 0717-24 and 0729-31, are placed in
the argument by Paul in order to stress his view of the basic problem: the
relation between status in the world and eschatological Christian existence.

---

[20] This dissertation was written under the direction of Hans Conzelmann
in Göttingen and published in typescript in 1965. Doughty's purpose was to
treat 1 Cor. 7 in light of H. von Soden's treatment of 1 Cor. .8-10 ("Sakrament
und Ethik bei Paulus," *Marburg Theol. Stud.* 1 [1931] 1-40 = *Das Paulusbild in
der neueren deutschen Forschung*, (1964) 338-379) and E. Dinkler's treatment
of 1 Cor. 6:1-11 ("Zum Problem der Ethik bei Paulus: Rechtsnahme und
Rechtsverzicht," *ZThK* 49 [1952] 167-200), both of whom were using a method
stressed by R. Bultmann.

[21] For a brief introduction to these various "opponents" and their places
in early Christianity, see H. Köster, "Häretiker im Urchristentum," *RRG*3
III, 17-21. See Doughty, pp. 5-8.

This understanding of the purpose of chapter 7 leads Doughty correctly to conclude that it was not Paul's intention to write a theoretical discussion of the question of slavery as such in 0720-24, and that to interpret 0721 as if Paul were addressing the slaves in the Corinthian congregation would be to miss the real point of the passage.[22] Doughty thus identifies 0720-24 as an illustration of the larger argument in ch. 7, and he suggests that 0721cd may be a parenthesis in this illustration; that is, he favors the interpretation: "take freedom."

Doughty did not intend to solve the riddle of 1 Cor. 0721 (he wrote with particular reference to marriage and celibacy), but his work reinforces my own conclusion that this verse and the pericope in which it stands, 0717-24, can only be understood in the broad context of the basic difference between Paul's theological-ethical position and those of the Corinthians.

With regard to Doughty's work and 0717-24 and 0721, the following observations are pertinent:

1) Although Doughty correctly sees that 0720-24 functions as an illustration of the larger argument and that 0721cd may be a parenthesis in this illustration, he does not set his consideration of slavery in its social-legal context.[23] Chiefly because he did not investigate the actual possibilities for action open to a slave in Corinth in the first century A.D., his interesting conclusions regarding 0721 remain unconvincing.[24]

2) Although he rightly insists on the unity of ch. 7, he does not inquire about the structure of the chapter. Thus he is not able to explain why Paul chose precisely "circumcision/uncircumcision" and "slave/free" as illustrations of his fundamental point in ch. 7.

3) Although Doughty insists correctly that ch. 7 must be interpreted in the light of the theology of the Corinthians, he does not establish a clear connection between this theology and the asceticism which many of the Corinthians were trying to practice.

---

[22] Doughty, p. 67.

[23] Doughty does include a ten page excursus on the problem of sacral manumission ("Exkurs zur Frage des Sklavenfreikaufs") in which he considers the appropriate literature available up to 1965. This research is a major assistance in his exegesis of 0722. But he undertook no comparable research with reference to 0721.

[24] For example, in his commentary on 1 Cor. published in 1969, Doughty's teacher, Hans Conzelmann, writes regarding 0721ab: "Getröstet werden muß der Sklave." And this consolation is reinforced in 0721cd, "durch die zunächst überraschende Aufforderung, von der Möglichkeit, frei zu werden, keinen Gebrauch zu machen." *Der erste Brief an die Korinther*, Meyers Kommentar V, (Göttingen, 1969), p. 152.

Many of Doughty's observations are very important for understanding
the context of 0721, and they will be noted below, especially in connection
with the discussion of the Corinthian "opponents" and the exegesis of 0722.

In another, recent dissertation written in Germany, Liem Khiem Jang
considers 1 Cor. 0721 in his attempt to exegete Paul's letter to Philemon.[25]
Regarding the fate of Onesimus, Jang concludes that Paul recommended to
Philemon that he set this slave free and then send him back to minister with
Paul. Such a manumission was not necessary to the Christian life of either
Philemon or Onesimus. But it would be a sign of the new reality in Christ,
a sign of the agape-love which was already available in the church of Christ.[26]
Jang does not, however, find that 1 Cor. 0721 supports Paul's preference for
freedom in the case of Onesimus.

Although Jang correctly observes that it makes no apparent difference to Paul if a Christian is a slave or a freeman, that in one sense a
Christian is independent of every kind of social circumstance, he nevertheless
says that in 0721 Paul is urging slaves to remain in slavery, even if they
could become free--as if there were some special value in remaining a slave
in the "last days." In interpreting 0721, Jang stresses the context, claims
that εἰ καί unambiguously (!) means "even if," translates κλῆσις with "Stand,"
connects the reason given in 0722 with the exhortation in 0721cd, and asserts
that 0723 was addressed to slaves (the slaves would become slaves of men if
they surrendered to the cares and desires which men usually have--such as becoming free). For these reasons he concludes that Paul was urging the slaves
to use "das Sklavensein."[27] Jang sees here a call by Paul to a renunciation of any disturbance of the social order or change in social status.[28]

Jang covers the apparent contradiction between his interpretation
of Paul in 1 Cor. and in Philemon as follows: 1) In 1 Cor. Paul is speaking
to slaves, not to masters. In the letter to Philemon the problem is not that
of what the slave Onesimus should do in view of his social position, but

---

[25] *Der Philemonbrief im Zusammenhang mit dem theologischen Denken des
Apostels Paulus*, written under the direction of E. Dinkler and Ph. Vielhauer,
printed in typescript, Bonn, 1964. Jang's treatment of 1 Cor. 0721 is on
pp. 53-57.

[26] Jang, p. 62.

[27] Jang, pp. 54-55.

[28] In this connection Jang makes the interesting comment that one could
hardly call Paul a "conservative," even if his exhortation denies a revolution. For Paul had no intention of preserving or protecting his society.
Why should he, asks Jang, since he viewed the society that he knew as being
"on the way out" (0731). Jang does not make clear, however, why in this
situation Paul would have any particular interest in a slave's manumission,
in the stability of marriage or in a preferred state such as celibacy.

14

rather what the master, Philemon, should do. 2) In both passages the statements of Paul are completely non-programmatic. In no way can either of them
be taken as indicating a realization of a social program of some kind.[29]

I take these two judgments about the relation of the interpretation
of 1 Cor. 0721 to that of the letter to Philemon to be entirely correct. Indeed, they are fitting no matter how 1 Cor. 0721 is read. The validity of
Jang's exegesis of 0721 remains completely independent of his conclusions
regarding Philemon, and his work must be viewed in terms of his own claim
that 1 Cor. 0720-24 is an important piece of Paul's "theological thinking."

Unfortunately, even if Jang's treatment of the grammatical and syntactical problems of 0720-24 were convincing, his arguments for "using your
existence as a slave" would still remain very weak in terms of his own choice
of final criteria: theological reasons.

Jang, of course, takes note of the "eschatological situation." But
in view of the changes in status which are noted throughout ch. 7, he does
not seek to clarify why it would be "better" or preferred by Paul for a slave
to remain in slavery.[30] Would it have been more difficult for a Christian
slave to endure the travail of the "last days" as a freedman? Would it have
been to the slave's "benefit" to remain in slavery, or could he more single-

---

[29]Jang,· pp. 56-57.

[30]A variety of reasons have been offered to clarify why Paul would advise
a slave to remain in slavery. For example, Severian, bishop of Gabala (c.
400) and an exegete in the Antiochene tradition, said that the slave should
stay in slavery in order to show the world that it is no disadvantage for
a Christian to be a slave (Cramer, *Catenae Graec. Patr. in N.T.* V, 141).
Cyril from Alexandria (d. 444), an important representative of the Alexandrian
tradition of exegesis, said to remain in slavery because bearing the yoke
of slavery will bring a reward in the future, especially if this yoke is
carried with a good attitude (Migne, 74, 878). Hervaeus of Bourgdieu, an
important 12th cen. monastic exegete (whose commentary was circulated under
the name of Anselm of Canterbury), said to remain in slavery because it is
a good and useful thing in that it encourages humility and patience; the person who serves well in earthly things, with the intent to preserve righteous-
ness and humility will earn a great reward from God, who does not see the
external condition of a man but the inner disposition and actions (Migne, 181,
880 f.). Peter Lombard (d. 1146) and Thomas Aquinas also stress the development of humility as the reason for staying in slavery. Hugh of St. Cher,
a Dominican Cardinal (d. 1264), said to stay a slave in order to nurture
humility, and he attached to his exegesis a series of quotes from authors
who praise the moral value of serving (See Kiefl, *Die Theorien*, p. 69).
More recently, E. von Dobschütz said that the slave should remain
in slavery, because as a slave the Christian could show that despite his
slavery he had the power of a new Christian Spirit, and that this Spirit
made him a true, obedient, reliable slave. (*Die Urchristlichen Gemeinden:
Sittengeschichtliche Bilder*, [1902], p. 32). J. Weiß, apparently referring
to 0722, thinks that Paul urged the slaves to remain in slavery "for the
highest religious motives." (*Der erste Korintherbrief*, [1910], p. 188).

mindedly serve the Lord as a slave? These questions are appropriate because Paul, when urging the Corinthians to remain unmarried, does not simply point to his conviction that the "frame of this world is passing away." Rather he has a variety of specific reasons which he uses to support his admonitions, either for remaining unmarried or for remaining married. Jang does not suggest any reasons for a Christian slave to stay in slavery if he has the opportunity to have freedom.

In short, Jang's work does not bring any light to our understanding of 1 Cor. 0721. At least four factors have limited the value of his exegesis: 1) He overlooks many of the grammatical and syntactical problems. 2) He tries to understand vv. 20-24 without close reference to the whole of ch. 7 and the function of 0717-24 within the chapter. 3) He does not inquire about the actual possibilities facing the slaves in Corinth. 4) Most important, in terms of his own interests, Jang does not consider Paul's theological thinking against the background of the theology of the Corinthian Christians.[31]

A large scale attempt to deal with Paul's theological thinking with particular reference to slaves and slavery is made by Kenneth C. Russell in his recent dissertation: *Slavery as Reality and Metaphor in the Pauline Letters*.[32] Russell argues that "slave" as a concept used in Scripture is a title which has kept close to its roots, i.e., real bondage. From this conclusion he claims: "St. Paul, in viewing the condition of Christian slaves saw in it a unique and important opportunity for the imitation of Christ in

---

[31] Jang's treatment of the letter to Philemon *also* lacks precision, principally because he falsely assumes that Roman law was in effect in Asia Minor during the 1st cen. A.D. Only if Philemon had been a Roman citizen could the fugitive laws which Jang describes have been applied in the case of Onesimus. As it is, we know nothing about Philemon's status, except that he himself was not a slave. He was probably a provincial, and as such he did not come under the provisions of the *ius civile*. Therefore it seems that Paul was not legally obligated to send Onesimus back to his master. That is, any Roman citizen (as was Paul) could legally retain a provincial's slave who had sought refuge with him. To be sure, we have no evidence that Onesimus had actually sought "refuge" with Paul. See P. R. Coleman-Norton, "The Apostle Paul and the Roman Law of Slavery," *Studies in Roman Economic and Social History in Honor of Allan Chester Johnson* (Princeton, 1951), pp. 166-177.

[32] Presented to the Theological Faculty of Pontifical University, Rome, 1968. The dissertation consists of five chapters, the last two of which have been published and were made available to me by the author. These chapters treat: "St. Paul's Use of the *Ebed* Theme" and "St. Paul's Application of His Servant Theology to Enslaved Christians."

union with him in his work of salvation."[33] This claim leads him rightly to
reject the argument that Paul advised slaves to keep their places and their
silence in order to avoid the "public image of the church as a revolutionary
society."[34]

With this discussion in mind, Russell considers the various grammatical problems to be found in 1 Cor. 0721. In light of the many difficulties,
he comes to no conclusion, saying that a solution "cannot be given until the
other passages where Paul speaks of slaves have been analyzed."[35] Unfortunately, Russell never returns to 0721!

Nevertheless, in light of his conclusions that "Paul called the
slave to an heroic emptying of self in imitation of Christ, who like him was
a slave of others" (p. 85), it seems fairly clear that Russell would prefer
"rather use your slavery" as the conclusion of 0721.

The following observations regarding Russell's work are pertinent:

---

[33]Russell, p. 17. In his dissertation, Russell poses three questions:
1) "Did the title 'slave' become purely a title of honour and the description of a function or did it retain its original vitality throughout the
centuries and describe a fundamental condition?"
2) "Did Paul limit his servant theology to Christ, himself and his fellow
apostles, or did he see the ordinary Christian as a slave?"
3) "Did he see the enslaved Christian sharing in a privileged way in the
humiliations and sufferings of Christ? ... And if so, are the slave passages
simply specific applications to one social class of attitudes common to all
faithful Christians?" p. 17.

Russell's conclusions, in short:
1) "The title 'slave' never became purely a title of honour or simply the
description of a spiritual function but always described a fundamental condition of complete dedication to the divine will. It is hard to think of a
metaphor which has kept the sense of its root meaning more strongly." p. 88.
2) "An examination of St. Paul's use of the servant theme which looks beyond
functions, shows that he exploited the O.T. image to describe the situation
of every Christian ... including those designated slaves by society. But it
is in the case of the latter that the metaphor, which was never far from its
secular root, is united to it." pp. 88-89.
3) "Each Christian's *ebed*hood (spiritual attitude of dependence on God and
readiness for obedient service) is marked by the *ebed*hood of Christ into whom
he is incorporated at baptism ... The enslaved Christian who takes on the
burdens of his state in union with Christ unites his religious commitment to
his social condition and makes his social bondage the vehicle of his spiritual
*ebed*hood." p. 89.

[34]Russell correctly stresses that it was not the case that Paul had "the
desire to keep them in their subservient position for the sake of peace between the infant church and the Roman Empire." Rather, he says that it was
the poor attitudes of the slaves caused by their enslavement which moved
Paul to "show the slave the way to Christian living." p. 53.

[35]Russell, p. 48. Russell has such books as W. L. Westermann, *Slave Systems in Greek and Roman Antiquity*, M. Rostovtzeff *Social and Economic
History of the Roman Empire*, and I. Mendelsohn, *Slavery in the Ancient Near
East* in his bibliography, but there is no evidence that he used them when
considering slavery in Paul's time.

1) Although he has given a great deal of attention to the Old Testament and Intertestamental background of Paul's theology (chs. 1 and 2), Russell says nothing either about the Corinthian Christians' theological views or about their backgrounds.

2) Although the unpublished parts of his dissertation deal with slavery in the Old Testament, the Intertestamental literature, and the early Rabbis, he does not investigate slavery in the Greco-Roman world and he gives no historical-social background for his interpretation of 1 Cor. 7.

3) Although he expresses concern for the whole of Paul's theology, Russell uses neither the whole of ch. 7 nor the evidence of the whole of 1 Cor. for his consideration of 0721.

These errors in method lead to the fact that Russell does not contribute to a better understanding of 1 Cor. 0721.

The most recent scholarship on 1 Cor. 0721 known to me appears as an excursus in Henneke Gülzow's book, *Christentum und Sklaverei in den ersten drei Jahrhunderten*.[36] Gülzow begins with the assumption that in 0721c Paul is *not* speaking to a slave who might receive his freedom as a gift from his owner, but rather to a slave for whom manumission would involve some effort or burden on his part, or perhaps some post-manumission duties.[37] And it is a short step from this assumption to his conclusion that Paul is admonishing slaves to "use slavery."

Gülzow supports this judgment by arguing that the reasons given in 0722 apply to the admonition in 0721d on the ground that 0722 does not project the slave into a new legal situation as a freedman, but rather continues to speak of him as a slave who is now a "freedman in Christ." Gülzow finds the decisive support for his exegesis, however, in the context, ("Jeder soll in seinem Stand bleiben.") which he says would be enough in itself to demand

---

[36] Habelt Verlag, Bonn, 1969. Gülzow examines especially the relationships between the Christian congregation in Rome and the economic, political, legal, philosophic and religious life of that great city. He presented an earlier form of this work to the Protestant Theological Faculty in Kiel as a dissertation in 1966, writing under the direction of Heinrich Kraft. The excursus is on pp. 177-181.

[37] Gülzow takes this view from J. Weiß, who wrote: "Voraussetzung ist hierbei natürlich, daß die Freiheit dem Betreffenden nicht etwa geschenkt wird, sondern daß er nur die Möglichkeit hätte sich selbst loszukaufen." *Der erste Korintherbrief*, Meyers Kommentar V (Göttingen, 1910), p. 188. Against this view H. Greeven is correct in stating: "So bedeutet das eine Modifizierung von εἰ καὶ δύνασαι die am Text keinen Anhalt hat." *Das Hauptproblem der Sozialethik in der neueren Stoa und im Urchristentum* (Gütersloh, 1935), p. 51 n. 3. Very few exegetes have commented on this phrase, 0721c. A closer examination of its meaning in terms of the social-legal options will help solve the riddle of the entire verse.

the "stay in slavery" interpretation.[38] He further comments that in 0721d
Paul is not making an exception such as he makes in the case of mixed marriage
(0715), and he apparently bases this conclusion on the observation that Paul
does not refer to any ethical threats or difficult situations which might
come to a slave who became a Christian.[39]

Gülzow correctly stresses his view that Paul's main point in 0721ab
and 0722 is that a Christian slave is already "free in Christ," and that
Paul's admonition in 0721cd is determined neither by a timidity to allow
change nor by the influence of slave-owning members of the Corinthian congregation.[40] For the following reasons, however, Gülzow has not satisfactorily
interpreted 1 Cor. 0721:

1) He mistakenly thinks that the overwhelming majority of exegetes have
favored "stay a slave," which leads him to write as if the grammatical and
syntactical problems of 0721 have been solved.[41]

2) He offers no reasons to support his assumption that Paul is speaking only
to slaves who were having to *strive* to obtain their legal freedom, and this
assumption falsely determines the meaning of 0721c before any investigation
is undertaken of the options for slaves which existed in first-century
Corinth.

3) His claim that 0721d is not an "exception" in the immediate context is

---

[38]Gülzow follows very closely the exegesis of H. Greeven, *Sozialethik*, pp.
49-52. He also follows Greeven in the assumption that Paul means to address
an important word to slaves as such in all parts of 0721-22. See Greeven's
comment that 1 Cor. 0721 shows that the mention of slaves in the Haustafeln
is not just a taking over of a schema which included admonitions to slaves
but rather appears because of a real need to address slaves as such. "Evangelium und Gesellschaft in Urchristlicher Zeit," *Festschrift zur Eröffnung
der Universität Bochum*, eds. H. Wenke and J. H. Knoll (1965), p. 116.

[39]Gülzow, p. 179.

[40]Gülzow, p. 178. He suggests on the basis of the conversion of "households" that most Christian slaves in the first century had Christian masters
(pp. 42-44). Nevertheless, he notes that Paul does not want to restrict his
message to such slaves as is indicated by his speaking directly to any slave
who was a Christian--0721. But Gülzow then finds the parallelism of Christian
slave and Christian master in 0722 to be evidence in favor of Christian masters in the case spoken to in 0721.
    Note also that Gülzow (p. 179 n. 5) mistakenly objects to Greeven's
view of this matter (*Sozialethik*, p. 52), i.e., they *agree* that Paul's speaking to the individual slave means that we hear nothing about the relationship
between owner and slave.

[41]In favor of "take freedom," Gülzow knows only the work of J. von Walter
and A. Steinmann, which means that he did not read A. Schlatter, W. Foerster,
nor such English scholars as J. H. Moulton, W. D. Davies, D. Daube, C. F. D.
Moule or N. Turner. See "Table I" above, p. 6.

not persuasive because he does not analyze Paul's pattern of arguing throughout ch. 7.

4) He assumes that Paul was motivated to speak to Christian slaves as such
in 0721 because of their striving after freedom motivated by religious
"enthusiasm"--and this assumption is open to question.[42]

5] He tries to interpret this verse without close reference to the *whole* of
ch. 7 and without any reference to the theology of the Corinthians.

In addition to these six, more or less lengthy treatments of 1 Cor.
0721 (Lappas, Bellen, Doughty, Jang, Russell, Gülzow), the following four,
recent and brief comments on this text should be noted (Neuhäusler, Barrett,
Conzelmann, Bornkamm).

In his article, "Ruf Gottes und Stand des Christen: Bermerkungen
zu 1 Kor. 7,"[43] E. Neuhäusler is principally interested in explaining the
meaning of 0720, and he considers 0721 in that context. Without mentioning
any of the grammatical difficulties in 0721, Neuhäusler argues from the context of 0720 and 0724 that "use slavery" must be the correct completion of
0721d. He makes the interesting, but unsupported, suggestion that Paul does
not mean that a Christian slave *should* remain in slavery, but only that he
could do so.[44] He translates 0721d: "Mache dir deinen Sklavenstand nur um
so mehr und intensiver zunutze."[45]

Neuhäusler's treatment of 0721 is marred by his lack of attention
to the meaning of 0721c as well as by his unconcern for the grammatical and
syntactical problems of the verse. He does raise some very important questions about the relationship between the call from God and the earthly circumstances of the one who is called. But his answers remain incomplete or in-
correct because he considers neither the larger context of Paul's theology in
the entire letter nor the understanding of "calling" in the theology of the
Corinthians.[46]

---

[42]Gülzow writes: "Paulus will hier mahnén, trösten und ermutigen." And he
claims that Paul is replying to the "starken Freiheitsdrang der Sklaven."
p. 180.

[43]*Biblische Zeitschrift* (Neue Folge) 3/1 (1959), 43-60.

[44]Neuhäusler, p. 49. Compare with this the equally unsupported proposal of
A. Juncker that Paul is advising against the attainment of freedom, but not
strictly forbidding it. *Die Ethik des Apostels Paulus* II (Halle, 1919),
176-177.

[45]Neuhäusler, p. 51.

[46]Neuhäusler's arguments, as well as those of W. Bieder, *Die Berufung im
N.T.* (Zürich, 1961) and D. Wiederkehr, *Die Theologie der Berufung in den
Paulusbriefen* (Freiburg, Switzerland, 1963),are closely considered in my
exegesis of 0720 in ch. 3 below.

In his commentary on 1 Cor., C. K. Barrett begins his treatment of
0721 by asserting that it would be wrong to introduce in 0720 the meaning of
κλῆσις which he notes that it has in every other Pauline usage, namely, the
call of God in Christ.[47]

> "Calling" in this verse is not the calling *with* which, *to* which,
> or *by* which a man is called, but refers to the state in which he
> is *when* he is called by God to become a Christian. Since Paul in
> the same sentence, and repeatedly in the context, declares that it
> is the will of God that the Christian should continue in this
> state, it acquires new meaning: the slave, for example, becomes
> the Lord's freedman.[48]

So Barrett translates 0721cd: "But even though you should be able to become
free, put up rather with your present status."[49]

Although he finds in the grammar of 0721 evidence for the "take
freedom" interpretation, especially the aorist tense of χρῆσαι, he argues
that the context demands "use slavery." In addition the γάρ at the beginning
of 0722 is taken as the introduction of a reason for such a phrase as, "You
need not hesitate to put up with your servile conditions."[50] Thus for Barrett, 0721cd has a consoling and encouraging function, much like that of
0721b.

Barrett's exegesis stimulates the following observations:
1) He points again to the importance of clarifying the meaning of "calling"
throughout 0717-24 with reference to 0721. 2) He highlights the problem of
the relation of 0721 to its context: is it the most extreme example of

---

[47] *A Commentary on the First Epistle to the Corinthians*, Black's N.T. Commentaries (London, 1968), p. 169.

[48] Barrett, pp. 169-170.

[49] Barrett, p. 170.

[50] Barrett refers to the comments of J.N. Sevenster, who thinks for the following reasons that δοῦλος εἶναι is "the most promising" completion of 0721d:
1) The position of καί in the sentence favors reading it with εἰ rather than
with the rest of the phrase. 2) μᾶλλον would be "virtually meaningless" if
Paul were advising using the opportunity to become free. "It fits in very
well if he is advising those who are slaves to do instead the unexpected,
namely to remain in bondage despite the fact that there is an opportunity of
their gaining their freedom." 3) The train of thought in 0720-24. *Paul and
Seneca*, Supplement to *Novum Testamentum* IV (Leiden, 1961), pp. 189-190.

"remaining" in the status quo,[51] an "exception" to Paul's trend of thinking
in 0717-24, or does some other relationship exist, perhaps in connection
with a different understanding of "calling"? 3) Barrett's exegesis does not
reflect a concern for Pauline theology as a whole nor any awareness of the
theological situation *to* which Paul is speaking.[52]

Hans Conzelmann, in his recent commentary on 1 Cor., sets the stage
for his comments on 0721 by claiming that the exhortations to "remain" found
in 0717-24 are dialectic: even the "remaining" is not a method for obtaining
salvation. The meaning of "remaining" is understood eschatologically, i.e.
the worldly differences are to be overcome in the new eschatological community,
but not in the world.[53]

So Conzelmann judges 0721 to be a special example needed to clarify
0720, because eschatological equality is not, to be sure, the same as psychological equality. That is, the slave must be consoled because he is still a
slave in the eyes of the world. And Paul does this not by giving the slave
the hope of a better future beyond death, but rather by pointing to a situation which goes beyond the need for consolation, namely, by urging the slave
not to make use of freedom, even if it becomes a possibility.

Conzelmann also notes the force of the aorist, χρῆσαι, but he says
that in spite of it, τῇ δουλείᾳ is to be supplied because the verse is a consolation. He emphasizes that Paul neither calls the slave to Stoic indifference nor does he encourage any feelings of *ressentiment* nursed by the

---

[51]Claus-Hunno Hunzinger comments that if Paul had meant to say that slaves
should stay slaves even if they could become free: "Darin fände dann die
Gleichgültigkeit gegenüber der gesellschaftlichen Situation ihren aufs
äußerste zugespitzten Ausdruck." And he adds that for Paul to have done so
would have been "seine eigenen Prinzipien zu Tode zu reiten." "Paulus und
die politische Macht," *Christentum und Gesellschaft*, eds. W. Lohff and B.
Lohse (Göttingen, 1969), p. 125.
But, in contrast to Hunzinger's first comment, unless 0721c is
understood as referring to "striving" after freedom, 0721d would not be the
"height of indifference." Rather, "remaining" in the status quo would presuppose some *positive* theological basis.

[52]In his review of Barrett's commentary, D. Doughty correctly criticizes
Barrett's method, noting that "the relationship between Christology and
ethics never becomes defined. What we have, in general, is a careful elaboration of the biblical text, but not really an interpretation which opens up a
theological understanding of the ethical situation to which the text is directed." "Elaboration over Understanding," *Interpretation* 23 (1969), 475-476.

[53]*Der erste Brief an die Korinther*, Meyers Kommentar V (Göttingen, 1969),
p. 151.

oppressed. By this verse Paul makes clear that civil freedom has worth only in *this* world: "in der Kirche ist sie kein Wert."[54]

The format of a commentary may be ill-suited for settling such difficult problems as the exegesis of 1 Cor. 0721. Conzelmann's comments, however, have the following positive results: 1) the importance of the larger theological context for understanding 0721 is stressed. 2) the question is sharply raised: is 0721 an "example" or is it a direct word (a "consolation") to the slaves in the Corinthian congregation? 3) and two other questions are also stimulated: in *what* is the Christian to "remain" and *why* is this "remaining" so important?

Günther Bornkamm, in his recent book, *Paulus*, takes up the interpretation of 1 Cor. 0721 in his section entitled, "Stand und Abstand des Christen."[55] In this context he correctly stresses that in contrast to the thinking of Paul's "opponents" in the Corinthian congregation, the Christian does not have to change any of his relationships in this world in order to remain a Christian. These relationships, such as marriage or slavery, have no significance for salvation. The important thing to Paul is how the Christian conducts himself, wherever he finds himself. As Bornkamm says:

> Leitmotiv und Maßstab der paulinischen Weisung ist allein das Verhältnis der Glaubenden zu dem kommenden Herrn. Wie die Glaubenden konkret ihr Christsein verwirklichen und bewähren sollen, dafür nimmt Paulus dem einzelnen die Entscheidung nicht ab.[56]

But in spite of this excellent observation regarding Paul's evaluation of earthly "relationships," Bornkamm insists on translating κλῆσις with "Stand." And he concludes that Paul is answering a question of the Corinthians in 0721, and that his reply is "take slavery."[57] Bornkamm supports this conclusion with the unconvincing assertion that the verse refers to relationships within the congregation and not to problems of the social structure.

---

[54]Conzelmann, p. 153. Conzelmann further comments that it would be absurd to refer to the problematic character of some manumissions, e.g. that a slave might not want to be freed because he preferred the security (board and room) of his slavery. Yet, his lack of attention to 0721c and the options which Paul may be referring to there makes his exegesis of 0721 very questionable. He allows theology to decide the issue before the historical circumstances are closely examined.

[55]*Paulus* (Stuttgart, 1969), pp. 212-216. On the one hand, Paul in 0729-31 speaks of the *distance* or *difference* of the Christian from the world. On the other hand, in 0717-24 he speaks of the *place* or *presence* of the Christian in the world.

[56]Bornkamm, p. 214.   [57]Bornkamm, p. 215.

In line with his suggestive understanding of "relationships" as Paul treats them in ch. 7, Bornkamm observes that Paul accomplishes two things in 0717-24: 1) He shows that in relation to the question of salvation, every circumstance of living is radically relativized and de-sacralized. 2) At the same time, Paul shows that the circumstances of life are of decisive importance because they are precisely those earthly, historical, concrete places in which Christ has already set the believer free for a new kind of existence.[58]

Bornkamm does not make clear the connection between his insightful interpretation of 0717-24 and his translation of 0721. Indeed, his analysis of Paul's theology in this passage could just as easily support the opposite reading of 0721.[59] Thus, Bornkamm has not solved the riddle of 0721, but he has suggested a very persuasive way of understanding Paul's intent in the context. His statements regarding the particular and abiding importance of earthly circumstances now need to be tested and developed with reference to the theology of Paul's Corinthian "opponents."

This survey of recent scholarship on 1 Cor. 0721, as well as a close acquaintance with the history of this text's interpretation, make it possible for me to summarize the current state of research as follows:

No thoroughly convincing case has been made on the basis of grammar and syntax alone for the correct interpretation of 0721. In various ways, this grammatical ambiguity has resulted in special stresses on the *context* as decisive for a correct interpretation. Yet, the work on 0717-24 as such has not resulted in a convincing interpretation, because scholars have been able to draw on a variety of themes in Paul's writings and his background in order to find theological support for both of the prevailing, contradictory interpretations.[60] Most of those scholars who stress the grammatical considerations prefer the "take freedom" interpretation (such as J.H. Moulton, C.F.D. Moule, M. Thrall, N. Turner), and most of the scholars who stress the importance of the context prefer the "use slavery" interpretation (such as J. Weiß, H. Greeven, J.N. Sevenster, E. Käsemann).

---

[58] Bornkamm, pp. 215-216.

[59] If the "freedom" to which Paul refers in 0721c is not related to "striving" on the part of the slave but rather is the result of the owner's action, then Paul could be saying that he, of course, has no objection to the slave becoming a freedman, for all earthly positions have been relativized. Bornkamm and many other exegetes seem to have assumed that 0721c must be referring to some action by the slave which Paul is disapproving of in 0721d. This assumption must be carefully tested.

[60] Seldom has 0721 been considered in the context of ch. 7 as a whole (see Bellen, above pp. 10-11). And to my knowledge, no attempt has been made to relate 0721 to the whole of 1 Cor. and the theology of the Corinthians to which this letter speaks.

Indeed, those scholars whose primary interest has been in theological considerations have most often preferred the "use slavery" solution, and for a variety of reasons. For example, this interpretation seems to present Paul as one who encourages the theological virtue of "humility." Such an interpretation seems to be "more religious."[61] And recently, some of the exegetes who argue that 1 Cor. is Paul's reply to the theology and ethics of the Corinthian "enthusiasts" have found in 0721 an admonition intended to dampen the "enthusiasm" which supposedly heightened the Christian slave's dissatisfaction with his lot.[62] On the other hand, some interpreters conclude that a voluntary "remaining in slavery" would be motivated by the false religious pride against which Paul is arguing in 1 Corinthians.[63]

In an attempt to overcome the grammatical, contextual and theological ambiguities of 0721, some scholars have referred to the institution of slavery in the ancient world. And their interpretations have varied, especially of 0721b and 0721c (and then consequently of 0721d), directly with their assumptions about the relative severity of dependence and deprivation suffered by slaves in the first century. That is, scholars who have read of the terrors of slavery in the ancient world urge that Paul was allowing, indeed encouraging, a slave to take his freedom, if he could get it.[64] But those who judge first-century slavery to have been a relatively benign institution, affirm Paul's own indifference to this social condition.[65]

Unfortunately for the understanding of this verse, New Testament scholars do not seem to have been concerned to establish the actual social and legal situation of the slaves in Corinth in the middle of the first century A.D., as a prerequisite for a correct exegesis. The term δοῦλος seems to gain its content from "general knowledge" rather than from an historical investigation,[66] and the possibilities that Paul might be referring to in

---

[61] See above pp. 10-11 and p. 14 n. 30.

[62] See, e.g., E. Käsemann's discussion of 1 Cor. 0721 in "Principles of the Interpretation of Romans 13," *New Testament Questions of Today* (London, 1969), pp. 208-210 (trans. W.J. Montague from *Exegetische Versuche und Besinnungen* II² [Göttingen, 1965] 215-217).

[63] See, e.g., A. Schlatter, *Paulus der Bote Jesu: Eine Deutung seiner Briefe an die Korinther* (Stuttgart, 1956), pp. 230-236.

[64] Even when 0720 is read as a re-enforcement of the status quo, an interpreter may read 0721 as an exception because of the terrors of slavery.

[65] In this case it has been assumed that "use your slavery" would not only develop "humility" but also be an opportunity to carry on evangelism within the family circle of the owner.

[66] For example, in contrast to the actual situation in the first century A.D., E. Käsemann speaks of the "slave revolts" and the "armies of runaway slaves" which supposedly are the background for what Paul says in 1 Cor. 0720-24. Käsemann, *New Testament Questions*, p. 208 (*Exegetische Versuche*, p. 215).

0721c ("But [even] if you are [indeed] able to become free") have never been researched.[67]

On the other hand, those historians and philologians who have commented on 1 Cor. 0721 have done so both without reference to the context in which this verse is anchored and without challenging the assumption that Paul intended to make a major declaration of his views of slavery in 0721.[68]

In this fashion the disagreement about the meaning of 1 Cor. 0721, which was first noted by J. Chrysostom (between himself and his "unnamed opponents") and which reached a lively peak in the debate between Steinmann and Kiefl, continues in the most recent commentaries, monographs and articles. It seems clear, therefore, that in order to solve the riddle of this passage not only must the grammatical and contextual problems be thoroughly re-examined but also the prevailing assumptions with which this text has been approached must be carefully tested.

For example, did the Corinthian congregation include a large number of slaves, and did Paul intend to speak to them in 0720-24? Indeed, what did it mean to be a slave in Corinth in the first century A.D.? What was the relationship between a slave's hopes and his becoming a Christian? Did a question from the Corinthians about slavery stimulate 0720-24? Or did the behavior of the slaves themselves demand such a reply from Paul? And if neither of these assumptions is correct, why does Paul mention slavery at all in his extended reply to the Corinthians' questions about male-female relationships? In the light of Paul's manner of arguing in the rest of chapter 7, does 0721c refer to an action by the slave of which Paul disapproves?

In this dissertation I seek to answer these questions as necessary background for the exegesis of 1 Cor. 0721.

C. *The Approach to the Exegesis of 1 Cor. 0721 Taken in this Dissertation.*

In full view of the unsatisfactory and inconclusive results of previous attempts to explain the meaning of 1 Cor. 0721, I approach the task of exegeting this verse in the following manner:

In the next chapter I examine the institution of slavery in the first century A.D., limiting my discussion to those aspects of this legal-

---

[67]In his commentary, James Moffatt does discuss at some length the social make-up of the Corinthian congregation, but he does not give any special attention to the meaning of 0721c. *The First Epistle of Paul to the Corinthians*, Moffatt's N.T. Commentary (London, 1938), pp. xix-xxi.

[68]See, e.g., P.R. Coleman-Norton, "The Apostle Paul and the Roman Law of Slavery," (above, n. 31), pp. 161-163; W.L. Westermann, *The Slave Systems of Greek and Roman Antiquity* (Philadelphia, 1955), p. 151; J.H. Moulton, *A Grammar of New Testament Greek* I (Edinburgh, 1908), 247, and II (1919-1929), 165.

social state which are suggested directly by 1 Cor. 0721. That is, under
0721a ("Were you a slave when you were called?") I discuss the definitions
of slavery in Greek and Roman law, how persons became enslaved, what Paul
probably knew about slavery, and the slaves in the Christian congregation at
Corinth. Under 0721b ("don't worry about it") I discuss first century attitudes toward slavery, the treatment of slaves and their place in society, the
aspirations held by slaves and the level of their discontent and unrest.
Under 0721cd ("But [even] if you are [indeed] able to become free, rather
you should use ? .") I discuss the owner's reasons for manumitting his
slaves, his methods for doing so, and the options which the slave himself
could exercise in an attempt to obtain freedom or to remain in slavery.

It should now be quite clear that the exegesis of 0721 cannot be
isolated successfully from its context, and in chapter three I extend this
context to include Paul's response throughout 1 Cor. to the theology and
ethics of the Christians in Corinth, his "pneumatic opponents."[69] I seek to
clarify the religious self-understanding of these Corinthians, especially
with regard to their understanding of the "call from God" and the ethical and
social consequences they drew from this call. Then I analyze Paul's polemic
and varied response to this pneumatic view of Christian faith and life, especially as expressed in his teaching about the relation of the Christian's
σῶμα to Christ and the Holy Spirit (0616-20), in the reasons he gives for
his preference for celibacy (ch. 7), in his theology of "calling" (0717-24
and 0126-29), in his ὡς μή ethics (0729-31) and in his claim that ἀγάπη is
the most important spiritual gift (chs. 13-14).

1 Cor. 0721 appears in the midst of a long and careful discussion
of problems which existed in the relations between men and women in the

---

[69] I have found no compelling reasons to abandon the view that "1 Corinthians" is a literary unity. Brief reviews of the chief literary and historical
objections to this view can be found in C.K. Barrett, *First Epistle to the
Corinthians* (1968), pp. 11-15 and H. Conzelmann, *Der erste Brief an die
Korinther* (1969), pp. 13-15. A more detailed presentation of these objections
is made by Wolfgang Schenk, "Der 1. Korintherbrief als Briefsammlung," *ZNW* 60
(1969) 219-243.
    Our "1 Corinthians" is not the first letter which Paul wrote to the
Corinthians (see 0509: "I wrote to you in my letter not to associate with
immoral men"). Our letter was written about three years after Paul himself
had served the congregation as evangelist and pastor for a period of about
eighteen months, a period which can be dated with some precision: it was in
the proconsulship of L. Junius Gallio Annaeanus, a brother of Seneca. This
fact is established by an inscription from Delphi (for the text and recon-
struction see W. Dittenberger, *SIG* II 801D) with the help of other inscriptions from 51/52 A.D. Our letter, "1 Corinthians," was written from Ephesus
in the spring (see 1 Cor. 1608) of the year, between 53-56 A.D. Paul wrote
in response to a letter written to him by the Corinthian congregation and to
reports from the household of Chloe. For Pauline chronology in general (and
an early dating of 1 Cor.) see D. Georgi, *Die Geschichte der Kollekte des
Paulus für Jerusalem* (Hamburg, 1965), pp. 91-94.

the Corinthian congregation. In addition, this verse is part of a pericope (0717-24) that appears to be out of place in this discussion. Thus in the fourth chapter I analyze Paul's style of arguing in ch. 7, discuss the form and unity of the chapter, and clarify the function of 0717-24 within this chapter and of 0721 within this pericope.

The exegesis of 0721-24 and my conclusions appear in chapter five.

Before turning to chapter two dealing with slavery in the first century, I discuss in an excursus the topic: Biblical scholarship and slavery in the ancient world.

BIBLICAL SCHOLARSHIP AND SLAVERY IN THE ANCIENT WORLD

A. *Scholarship on Ancient Slavery.*

Slavery, as an essential element in the social structure of antiquity, has been investigated closely since the advent of modern anti-slavery
movements at the beginning of the last century. The earliest, known monograph
on slavery was written already in 1789 by a historian of Roman law, J.F.
Reitemeier, *Geschichte und Zustand der Sklaverei und der Leibeigenschaft in
Griechenland*, Berlin. The real beginning of historical research, however,
was made by Henri Wallon, *Histoire de l'esclavage dans l'antiquité*, I-III,
1847.[70]

Building upon the work of Wallon, Paul Allard, *Les esclaves
chrétiens*, (Paris, 1876), tried to prove the influence of early Christianity
on the transformation of slavery. Allard's emphasis on the religious life
and ethical problems was strongly challenged by Ettore Ciccotti, *Il tramonto
della schiavitù nel mondo antico* (Turin, 1899), who gave very little credit
either to Christianity or to Stoicism for the removal of slavery from ancient
culture.[71] According to Ciccotti, only the changes in economic life could
have made possible the amelioration of slavery. One year earlier, Eduard
Meyer had given his very important lecture, "Sklaverei im Altertum," in which
he presented the ancient period as a social and political unity in which the
origin, preponderance and abolition of slavery are explained principally by
political factors.[72] Meyer influenced strongly two scholars in this century
who wrote standard works which treat slavery: M. Rostovtzeff, *The Social
and Economic History of the Roman Empire* (Oxford, 1926), and W.L. Westermann,
The Slave Systems of Greek and Roman Antiquity (Philadelphia, 1955).[73]

---

[70]For a very illuminating history of scholarship about ancient slavery, see
Joseph Vogt, "Die antike Sklaverei als Forschungsproblem--von Humboldt bis
Heute," *Gymnasium* 69 (1962), 264-278 (also in his *Sklaverei und Humanität:
Studien zur antiken Sklaverei und ihrer Erforschung* [Wiesbaden, 1965], pp.
97-111).

[71]The fifth edition of Allard's book was published in 1914. Ciccotti's
book was translated into German, *Der Untergang der Sklaverei im Altertum*, in
1910.

[72]In his *Kleine Schriften* I (Halle, 1910), 169-210.

[73]A second edition of Rostovtzeff's work, revised by P.M. Fraser, appeared
in 1957. Westermann's book is an expansion of his 1935 article on "Sklaverei"
in Pauly-Wissowa, *RE*, Suppl. VI, 894-1068. See also W.W. Buckland, *The Roman
Law of Slavery* (Cambridge, 1908) and R.H. Barrow, *Slavery in the Roman Empire*
(London, 1928).

Since the death of Rostovtzeff in 1952 and of Westermann in 1954, the most striking feature of research about slavery in the ancient world is its intensity. Within a few years, scholars from many different lands have produced more titles on slavery than were seen in the previous forty years. There is now a concern for observing ancient society on its own terms, with sensitivity to the presuppositions of the writers of that time and of our own forms of thinking. S. Lauffer writes:

> Die Antike in ihrer Eigenart anerkennen, das heißt hinsichtlich der Sklaverei in erster Linie, jede irreführende Modernisierung zu vermeiden. Darin sind sich wohl alle heutigen Beurteiler einig.[74]

Nevertheless, much work has yet to be done before scholars will be able to present a complete and convincing picture of slavery in ancient culture. Preparing this dissertation was made more difficult by the lack of any serious, full-scale history of slavery in the Greco-Roman world.[75] However this gap may be filled, research which directs its attention less to the abolition of slavery and more to its function in the Greco-Roman world will certainly convincingly demonstrate that no aspect of ancient culture can be fully understood without reference to the institution of slavery.[76]

B. *The Study of Slavery and Biblical Scholarship.*

It is argued that slavery "has always been a source of social and psychological tensions, but that in Western culture it was associated with

---

[74]S. Lauffer, "Die Sklaverei in der griech.-röm. Welt," *Gymnasium* 68 (1961), 373.

[75]The only recent book dedicated to slavery in this period, Westermann's *The Slave Systems of Greek and Roman Antiquity* (1955), is widely recognized to be unsatisfactory. Many historians and jurists have made strong objections to various points of his work. J. Vogt notes that he overlooked the connection between the political and social constitution of the state and the contemporary phases of the slave systems, and that the wide variety of gradations of freedom and half-freedom are neglected. "Die antike Sklaverei als Forschungsproblem," p. 274-275.
See also the reviews by P.A. Brunt, *JRS* 48 (1958), 165-68; H.J. Wolff, *Iura* 7 (1965), 307-315; G.E.M. de Ste Croix, *CR* n.s.7 (1957), 54-59; H. Strasburger, *HZ* 186 (1958), 600-608; and C.B. Welles, *AJP*, 77 (1956), 316-318. See also the comments by M.I. Finley, *International Encyclopedia of Social Sciences* (1968) XIV, 312.

[76]J. Vogt notes that the ancient philosophers never proposed the abolition of slavery, even when they had objections to various aspects of it. The concepts of philanthropy and humanity were valid essentially for the politically enfranchised citizenry. Vogt urges that we humanists of the twentieth century should take cognizance of this fact without reservation. "Die antike Sklaverei," p. 278.

certain religious and philosophical doctrines that gave it the highest sanction."[77] Such tensions may well lie behind the fact that in neither the *Lutherbibel* nor the *Authorized Version* does the word *Sklave* or *slave* appear.[78] Readers of these translations could have concluded that no actual slavery existed in the Biblical era, whereas more than 190 instances of Greek words referring to slavery or slaves can be found in the New Testament alone! Words like *bondage, service, maiden, bondsman* and *servant* are used. On this account E.J. Goodspeed observed: "Slavery is so disagreeable a subject that it has been almost obliterated from the English New Testament."[79]

Only recently have Jewish scholars begun to admit that any slavery at all could be found in Palestine or among Jews in the Diaspora after the return from the Exile in the fifth cen. B.C.; many Christian scholars accepted the earlier, apologetic claim that no slavery existed in the Second Commonwealth. For example, S. Krauss accepted *b. Arak.* 29a and parallels *b. Kidd,* 69a, *b. Gitt* 65a, which claim that there had been Jewish slaves only as long

---

[77]David B. Davis, *The Problem of Slavery in the Western World* (Cornell U. Press, 1966), p. ix. "Slavery had always been more than an economic institution; in Western culture it had long represented the ultimate limit of dehumanization, of treating and regarding a man as a thing." p. 10.

[78]Luther used the word *Knecht*. The word *Sklave* was in general use in Luther's time, often being employed to designate Turkish boys and girls. See the *Deutsche Wörterbuch* by J. and W. Grimm (Leipzig, 1905) X, 1313, quoted by G. Kehnscherper, *Die Stellung der Bibel und der alten christlichen Kirche zur Sklaverei* (Halle, 1957), p. 14.

A. Steinmann complained about the confusion that the translation with *Knecht* has caused. *Sklavenlos und alte Kirche: eine historisch-exegetische Studie über die soziale Frage im Urchristentum*[4] (M. Gladbach, 1922), p. 47. And A. Deissmann also remarked: "the word *slave* with its satellites has been translated *servant*, to the total effacement of its ancient significance, leading to our misunderstanding of many passages in the N.T." *Light from the Ancient East* (1927) p. 319 (trans. L.R.M. Strachan from *Licht vom Osten*[4], 1922, p. 271).

For a striking example of the false conclusions drawn by some historians from the fact that the *Authorized Version* never uses the term *slave* in translating δοῦλος in the New Testament, see E.J. Goodspeed, "Paul and Slavery," *JBR* XI (1943), 169-170. The word *slave* does appear in the A.V. two times: in Jer. 0214 and in Rev. 1813 for σῶμα.

[79]*The Meaning of Ephesians* (Chicago, 1933), p. 7 n. 4. Noting that slavery was an institution whose appropriateness was never questioned in ancient culture, E.J. Görlich has called upon translators of the Bible to accept this fact and to stop trying to disguise the actual situation by the use of the term *servant* instead of *slave*. "Sklaveco en la Antikva Proksima Oriento," *Biblia Revuo* 1 (1954), 46-51. It is very interesting that the term which does express the actual legal relationship, namely "slave," was avoided in translations which were made when very little was known about the varieties of slavery in the first century A.D.

as the Jubilee Year was observed, i.e., in the time of the first temple.[80]
George Foote Moore agreed with Krauss and concluded: "The rules found in
rabbinical sources about the Hebrew slave are purely theoretical....we may
safely infer that servitude had become obsolete long before the age of the
Tannaim."[81] As recently as 1966, Boaz Cohen wrote: "The institution of civil
bondage had completely disappeared already before the Babylonian exile."[82]

Already in 1923, Joachim Jeremias challenged this view, calling the

---

[80]*Talmudische Archäologie* II (Leipzig, 1911), 83. This conclusion is
reached not only in studies of a clearly apologetic character, which describe
the attitude of Judaism towards slavery in terms of a kind of abolition movement, such as M. Mielziner, *Die Verhältnisse der Sklaven bei den alten
Hebräern*, 1859; Z. Kahn, *L'Esclavage selon la Bible et la Talmud*, 1867; Jacob
Winter, *Die Stellung der Sklaven bei den Juden in rechtlicher und gesell-
schaftlicher Beziehung nach talmudischen Quellen* (Halle, 1886); Lazar Gulko-
witsch, "Der kleine Talmudtraktat über die Sklaven," *Angelos*, ed. Joh.
Liepoldt (Leipzig, 1925) I, 89; it is also the case in research primarily concerned with Jewish laws of slavery and the explanation of the legal processes,
such as S. Rubin, *Das talmudische Recht* (Vienna, 1920) and Boaz Cohen, *Jewish
and Roman Law: A Comparative Study* (N.Y.: The Jewish Theological Seminary,
1966).

In principle the Jubilee Year, the final year in a cycle of fifty
years, was the occasion for the automatic emancipation of a Jew who had become the slave of a fellow Jew sometime in the previous forty-nine years.
Not only does this Jubilee legislation, which first appears in the Holiness
Code (late sixth cen. B.C.), contradict absolutely the earlier, pre-exilic
legislation (Exod. 2102-6; Deut. 1512-18), but also "abundant evidence indicates unmistakably that this legislation never became effective in any manner." J. Morgenstern, "Jubilee, Year of," *The Interpreter's Dictionary of
the Bible*, ed. G. A. Buttrick, II (N.Y., 1962), 1001-1002. See also Robert
North, *Sociology of the Biblical Jubilee*, esp. the ch. on "Slave Release"
(Rome, 1964), pp. 135-157.

[81]*Judaism in the First Centuries of the Christian Era: the Age of the
Tannaim* (Cambridge, Mass., 1962; first published 1927) III, 185. See II,
138. In strong contrast P. Billerbeck wrote: "Die Frage, ob es in der n.t.
Zeit hebräische Sklaven bei den Juden gegeben habe, ist unbedingt zu bejahen."
"Das altjüdische Sklavenwesen," *Kommentar zum Neuen Testament aus Talmud und
Midrasch* IV (Munich, 1928), 698.

[82]*Jewish and Roman Law* I, 329. Roland de Vaux notes: "Certain writers,
and especially Jewish scholars, have denied that real slavery ever existed in
Israel; at least, they maintain, Israelites were never reduced to slavery.
... By *slave* in the strict sense we mean a man who is deprived of his freedom, at least for a time, who is bought and sold, who is the property of a
master, who makes use of him as he likes; in this sense there were slaves in
Israel, and some were Israelites." *Ancient Israel, Vol. 1: Social Institutions* (N.Y. 1965; trans. J. McHugh, *Les Institutions de L'Ancien Testament*,
1957), p. 80.

texts cited by Krauss "pure speculation."[83] He wrote:

> What is certain is that Josephus assumes that the Old Testament
> precept (Ex. 22.2), by which a Jewish thief who could not pay
> the necessary compensation had to be sold as a slave, is valid
> for Herod the Great's time; he reports how the king tightened
> up the regulation concerning this (*Ant.* 16.1f).[84]

Then in 1959, E.E. Urbach published an excellent major article in which he
argued that in the whole of ancient society "slavery was taken for granted
as a factor basic to political, economic, and social life. From this point
of view, the Jewish people formed no exception."[85] Urbach rejects the
opinion that most laws regarding Jewish slaves are purely theoretical, arguing that precisely these slave laws mirror faithfully the various conditions
of the three periods he distinguishes in the time between the Second Temple

---

[83]*Jerusalem in the Time of Jesus: an Investigation into the Economic and
Social Conditions during the New Testament Period* (Philadelphia, 1969), p.
110. Trans. F.H. and C.H. Cave, *Jerusalem zur Zeit Jesu*[3] (Göttingen, 1962),
with author's revisions to 1967. Even though Jeremias usually calls a *slave*
a *slave*, J. Vogt faults him for confusing real slaves with bondsmen and for
wanting to describe the slaves in the country settings of Jesus' parables as
"day labourers." "Sklaventreue," *Sklaverei und Humanität: Studien zur
Antiken Sklaverei und ihrer Erforschung*, p. 93, referring to Jeremias,
Jerusalem zur Zeit Jesu[3], p. 125, n. 3 (Eng. p. 110, n. 5).

[84]*Jerusalem in the Time of Jesus*, p. 111. Whether or not a slave was of
Jewish extraction is not very important, since most Gentile slaves accepted
circumcision and so became Jews (they were given a year in which to decide
to become Jews, and if they refused, they were sold to non-Jews).
  Note also that Flavius Josephus was himself a freedman of the
Emperor. Assuming the correctness of the standard text for Acts 0609, there
was a specific synagogue in Jerusalem made up of Jewish freedmen who were
former captives of Rome (or children of former captives), who had been manumitted and had returned to Jerusalem.

[85]E.E. Urbach, "The Laws Regarding Slavery as a Source for Social History
of the Period of the Second Temple, the Mishnah and Talmud," *Papers of the
Institute of Jewish Studies, London*, ed. J.G. Weiss (Jerusalem, 1964) I, 1-94.
The citation is from p. 4. This article appeared originally in Hebrew in
Zion XXV (1959/60), 141-189; trans. R.J. Loewe.
  Against those scholars who have said that there was never any slavery in Israel (see n. 82 above), R. North writes: "We shall maintain that
there was countenanced in the Bible a *true slavery* but a humane one. It was
a paternal refuge for the impoverished and a sanctuary for conquered aliens.
Its restriction was not primarily in the interest of the individual but to
preserve a wholesome distribution of independent ownership, operating in connection with the tribal customs of marriage and inheritance." *Sociology of
the Biblical Jubilee*, p. 135.

and the end of the fourth century A.D.[86]

Before Urbach's work appeared in English, Solomon Zeitlin also published a long article against the previous, apologetic scholarship, writing that the claim that there were no Jewish slaves during the Second Commonwealth "contradicts everything that we learned from the tannaitic literature....During the Hellenistic period, slavery was an important institution upon which the social and economic structure of the country was based."[87]

Urbach, Zeitlin and Jeremias have made major breakthroughs in clarifying the intimate connection between real slavery as an institution and the social and political conditions in Palestine and the Diaspora in the first century A.D. Lauffer, Vogt and others have emphasized the high importance of understanding the functions of slavery in the Greco-Roman world, if ancient culture in general is to be correctly understood. The work and admonitions of these scholars should now be heeded seriously by New Testament scholars, especially in the English-speaking world, in order that their own presuppositions and conclusions might reflect an increasing awareness of those social realities in which the first Christians acted and thought.[88] Such research

---

[86]Urbach concludes: "It cannot be said that the juridical treatment of slavery in halakhic texts is such as to add any very glorious chapter to the history of Jewish ethics; but insofar as it does constitute a reflection of social realities in the period of the Second Temple and that of the Mishnah and Talmud, the student of ethics in Israel has no more right than has the social historian to close his eyes to it." p. 94.

[87]S. Zeitlin, "Slavery during the Second Commonwealth and the Tannaitic Period," *JQR* 53 (1962/63), 185-218. Citations from pp. 194, 198. Zeitlin concludes: "In this essay it was demonstrated that slavery existed in Judea during the Second Commonwealth and the tannaitic period. The sages like the Stoics did not condemn the institution but endeavored to ameliorate the condition of the slaves by improving their status. They strove to impress the people that slaves are human beings and should be treated humanely. The sages were opposed to the sale of Judaean slaves outside of Judaea and to foreigners and favored the manumission of gentile slaves." pp. 217-218.

[88]The lack of helpful scholarship in English is emphasized by the fact that no articles on "Slavery in N.T. Times" or any thing similar appear in the recent and usually quite reliable *Interpreter's Dictionary of the Bible*, 1962. Important German contributions, corresponding to the advances in understanding made by the ancient historians, have been: Franz Overbeck, "Über das Verhältnis der alten Kirche zur Sklaverei im Römischen Reich," *Studien zur Geschichte der alten Kirche* (Chemnitz, 1875), pp. 158-230; Th. Zahn, "Sklaverei und Christentum in der alten Welt," *Skizzen aus dem Leben der alten Kirche* (Erlangen, 1898), pp. 116-59; Adolf Deissmann, *Licht vom Osten*[4] (Tübingen, 1923), pp. 270-281 and *passim* (*Light from the Ancient East*, pp. 318-330 and *passim*); K. H. Rengstorf, art. "*doulos*," *ThWNT* (1935), II, 264-283 (*TDNT*, II, 261-280); Henneke Gülzow, *Christentum und Sklaverei in den ersten drei Jahrhunderten*, (Bonn, 1969). See also Gülzow, "Kallist von Rom: ein Beitrag zur Soziologie der römischen Gemeinde," *ZNW* 58 (1967), 102-121.

is not only indispensable for a better understanding of texts such as 1 Cor. 0721, which deal directly with the institution of slavery, but also for a more accurate perception of the entire social, economic, legal and political fabric of the first century A.D.

CHAPTER II

THE INSTITUTION OF SLAVERY IN FIRST-CENTURY GREECE

In distinction from the treatments of 1 Cor. 0721 which have already been published, I seek in this chapter to define with some precision what it meant to be a slave in Corinth in the middle of the first century A.D. This intention to be specific forces me to avoid any attempt at a general definition of slavery, and it challenges the reader to put aside his ideas about Negro slavery in the nineteenth century, ideas which pervasively distort the modern comprehension of slavery in other periods and cultures.

Fortunately, we have a large amount of primary evidence on which to base a description of slavery in the first century A.D.[89] Of exceeding importance for understanding what slavery was like in Corinth are the records, taken from various walls of the sacred precinct of Apollo at Delphi, of more than one thousand manumissions of slaves which took place between 200 B.C. and A.D. 75.[90]

It is not the purpose of this chapter to discuss every topic which might be thought pertinent to a full treatment of the institution of slavery in this period. Rather, I describe only those aspects of slavery which are necessary for understanding the situations from which and to which Paul was speaking, especially in 1 Corinthians. The manner in which the relevant features of the institution of slavery are introduced is ordered by 1 Cor. 0721 itself:

A. "Were you a slave when you were called?"

   1. Definitions of "slave" and "slavery."

   2. Sources of slaves.

   3. Paul's knowledge of slavery.

   4. Slaves in the Corinthian congregation.

---

[89] For a comprehensive listing of the important references by historians, satirists, philosophers and other writers as well as in the Latin inscriptions see R. H. Barrow, "Appendix I," *Slavery in the Roman Empire*, pp. 237-246. For a very helpful listing of the reliable secondary literature see M. I. Finley's "Bibliographical Essay," in *Slavery in Classical Antiquity*, ed. M.I. Finley, 2nd edn. (New York, 1968), pp. 229-236.

[90] Most of these inscriptions can be found in Collitz-Baunack-Bechtel, *Sammlung der griechischen Dialektinschriften (GDI)* II (Göttingen, 1899), nos. 1684-2342; *Bulletin de correspondance hellénique* XXII (1898) 9-140 (121 documents, ed. G. Colin); and *Fouilles de Delphes III: Epigraphie*, parts 1,2,3, and 6 (Paris, 1929-39), eds. E. Bourguet, G. Colin, G. Daux, A. Salač, and N. Valmin. A full discussion of the manumission inscriptions can be found in G. Daux, "Delphes au IIème et Ier siècle," *Bibliothèque des écoles françaises d'Athènes et de Rome* CXL (Paris, 1936), esp. pp. 46-209.

B. "Don't worry about it."

   1. First-century views of slavery.

   2. The treatment of slaves.

   3. The positions of slaves and freedmen in society.

   4. The slave's view of his situation.

C. "But [even] if you are [indeed] able to become free ..."

   1. The owners' reasons for manumission.

   2. The owners' methods of manumission.

   3. The options open to the slaves.

An excursus on "sacral manumission" is included in this chapter as background for 1 Cor. 0722.

A. "Were You a Slave When You Were Called?"

   1. *Definitions of "slave" and "slavery."*

     No single definition has succeeded in comprehending the historical varieties of slavery or in clearly distinguishing them from other types of involuntary servitude.[91] With regard to slavery in the Greco-Roman Empire, no ancient writer suggests a general definition of slavery, either as an institution or as a status.[92] For example, even Aristotle's famous phrase, "the slave is a living tool and the tool a lifeless slave,"[93] is not a definition but rather a description by metaphor which occurs in a closely-knit argument regarding friendship and justice in political relations.[94] Aristotle's phrase, however, does raise sharply the chief question in the legal definition of a slave: is it a thing or is he a person?

     In Roman society the answer is ambiguous; in Roman law the answer is clear: the slave is a "thing" (*res*), a "chattel" (*mancipium*), a "mortal

---

[91] David B. Davis, *The Problem of Slavery in the Western World*, p. 35.

[92] Westermann comments: "The Romans did no better than the Greeks in maintaining distinctions between the political, and the individual and legal, applications of their terms *servitus* and *libertas*." "Between Slavery and Freedom," *American Historical Review* 50 (1945), 214. Furthermore owning and using slaves were such normal parts of daily life in the Greco-Roman world that the slave as a social phenomenon hardly became an object of reflection. No distinct literature περὶ δούλου or περὶ δουλείας has come down to us. Will Richter notes that the writing of Antisthenes entitled περὶ ἐλευθερίας καὶ δουλείας does not deal with the institution of slavery as such. "Seneca und die Sklaven," *Gymnasium* 65 (1958), 198.

[93] *Nicomachean Ethics* VIII.11, (Bekker, 1161^{a}30-^{b}19).

[94] This friendship cannot exist between an owner and his slave *qua* slave; but *qua* man the slave can be a friend. "For there seems to be some justice between any man and any other who can share in a system of law or be a party to an agreement." *The Nicomachean Ethics of Aristotle*, trans. Sir David Ross (London, 1925), p. 212. (See Bekker,^{b}1161 3-6.)

object" (*res mortales*).[95] In this law, slavery is defined as an institution in which someone is subject to the *dominium* of another person "contrary to nature" (*Digest* 1.5.4.1).[96] *Dominium* was full legal power over a corporeal thing, the right of the owner to use it, to take proceeds from it and to dispose of it freely.[97] Thus the slave of a Roman was an object of buying, renting and selling; damage to this slave was damage to property; and several persons at once could own him, as if he were a field.[98]

The slave himself had no rights or duties. If he committed crimes, his owner could pay the damages or give him to the injured party. He had access to the courts only through a freedman or freeman acting as his mediator (and then only with regard to his slave status). The penalties inflicted on him were generally severer than those to which freemen were exposed. He could neither enter public life nor join the army. He could have no real family. Any children born to a female slave belonged to her owner, and slave "marriages" were considered *contubernia* and not *matrimonia*.[99] In short, that which separated the Roman slave from all other employees was the totality of his powerlessness in principle.[100]

---

[95]*Digest* 21.1.23.3. Although the *Digesta Iustiniani* first appeared in fifty books in 533, it can be referred to the first century A.D. in most cases because it summarizes the entire Latin legal tradition. See the article by this title in Adolf Berger, *Encyclopedic Dictionary of Roman Law*, Transactions of the American Philosophical Society, New Series Vol. 43, Part 2 (Philadelphia, 1953), pp. 436-437. See also the "introduction" to Roman law written by Gaius, a learned lawyer of the second century A.D. The essential text, translation and commentary are by F. de Zulueta, *The Institutes of Gaius*, I (1946), II (1953). Roman slave law is expounded with massive erudition by W.W. Buckland, *The Roman Law of Slavery* (The Condition of the Slave in Private Law from Augustus to Justinian), Cambridge, 1908.

[96]As the one institution which was common to all peoples of the Mediterranean world, slavery was reckoned as *iuris gentium*. Yet, contrary to Aristotle, Roman law held all men to be free by nature, and therefore judged slavery (the result of war) to be contrary to nature. H.J. Jolowicz notes that slavery is the only case in Roman law in which a discrepancy between "nature" and the *iuris gentium* can be found. *Historical Introduction to the Study of Roman Law* (Cambridge, 1952), p. 105.

[97]The term *dominium* first appears at the end of the Republic. See Berger, *Dictionary of Roman Law*, p. 441.

[98]John Crook, *Law and Life of Rome* (Cornell U. Press, 1967), pp. 55-56.

[99]See Berger, "Servus" in *Dictionary of Roman Law*, p. 704.

[100]M.I. Finley notes that while the law may declare a man powerless and rightless in a formal way, one reason such a law is enforceable is that the slave lacks any counterweight or support, whether from a religious institution, from a kinship group, from his own state or even from other depressed groups in the society in which he has become a slave. "Slavery," *International Encyclopedia of the Social Sciences*, ed. D.L. Sills (Macmillan Co., 1968), XIV, 307-308.

Yet a slave was also a man. In many ways there was little difference between a slave and a son in the household of a Roman citizen with respect
to the legal power of the father, except in ultimate expectations. That is,
the father had "the power of life and death" over son and slave alike; and
neither of them could own anything. They both acquired a *peculium* only with
the permission of the *paterfamilias*. Deliberate killing of either son or
slave was murder.[101]

At his manumission the slave of a Roman citizen could become a
citizen himself. Likewise, a Roman citizen could be reduced to slavery if
convicted of certain crimes.[102] Many slaves had Roman citizens as their
fathers. Thus Crook concludes:

> In spite of the Roman law's insistence on sharply distinguishing
> between slave and free, the evidence suggests that in social,
> cultural and economic terms there was something much more like
> a 'continuum' of statuses, quite apart from labour conditions
> in which the free worker might be worse off than the slave.[103]

This "continuum" between slave and free which was regularly experienced in
Roman circles had been made a regular part of the Greek law under which many
slaves at Corinth lived.[104]

---

[101] Crook, *Law and Life at Rome*, pp. 56-57.

[102] See Crook, pp. 272-273.

[103] Crook, p. 58.

[104] In order to understand slavery in first-century Corinth we must take
account of *two* legal systems. For as Fritz Pringsheim comments: "Greek
notaries did not merely ignore Roman law, but openly rejected it." He calls
attention to the "tough resistance of popular Greek conceptions to Roman influence." *The Greek Law of Sale* (Weimar, 1950), pp. 481, 483. For example,
Pringsheim has shown that the eastern provinces rejected Roman laws concerning
buying and selling slaves and animals. "Ausbreitung und Einfluss des Griechischen Rechtes," *Sitzungsberichte der Heidelberger Akademie der Wissenschaften*,
Philosophisch-Historische Klasse (1952), p. 14. See also Hans Volkmann, "Die
römische Provinzialverwaltung der Kaiserzeit im Spiegel des Kolonialismus,"
Gymnasium 68 (1961), 406-407.

For example, a slave living under this peregrine law during the first century A.D. was often granted the right of private ownership, and to this extent he was considered a person.[105] While the domestic slave living under Greek law quite often had no possessions, this was not the result of his inability to own property but rather of the unfavorable situation of his kind of slavery. That is, as a domestic slave he was rewarded not with money but with food and shelter.[106] Thus some domestic slaves sought and obtained

---

Ever since the work of Ludwig Mitteis, *Reichsrecht und Volksrecht in den östlichen Provinzen des römischen Kaiserreiches* (Leipzig, 1891; reprinted 1935), jurists have concerned themselves with the problem of clarifying the relations between the provincial and Roman laws. John Crook notes that "it would be desirable to distinguish, even in our period [early Empire], in the provinces, between Roman law proper between citizens, provincial Roman law when peregrines came into the Roman courts, 'provincial practice' (*i.e.* the adoption of local institutions by the Roman courts), peregrine law proper as between peregrines in their own courts, and 'peregrine practice' (*i.e.* the adoption of Roman rules by peregrines). *Law and Life of Rome,* p. 284; see also pp. 29-30.
Note that there is nothing comparable to Gaius (see above, n. 95) for Greek law. Mitteis has shown that every Greek *Polis* had its own law, but that we are justified in referring to "Greek Law" as long as we are aware that significant and unknown differences probably existed from city to city. Pringsheim ("Ausbreitung und Einfluss," pp. 6-7) concludes that just as we speak of a "koine" language so we may speak of a "koine" law. For Athens, then, the best work is G.R. Morrow, *Plato's Law of Slavery in its Relation to Greek Law* (U. of Ill. Press, 1939). For slavery in Greco-Roman Egypt we have R. Taubenschlag, *The Law of Graeco-Roman Egypt in the Light of the Papyri (332 B.C.-A.D. 640)*, 2nd edn. (Warsaw, 1955), pp. 66-101. Specifically for manumission practices in Greece we now have Herbert Rädle, *Untersuchungen zum griechischen Freilassungswesen* (diss. Munich, 1969).
The fact that Roman law was not automatically used everywhere in the Empire, esp. in the East, has rarely been noted by N.T. scholars. See, e.g., L.K. Jang, who simply assumes (quite probably wrongly) that Roman law was applicable in first-century Asia Minor in the case of Onesimus and Philemon. *Der Philemonbrief,* pp. 16-18, 42-45. See above, p. 15, n. 31.

[105]Westermann, *Slave Systems,* p. 122. See also L. Mitteis, *Reichsrecht und Volksrecht,* pp. 71-72, and R. Taubenschlag, *The Law of Graeco-Roman Egypt,* pp. 87-89.

[106]H. Rädle, *Untersuchungen zum griechischen Freilassungswesen,* pp. 131-132.

permission to take employment beyond their normal assignments.[107] In addition, unique to Greek practice was the slave who lived apart from his owner,
held a job or conducted an independent business and was obligated to pay his
owner a certain percentage of his income.[108] On the other hand, Roman influence on first-century Greek practice can be seen by the use of the term
τὸ πεκούλιον (from the Latin *peculium*) in the manumission inscriptions from
Delphi.[109]

Nevertheless, because of their clear legal distinction between
slave and free, Roman citizens in Corinth must have found the Greek laws regarding slavery somewhat confusing. For in Greek law, slavery was not separated from freedom by a sharp dividing line. Furthermore, even the slave who
did receive full legal freedom did not gain any kind of citizenship with his
manumission.[110]

Under Greek law, freedom was broken down into four elements, as
Westermann has convincingly shown on the basis of the more than one thousand
manumission inscriptions found at Delphi.[111] He describes these elements as
follows:[112]

1. The freedman (ἀπελεύθερος or ἐξελεύθερος) is to be his own
representative, i.e., his own master in all legal matters, without need of

---

[107]Rädle, p. 133 and pp. 158-167.

[108]For example, a group of slave shoemakers worked for three obols a day
per person, two of which had to be handed on to their owner. Each one was
free to use his remaining obol as he wished. Such slaves as these were called
μισθοφοροῦντες ("pay-earners") or χωρὶς οἰκοῦντες ("those who live apart"),
between whom there was no legal difference. See Rädle, p. 8 and Westermann,
Slave Systems, p. 31.

[109]Mitteis, *Reichsrecht und Volksrecht*, pp. 382-383.

[110]In most cases the freedman of a Greek owner had the same legal status as
a metic. So, e.g., he could not go to court alone; he had to have a representative, often his former owner. See Rädle, *Freilassungswesen*, p. 135. In
first-century Corinth a person in slavery under Roman law who was set free
might become a Roman citizen (*civis*) if his owner was one, or a *Latinus
Iunianus* (in which state he was legally free but was not a citizen and could
not make a testament) if he was only informally manumitted, or a *dediticius*
(in which he had freedom but no public rights) if he had been enslaved because
of a crime. For more exact legal definitions of these terms, see Berger,
Dictionary of Roman Law, pp. 389, 427, 537.

[111]Rädle (p. 144) also thinks that Westermann is correct in using the four
characteristics of freedom mentioned in the Delphic documents as the basis for
deriving a general definition of Greek slavery.

[112]"Slavery and the Elements of Freedom in Ancient Greece," *Quarterly Bulletin of the Polish Institute of Arts and Sciences in America* I (1943), 341.
See also his "Between Slavery and Freedom," p. 216.

any intervention by a second party. (This is the legal expression of freedom.)

    2. The freedman is not subject to seizure as property. He cannot be taken into custody, except by due process of the laws applying to free men.

    3. He may do what he desires to do, i.e., he may earn his living as he chooses.

    4. He may go where he desires to go, or (in a variant form) he may live where he desires to live.

In order to understand the significance of slavery to the slaves of Greek owners in Corinth, it is especially important to notice that the granting of the first of these freedoms was enough to establish "freedman" status. As Westermann observes:

> Each of the three remaining freedoms, once the legal status was fixed, could be broken into, or impinged upon. A freedman might be in posession of any one, or any two, of the three elements other than legal recognition which were the necessary components of complete freedom.[113]

With his freedom the slave of a Greek owner received control of his person and his goods, even of those things that belonged to him when he was a slave (including other slaves).[114] But this freedom, which could be so comprehensive, was in fact quite often rigorously limited. Any of the last three elements of freedom could be restricted for a period of time as a condition of manumission. For example, a freedman could be obligated to pay a certain fee each month to his former owner, or to pledge to care for him or his family, or to provide a certain quantity of wine each month. At the death of his manumittor, the freedman might have to pay money into the inheritance. Such restrictions were regulated by a legally recognized contract.[115] Not seldom, these limitations were so severe that the situation of a freedman was

---

[113]"Slavery and the Elements of Freedom," p. 343.

[114]Rädle, *Freilassungswesen*, p. 83.

[115]This contract to remain within certain restrictions was called ἡ παραμονή. The precise nature of such contracts is debated and has provoked much scholarship; for a long footnote on the history of this scholarship, see C. Bradford Welles, "Manumission and Adoption," *Mélanges Fernand De Visscher II, Revue Internationale des Droits de L'Antiquité* III (Brussels, 1949), pp. 512-513.

as bad as when he had been a slave, or even worse.[116]

From the four "freedoms" mentioned above, we may conclude (following Westermann) that the major personal restrictions which determined full slave status under Greek law were as follows:

1. In all legal actions the slave must be represented by his owner or by some other person legally empowered by the owner.

2. The slave is subject to seizure and arrest by anyone (the Latin *manus iniectio*). (This applied with particular emphasis to fugitive slaves.)

3. The slave cannot do what he wishes, but must do what his owner orders.

4. He cannot go to those persons or places to which he may wish to go, or live in the domicile in which he desires to live, or determine to which community he belongs.

To be a slave under Greek law, then, was to be legally restricted in many ways. Yet, as we have seen above, such a slave could own property and might even become an independent handworker or businessman. In addition, the various degrees of legal freedom enjoyed by freedmen resulted in a continuum of statuses between "slave" and "free," which makes it difficult to formulate a short and simple definition of "slavery" in first century Corinth.

Even under Roman law, in which the distinction between "slave" and "free" is much clearer, the actual social and economic functions of those in slavery indicate that a continuum of statuses existed also in Roman society in Corinth. Furthermore, there were many slaves under both legal systems who enjoyed far more favorable living conditions than many free laborers.[117] There was no "color line" between slave and free in Corinth. Contrary to Aristotle, there was no single and clearly defined slave-race or slave-caste.

Westermann speaks of the "astonishing fluidity of status in both directions, from slavery to freedom as from freedom to slavery."[118] How the slave became free is discussed below. Understanding how free men became slaves will help clarify the meaning of slavery to the slaves in first-century Corinth.

---

[116] See M. Bloch, *Die Freilassungsbedingungen der delphischen Freilassungsurkunden* (diss. Strassburg, 1914), p. 25. Westermann notes that these limitations had the result of making "illusory in some degree a liberty which was unquestionably and legally granted." "Slavery and the Elements of Freedom," p. 343.

[117] For a description of many of the free poor people under Roman rule, see P.A. Brunt, *JRS* 48 (1958), 168.

[118] "Slavery and the Elements of Freedom," p. 346. Westermann attributes the lack of slave-revolts in the Greek classical period to this fluidity.

2. *Sources of slaves.*

Prior to the first century A.D., the chief means by which people were taken into slavery were by being captured in war or being kidnapped by pirates. The establishment of law and order within the Empire finally eliminated piracy and greatly reduced the stealing of persons for the purpose of enslavement.[119] With the cessation of the great wars of conquest after the death of Augustus, the primary source for slaves became breeding.[120] That is, under both Greek and Roman law, children born to mothers who were in slavery became slaves at birth. During the first century A.D., most of the people in slavery appear to have come from within the Empire, usually from the same area in which they were born. For example, all the slaves mentioned in the Delphic manumission inscriptions which date after 100 B.C. had been born in their owner's house.[121] These inscriptions also indicate that after 90 B.C. all slaves manumitted there came from Greece.[122]

The importance of breeding as a source of slaves in the first century A.D. has been stressed by P. Brunt, who concludes that this source alone would have been adequate to maintain the slave population of the previous century.[123] But being born to a mother in slavery was by no means the sole entrance into slavery in the first century. Many people sold themselves into slavery. Children were sold into slavery or were "exposed" and (if found) raised as slaves. Some freedmen made the final payment on their manumission by giving a child to their former owner. Some women became slaves because they insisted on living with men who were in slavery. Other persons became

---

[119]A.H.M. Jones, "Slavery in the Ancient World," *The Economic History Review*, 2nd ser., 9 (1956), 193 (also in Finley's *Slavery in Classical Antiquity*, p. 9).

[120]Note that just a few years after Paul wrote to Corinth, the Jewish War (A.D. 66-70) opened a new source of slaves for the Empire. Vespasian sent 6,000 Jewish prisoners to Nero as a labor force for the (unsuccessful) cutting of a canal through the Isthmus of Corinth. See Josephus, *History of the Jewish War*, Bk. III, 540.

[121]Rädle (p. 72) notes that at Delphi house-born slaves are listed as οἰκογενής (*GDI* 1692, 1693) ἐνδογενής (*GDI* 1684, 1695) ἐγγενής (*GDI* 2092) or as θρεπτός, θρεπτή (Colin 110, 113).

[122]Prior to the first century B.C. a number of Jews and Egyptians were among those manumitted at Delphi. The Jews were probably brought to Delphi after having been enslaved at the time of the Maccabean revolt. See Salo W. Baron, *A Social and Religious History of the Jews* I, 2nd edn. (New York, 1952), p. 259.

[123]*JRS* 48 (1958), 166. Brunt correctly challenges the commonly held assumption that the slave population declined in the first-century; he refers to the growth of slave numbers in nineteenth-century America--precisely by breeding. Approximately 600,000 Negroes had been imported up to 1860, yet the slave population at that time was 4,500,000.

slaves because they did not fulfill their contracts as freedmen. Some were enslaved for non-payment of taxes, and others as punishment for criminal acts. And on the borders of the Empire, kidnapping (man-stealing) continued to be a means of enslaving men.[124]

Slavery was by no means an ideal situation, but it was often much better than modern men are inclined to think, not only in the time of Homer and classic Athens, but also in the Empire. In both Greece and Italy, large numbers of persons even sold themselves into slavery; they did so for a variety of reasons, among which were to find a life that was easier than they had as freemen, to secure special jobs, and to climb socially.

Speaking to a Greek audience, Dio of Prusa remarked:

> Great numbers of men, we may suppose, who are free-born sell themselves, so that they are slaves by contract, sometimes on no easy terms but the most severe imaginable.[125]

The "contract" Dio mentions probably included a time limit and perhaps also provisions for the care of the slave's family. Greek law recognized the validity of selling oneself, and such sales were frequent in the eastern provinces in imperial times.[126] Temporary self-sale had been known in Jewish circles for centuries.[127]

---

[124]Stealing men and selling them into slavery had been practiced in the Near East for many centuries. For example, Albrecht Alt has shown (referring to Ex. 2116 and Deut. 2407) that the eighth commandment of the Israelites ("You shall not steal," Ex. 2015) originally prohibited not theft in general but kidnapping (the stealing of persons), specifically the kidnapping of a free Israelite man. (The waylaying of dependent persons, such as women, children, and slaves, was covered by the tenth commandment). "Das Verbot des Diebstahls im Dekalog," *Kleine Schriften zur Geschichte des Volkes Israel* I (Munich, 1953), 333-340. See also the recent discussion of this topic by J.J. Stamm and M.E. Andrew, *The Ten Commandments in Recent Research*, Studies in Biblical Tehology, 2nd ser. no. 3 (London, 1967), pp. 101-107. See also I. Mendelsohn, *Slavery in the Ancient Near East* (Oxford, 1949), p. 5.
The term ὁ ἀνδραποδιστής ("kidnapper" or "slavedealer") in 1 Tim. 0110 appears in a traditional "list of vices," indicating not only the evil reputation of such men but also the assumed knowledge of such activity at the end of the first century A.D. See Siegfried Wibbing, *Die Tugend- und Laster-kataloge im Neuen Testament* (Berlin, 1959), pp. 88-90.

[125]From Dio's 15th Discourse: "On Slavery and Freedom II," 23. English tr. J.W. Cohoon in the Loeb edn. of *Dio Chrysostom* II (Cambridge, Mass., 1939), 165. Dio also notes that there were men who were legally free who lived in the status of slaves because their so-called masters were not harsh with them. 15th Discourse, 13.

[126]See Barrow, *Slavery in the Roman Empire*, p. 12. Also Urbach, "The Laws Regarding Slavery," p. 9.

[127]See David Daube, *Studies in Biblical Law* (Cambridge, 1947), pp. 41-53. Also Urbach, "The Laws Regarding Slavery," pp. 9-15.

On the other hand, "temporary slavery" was a contradiction of terms in Roman law, and self-sale was continually questioned as a valid method of enslavement.[128] Yet during the first centuries of the Empire, increasing numbers of Roman citizens sold themselves into slavery in order to get some money and room and board.[129] The money such a citizen received for himself was the beginning of a peculium with which he might later enter freedom under more favorable circumstances, e.g., with his former debts extinguished.[130] There are also cases of self-enslavement in order to secure the position of *servus actor*, the chief accountant of a large private household. With normal luck this man could later become a freedman in the same post, finishing his life as a rich citizen with free-born children.[131]

The sources are so problematic that it is impossible to determine if a freeman could legitimately sell himself so as to make himself irrevocably a slave.[132] We can be certain, however, that Romans and Greeks did sell themselves into the practical situation of slavery; and if they were content to remain in slavery, no one ever knew the difference.[133]

Persons also sold themselves into slavery with the hope of finding later a place in Roman society as a freedman. For example, Trimalchio, the infamous freedman of the first century, had a guest who boasted:

> Actually my father was a king. Why am I only a freedman now?
> Because I handed myself into slavery of my own free will. I
> wanted to end up a Roman citizen, not a tribute-paying peregrine.[134]

---

[128] Barrow, *Slavery in the Roman Empire*, p. 12.

[129] M. Bang, *Mitteilungen des Deutschen Archäologischen Instituts, Römische Abteilung* 27 (1912), 221.

[130] A.H.M. Jones reports that during the early Empire, 500-600 denarii was the usual price for an unskilled adult. Much larger sums were paid for skilled men. Columella, writing under Nero, recommended paying 2,000 denarii for a trained vinedresser. "Slavery in the Ancient World," p. 194 (Finley, p. 10).

[131] Crook, *Law and Life of Rome*, p. 60.

[132] Crook (p. 60) comments: "the reason for this may well be that the law was not altogether in line with the facts of life at this humble level."

[133] Brunt notes that even those who had been stolen or exposed and taken into slavery might not attempt to establish their free origins, for not all would have wanted to recover "their freedom to starve." *JRS*, p. 167.

[134] Petronius, *Satyricon*, 57,4, trans. Crook, p. 60. For the text and commentary see Ludwig Friedlaender, *Petronius: Cena Trimalchionis* (Leipzig, 1906; reprinted Amsterdam, 1960), pp. 150-151, 293-294 (Bücheler, 4th edn., pp. 37-38). The prince continued: "I did my utmost to please my master, a splendid, dignified gentleman, whose little finger was worth more than the whole of you." After forty years in slavery, this prince bought his freedom and that of his partner in *contubernio*.

In addition, examples of self-sale by first-century Christians are found in the situation against which Paul speaks in 1 Cor. 0723 ("do not become slaves of men") and in 1 Clement 5502:

> We know that many among ourselves have given themselves to bondage (παραδεδωκότας ἑαυτοὺς εἰς δεσμά) that they might ransom others. Many have delivered themselves to slavery (ἑαυτοὺς παρέδωκαν εἰς δουλείαν) and provided food for others with the price they received for themselves.[135]

Selling one's children into slavery was also widely practiced, especially in the eastern part of the Empire.[136] In Roman society, the sale of children was frowned upon, but the seemingly less humane practice of abandoning infants in deserted places (*exponere filium*) was permitted.[137] If rescued, such children were usually raised as slaves. Their actual legal status was debated throughout the first century A.D., especially in the case of a later assertion of the child's freedom by the parents in view of the cost to the rescuer of raising and perhaps educating the child.[138]

Also in first-century Greece, many children whose parents had been slaves were handed into slavery by their fathers or mothers, who were

---

[135]Referring to 1 Cor. 0723, A. Robertson and A. Plummer claimed that a prohibition not to sell oneself into slavery "could not be needed." *A Critical and Exegetical Commentary on the First Epistle of St. Paul to the Corinthians*, International Critical Commentary, 2nd edn. (Edinburgh, 1914), p. 149. But in view of the frequent practice of self-sale, particularly in the eastern Empire, and in view of the straightforward meaning of 1 Clem. 5502, such a prohibition would indeed make good sense. Commenting on 1 Clem. 5502, Gülzow notes: "Der Selbstverkauf in die Sklaverei bedeutete in damaligen Zeiten nichts Außergewöhnliches." *Christentum und Sklaverei*, p. 79.

[136]With reference to Jewish society, Urbach states that "an extremely frequent phenomenon was the selling of daughters as slaves by their fathers" (when the girl reached 12 years she could no longer be sold). "The Laws Regarding Slavery," pp. 15-18.
   According to Philostratus, Apollonius of Tyana said that "with the Phrygians it is a fashion even to sell their children, and once they are enslaved, they never think any more about them." *The Life of Apollonius of Tyana*, VIII, 7, tr. F.C. Conybeare, Loeb edn. (Cambrdige, Mass., 1950), II, 337.

[137]Brunt, *JRS*, p. 167. A.R. Hands notes a series of quotations gathered by Stobaeus which suggest that the "cruelty" shown to those children who were "exposed" was viewed by their parents as a proper means for assuring that those who were allowed to survive would not have to endure poverty. *Charities and Social Aid in Greece and Rome* (London, 1968), p. 70.

[138]This problem is discussed in a rescript of Trajan in A.D. 112, replying to an inquiry by Pliny the Younger about the status of such children when free-born. See A.R. Hands, pp. 70-71, and Westermann, *Slave Systems*, p. 30.

obliged to "reimburse" their former owners with a child as the final condition of full manumission.[139]

At Delphi, the punishment for non-fulfillment of such a *paramonê*-contract (the terms of which could be quite varied) was physical chastisement or return to slavery.[140] That is, under Greek law the manumission could be declared void, resulting in re-enslavement. Under Roman law, a freedman who refused to maintain his poverty-stricken *patronus* (former owner), or who plotted against him, or who treated him with contempt could be charged with "ingratitude" (*ingratus*). If convicted, he could be fined, flogged, or exiled.[141] Shortly before Paul wrote to the Corinthians, Claudius declared that he would always give judgment against a freedman, and he is reported even to have ordered re-enslavement in certain cases.[142]

Although not a large number of Corinthians became slaves by "re-enslavement," this possibility points to the actual narrowness of the line separating many freedmen from slavery. One attempt to keep clear the distinction between slave and free, which nevertheless indicates that clarity was often lacking, is the *Senatusconsultum Claudianum* of A.D. 52. This formal decree by the Roman Senate contained a provision that a free woman living in a conjugal union with a slave (*conturbernium*) would become a slave of her lover's owner (along with her children) if after three warnings by his owner she continued her relation with the slave.[143] It was also a short step into slavery for those freemen in Greece who were convicted of non-payment of their taxes.[144]

In 1 Cor. 0721a, Paul asks, "Were you a slave when you were called?" The foregoing attempt to define the institution of slavery in first-century Corinth and the description of the variety of sources for slaves in this period have illuminated the complex and diversified nature of the legal status

---

[139]Rädle (*Freilassungswesen*, pp. 151-152) observes that in the time of Claudius and Nero, the freedmen on Calymna (an Aegean island) were regularly required to deliver a child born after manumission to their former owners. There is also evidence from Delphi that the deliverance of a child as a condition of a valid manumission was practised already by 40 B.C.; and in the second half of the first century A.D., such post-manumission "reimbursements" became very common.

[140]See Rädle, pp. 82-84, for the formulas used in these conditional manumissions.

[141]Barrow, *Slavery in the Roman Empire*, p. 192.

[142]*Digest* 37.14.5. The whole question of "re-enslavement" was raised anew in Nero's reign and became the subject of a debate in the Senate.

[143]See Berger, *Dictionary of Roman Law*, p. 697.

[144]Westermann, *Slave Systems*, p. 30.

to which Paul referred. Now it may be asked: how much personal contact with slaves and slavery did Paul have before asking this question?

3. *Paul's knowledge of slavery.*

In an attempt to delineate Paul's probable contact with slaves and his knowledge of the various laws regarding slavery, I describe briefly the kinds of slavery Paul saw from Tarsus to Corinth, the attitudes toward slavery with which he was familiar as a Jew and the evidence that he was aware of Greek and Roman legal procedures.

In Tarsus, the city of his birth, Paul probably saw relatively few men in slavery. Many of the tasks performed by slaves in other places, such as linen weaving, dyeing, leather cutting and carpentry, were the jobs of freemen in Tarsus.[145] His first contact with a major center of slavery may have been in Tyre, through which he passed on his way to Jerusalem. Indeed, most of the Gentile slaves of both sexes, from Syria and beyond, came to Jerusalem through Tyre's large slave-market.[146]

In Judea and Jerusalem, Paul undoubtedly saw many slaves working in a wide variety of activities, including positions of high responsibility in the court of Herod and the families of the high priests.[147] Around Jerusalem itself there seem to have been no industries requiring slaves nor many rural estates which used slave-labor in large numbers.[148] But within the city, Paul saw great numbers of domestic and civil slaves, both Jew and Gentile; and he probably was acquainted with the special stone (אבן הלקח), set close to the cattle market, from which slaves were auctioned.[149]

As he traveled through Asia Minor, Paul came upon increasingly large slave populations in the cities where "the total of the slave population may have been about one third of the entire body of residents, as

---

[145] Dio Chrysostom 34,23. Westermann assumes that the use of slaves in Cilicia remained small after the suppression of Cilician piracy by Gnaeus Pompey. Also inscriptions from eastern Phrygia show a very small number of slaves in private ownership. *Slave Systems*, p. 126.

[146] Jeremias, *Jerusalem in the Time of Jesus*, p. 36. See also J. Vogt, "Sklaventreue," p. 94.

[147] Zeitlin, "Slavery during the Second Commonwealth," p. 198. Also Urbach, "The Laws Regarding Slavery," p. 33.

[148] Jeremias, p. 345.

[149] Krauss, *Talmudische Archäologie* II, 87, 362. Zeitlin (p. 198) claims that no such stone ever existed in Judea; but Jeremias (p. 36) accepts Krauss's evidence, calling on *Siphra Lev.* 25.42; *Siphre Deut.* 26 on 3.23.

intimated by Galen for Pergamum."[150] In Ephesus, e.g., slaves were involved
in the widest thinkable range of activities, including working in the local
wholesale and distributing agencies and managing retail stores. When Paul
supported himself as a leather-worker in association with Aquila and Prisca
(1 Cor. 1619) in Corinth and Ephesus, he quite probably worked alongside
craftsmen who were slaves.[151]

The closer Paul came to Rome, the more he found the institution of
slavery to be an essential part of the economy and a normal part of the life
of most families.[152] How had his Jewish background prepared him to react to
this major aspect of Greco-Roman society?

That there were, in fact, many slaves in Jerusalem in the first
century A.D. has been shown above (pp. 31-34). In a major article, E.E.
Urbach has convincingly argued that much of the extensive Halakhic literature
dealing with slavery pertains directly to the social and political conditions
in first-century Jewish Palestine.[153] Thus, the complicated traditions and
laws which Paul learned, regulating the relationships between Jewish slaves
and Jewish owners, between Gentile slaves and Jewish owners, and between
Jewish slaves and Gentile owners, were *not* theoretical but were descriptive
of his immediate social and legal environment. Indeed, even when worshipping
in the Temple, Paul saw many slaves assisting the high priests in their minis-
trations.[154]

---

[150] Although household slavery persisted in the homes of the wealthy town-
dwellers and on large country estates, the number of slaves in the towns,
villages and rural areas was relatively small. Westermann, *Slave Systems*,
p. 127.

[151] In Tarsus Paul would have learned his craft from freemen, but in these
large coastal cities many slaves were used in the handicrafts.

[152] Paul was moving from a *slave-owning* economy to the edge of a genuine
slave-economy. See M.I. Finley "Was Greek Civilization Based on Slave
Labour," *Slavery in Classical Antiquity*, pp. 53-72, and Finley's good article
on "Slavery" in *International Encyclopedia of the Social Sciences*, ed. D.L.
Sills (New York, 1968), XIV, 308.

[153] "The Laws Regarding Slavery As a Source for Social History of the Period
of the Second Temple, the Mishnah and Talmud" (see above, p. 33 n. 85 for the
complete reference). This excellent article supersedes most of the previous
scholarship on Jewish slavery in this period. The complicated details of the
rabbinic controversies about slavery which took place between the Maccabean
wars and the destruction of Jerusalem in A.D. 70 are described on pp. 31-50.
See above, footnotes 81-85 (pp. 32-33), for references to other
works on Jewish slavery which are still valuable in specific ways.

[154] For example, according to one tradition, the men in the flute section of
the Temple orchestra were in slavery. See Urbach, p. 32 n. 8 for references.
Urbach also notes (p. 33) that some slaves reached eminent positions and seem
to have become assimilated into the priestly stock.

As a Jew, Paul was acquainted with self-sale into slavery, the sale of children into slavery, the enslavement of debtors who could not pay and of thieves who could not pay their fines.[155] He also knew about time-limited slave-contracts, for it was said that "one who sells himself into slavery may be sold for six years, or for more than six; one sold by order of the court may be sold for six years only."[156] Although the conveyance of the slave's person to the owner was not absolute in all cases, the Jewish owner did have complete control of a Jewish or Gentile slave's time, of his employment and of his freedom of movement.[157] In Jerusalem as well as in Corinth, Paul saw slaves whose special abilities made it favorable to their owners to rent them by the day or by contract.[158] In short, Paul was already acquainted with a variety of the sources and practices of real slavery before he left Jerusalem.

As he traveled west, however, Paul must have noticed that the slaves of Gentiles lacked the unusual legal protection granted to slaves under Jewish law. For under this law the Jew who became a slave was required to receive such good treatment that Jews who were anxious to sell themselves into slavery often could not find Jewish purchasers.[159] Because of these regulations it was said: "Whenever one acquires a Hebrew slave he acquires a master."[160] In contrast, a Roman proverb ran: "So many slaves, so many enemies."[161]

---

[155] See Zeitlin, "Slavery during the Second Commonwealth and the Tannaitic Period," pp. 186-195. Also Jeremias, *Jerusalem in the Time of Jesus*, pp. 312-314.

[156] *b. Qidd.* 14b. See Urbach, p. 9.

[157] Urbach, p. 30.

[158] Urbach, p. 28.

[159] The principal Old Testament texts pertaining to the status and treatment of slaves are: Ex. 2102-11, 20-21, 26-27; Lev. 2539-55; Deut. 1512-18, 2110-24, 2315-16. These texts are not consistent within themselves and for this reason encouraged a large amount of rabbinic commentary and controversy. Lev. 25 introduced a distinction between Hebrew slaves and Gentile slaves which strongly favored the Hebrew slave. (I. Mendelsohn speaks of this national distinction as "a new element" in the slave laws of the Ancient Near East, *Slavery in the Ancient Near East* [New York, 1949], p. 90.) The significance of this Pentateuchal distinction for the conditions of slavery in the first century is questionable. For "slavery became an influence contributing towards proselytism, and there were many who were accepted into the Jewish faith *via* this route." Urbach, p. 48. At the moment of his emancipation such a convert became a Jew in the fullest sense. Not infrequently such a freedman married his owner's daughter. See Urbach, p. 48.

[160] *b. Qidd.* 22a. See Urbach, p. 50. "In equating the law for the slave with that for the free man, the Pharisees were set apart fundamentally from all approaches to the subject known from hellenistic law." Urbach, p. 38.

[161] *Quot servi, tot hostes*; quoted by Seneca, *Ep.* 47,5, and others. See S. Lauffer, "Die Sklaverei in der griech.-röm. Welt," *Gymnasium* 68 (1961), 376.

53

As Paul went west, he was moving from societies in which the institution of
slavery was very useful and yet was questioned, into societies in which the
institution was necessary and thus apparently was unchallenged.[162]
The enslavement of Hebrews had been questioned on grounds that they
had become slaves of God at the Exodus. Thus to become slaves of men would
be to forsake their true service. Yet in the first century Jews were indeed
in real slavery to other Jews as well as to Gentiles. The tension which this
created is reflected in a notable explanation (*b. Qidd.* 22b) of the ceremony
of piercing the ear-lobe of a slave who preferred to stay with his owner beyond the six year period of his slavery (Ex. 2106, Dt. 1517).[163] It was with
his ear that the man in slavery had heard God proclaim:

> For to me the people of Israel are slaves, they are my slaves
> whom I brought forth out of the land of Egypt: I am the Lord
> your God. (Lev. 2555)

Because the ear heard these words and nevertheless broke the yoke of heaven
and substituted subjection to a human yoke, it was judged worthy of being
bored for not having observed what it had heard. The slave who forfeited his
freedom was said thereby to have violated the special relationship between
God and Israel.[164]

---

[162]How little Seneca thought about ever questioning the institution of slavery as such, e.g., can be seen from his *De tranqu. an.* 9,3. See Will Richter, "Seneca und die Sklaven," *Gymnasium* 65 (1958), 211.

[163]Urbach notes this interpretation of Ex. 2106, but he prefers the explanation of "ear-boring" given in a homily attributed to R. Yohanan b. Zakkai, in
which it is the ear that heard the commandment "do not steal" but which nevertheless allowed its possessor to steal (and thus to be enslaved as punishment)
that is to be bored if the slave wants to stay in slavery longer than six
years. See Urbach's discussion of the history of these traditions, pp. 10-13.
In any case, the explanation given in *b. Qidd.* 22b is a reflection of a real
tension in Jewish society and theology.

[164]In a very interesting article, "Concessions to Sinfulness in Jewish Law,"
Journal of Jewish Studies X (1959), 1-13, David Daube calls attention to the
Jewish practice of consciously building into the law institutions or practices
which were in conflict with the "ideal order." For example, the monarchy in
Israel was a detraction from God's rule, even though it was conceded by God
and introduced under his guidance; ideally there should be no king over Israel except Yahweh. Another example is polygamy, which for the rabbis was
legally correct, but which was widely rejected as below the standard set for
man by God. A third example is slavery, in that the children of Israel are
slaves of God who forsake their true service if they become slaves of men.
Daube concludes that "a Jew voluntarily continuing in slavery thereby repudi-
ates God who, by redeeming the people from the hand of Pharaoh, became their
master in a very special sense" (p. 4). From this viewpoint Daube remarks:
"Paul's argument in 1 Cor. 7:21, 23, it may be noted, is strictly parallel."
See the exegesis of these verses in chap. 5, below.

Whether or not Paul was aware of this explanation of Ex. 2106 on the basis of Lev. 2555 is not clear.[165] In any case, it is highly probable that Paul knew that the Essenes had rejected slavery and that they challenged this institution on the grounds that it tempted men to act unjustly.[166] Josephus reports that the Essenes "neither marry wives nor are desirous to keep slaves, thinking that the latter tempts men to be unjust and the former gives a handle to domestic quarrels."[167] These dangers, of course, are mentioned in the Old Testament; the Qumran sect, however, distinguished itself from the rest of Palestinian Judaism by a more thorough-going attempt to avoid them.[168]

---

[165] It is conceivable that this explanation (if it existed in the first century) might have influenced Paul's expression in Gal. 0501: "For freedom Christ has set us free; stand fast therefore, and do not submit again to a yoke of slavery" (RSV).

[166] It is less certain that Paul was aware of the rejection of slavery by the Alexandrian "Therapeutae," on the basis that it was against nature (παρὰ φύσιν). According to Philo, "they do not have slaves to wait upon them as they consider that the ownership of servants is entirely against nature. For nature has borne all men to be free, but the wrongful and covetous acts of some who pursued that source of evil, inequality (ἀνισότητα), have imposed their yoke and invested the stronger with power over the weaker." *De vita contemplativa* 70, tr. F.H. Colson in the Loeb edn., *Philo* IX (1941), 157 (Cohn-Wendland VI, 64,18-65,4). Philo's description of the Palestinian Essenes' attitude toward slavery also appears to reflect a Stoic influence: "Not a single slave is to be found among them, but all are free, exchanging services with each other, and they denounce the owners of slaves, not merely for their injustice in outraging the law of equality (ἰσότητα λυμαινομένων), but also for their impiety in annulling the statute of Nature (θεσμὸν φύσεως), who mother-like has born and reared all men alike, and created them genuine brothers (ἀδελφοὺς γνησίους)." *Quod omnis probus liber sit* 79, tr. Colson, Loeb edn., *Philo* IX, 57 (Cohn-Wendland VI, 23,2-6).
   The Essenes and the Therapeutae appear to be the only groups in the first century who challenged the institution of slavery in principle.

[167] Trans. W. Whiston of *Antiquities* XVIII,21: καὶ οὔτε γαμετὰς εἰσάγονται οὔτε δούλων ἐπιτηδεύουσιν κτῆσιν, τὸ μὲν εἰς ἀδικίαν φέρειν ὑπειληφότες, τὸ δὲ στάσεως ἐνδιδόναι ποιῆσιν. On the basis of the Qumran texts and Thucydides' style, John Strugnell has defended both the "substantial accuracy of the theological information of Josephus, in his explanation of the reasons for the attitude of the Essenes towards wives and slaves" and the many scholars, including Whiston, who "have rightly taken these reasons chiastically." "Flavius Josephus and the Essenes: *Antiquities* XVIII,18-22," *JBL* 77 (1958), 110.

[168] D. Daube suggests that the Essenes rejected slavery because the "perfect community of the end" was to return to the "ideal state of the beginning." "Concessions to Sinfulness in Jewish Law," p. 5. No such explicit claim, however, can be found in the Qumran texts themselves. Indeed, ownership of slaves is assumed in the Damascus Document (*CD*), according to which "no one

The Old Testament warnings must have been included in Paul's rabbinic education, for they were kept alive in such sayings as the one attributed to Hillel, which runs: "Whoever multiplies female slaves multiplies promiscuity and whoever multiplies male slaves multiplies thieving."[169] This saying expresses compactly that which Paul as a rabbinic Jew must have known and felt about slavery, namely an acquaintance with the enslavement of both Jews and Gentiles for a variety of reasons and in a variety of circumstances, a knowledge of the attempt in Jewish law to consider the slave as a person rather than a thing, and a dissatisfaction with the institution itself because of the injustices which it encouraged. This was Paul's background, then, when he asked, "Were you a slave when you were called?" What, then, did he know about the actual legal situation of the Corinthians?

By the time Paul wrote "1 Corinthians," he had been moving in Gentile circles for some years and had lived among the Corinthian Christians for at least eighteen months (Acts 1811). Persons in slavery were among the first converts in Corinth. Paul must have come to know something about their daily lives. Beyond the natural assumption that during this period Paul became acquainted with Greek and Roman manumission practices,[170] do we have any evidence that he was made aware of the Corinthians' legal circumstances? Many scholars have suggested that Paul was strongly influenced by legal ideas beyond those with which he was acquainted as a Pharisee.[171] In particular,

---

is to put pressure on his male or female slaves or hired help on the Sabbath" (11:12), "nor is he to sell to them (heathen) any of his male or female servants that may have joined him in the Covenant of Abraham" (12:20). On the other hand, nothing about social-legal slavery is mentioned in the other Qumran texts checked by K.G. Kuhn for his concordance. In these texts, the term עבד appears only in metaphorical usage; e.g., "God's slaves, the prophets" in *1QS* 1:3. See Kuhn, *Konkordanz zu den Qumrantexten* (Göttingen, 1960), p. 154 and "Nachträge zur 'Konkordanz zu den Qumrantexten'," *Revue de Qumran* 14 (1963), 213. This silence regarding legal slavery does allow room for the accuracy of Josephus' report. The apparent contradiction of *CD* may be accounted for by recognizing various "orders" within the Qumran congregation, each following slightly different rules. See Frank Cross, *The Ancient Library of Qumran*, 2nd edn. (New York, 1961), p. 83, n. 46.

[169] *Aboth* II,8. See the text, trans., and commentary given by R.T. Herford, *The Ethics of the Talmud: Sayings of the Fathers* (New York, 1962), pp. 48-49.

[170] Manumission was a frequent occurrence under both systems of law.

[171] See, for example, the long bibliography given by A. Deissmann in *Light from the Ancient East*, pp. 318-319 n. 2 (*Licht vom Osten*, 4th edn., pp. 270-271 n. 3).

three recent articles have been written to show that certain aspects of Paul's
linguistic usage are best explained by the assumption that he was familiar
with Roman legal concepts. Greer M. Taylor has argued that Paul's use of
πίστις in Gal. 0216, 0220, and 0322 indicates that he was aware of the testa-
mentary procedure called *fidei commissum*.[172] Taylor also maintains that *fidei
commissum* was a device familiar to non-Romans in Paul's era who had no particular technical competence in Roman law.[173] Taking up Taylor's suggestions,
Francis Lyall, an historian of Roman law, scrutinized Paul's uses of the notion of adoption in R 0815, 0823, 0904, Gal. 0405, and Eph. 0105.[174] He notes
that the concept which Paul uses was foreign to Jewish law, and he concludes
that Paul appeals in these verses to the concept of adoption current in Roman
law.[175]

In another article Lyall correctly concludes that the way in which
Paul uses the term ἀπελεύθερος ("freedman") in 1 Cor. 0722 also indicates
that he was familiar with Greek and Roman legal practice.[176] For according

---

[172]"The Function of ΠΙΣΤΙΣ ΧΡΙΣΤΟΥ in Galatians," *JBL* 85 (1966), 58-75.
After noting the parallels in Roman law to the relationship Paul describes in
these verses, Taylor brings his argument further by noting that "πίστις is
the Greek word both generally and technically used to translate *fidei commissum*" (p. 73).

[173]Taylor stresses that his argument does not depend on the assumption that
Paul was a citizen (although he does not dispute the fact) or that he was
specially trained in Roman law. Rather, Taylor emphasizes the wide-spread
knowledge of Roman law that existed among non-Romans in the first century,
especially regarding such matters as inheritance. See pp. 73-74. The Greek
and Roman laws regarding enslavement and manumission must have also belonged
to such "common knowledge."

[174]"Roman Law in the Writings of Paul--Adoption," *JBL* 88 (1969), 458-466.

[175]Lyall writes: "I conclude that Paul's use of the term 'adoption' in
Romans, Ephesians, and Galatians was a deliberate, considered, and appropriate reference to Roman law" (p. 466). In this case Greek law had only a
pale shadow of the Roman concept of *patria potestas*, which lies at the root
of Roman family law and best explains Paul's use of adoption-language.
    Lyall affirms that Paul was a Roman citizen and a Jewish lawyer, and
and he notes not only the tendency of lawyers "to pick up knowledge of systems other than that of their training" but also the fact that "Roman law was
the system having paramount jurisdiction over him as a citizen." Lyall, pp.
465-466. According to the Book of Acts (esp. 2225-28), Paul was born as a
civis Romanus and was acquainted with the legal rights which he possessed as
a Roman citizen. See Adrian N. Sherwin-White, *Roman Society and Roman Law
in the New Testament* (Oxford, 1963), pp. 57-68 and 151-156, for a thorough
and positive evaluation of the evidence in Acts regarding Paul's citizenship.
Note that Paul himself never mentions his citizenship; it is not clear from
1 Cor. 0901-19 if Paul meant to emphasize his status as that of an *ingenuus*
("free-born").

[176]"Roman Law in the Writings of Paul--The Slave and the Freedman," *NTS* 17
(1970), 73-79.

to Jewish law, the manumission of a slave effected his complete liberty, breaking all bonds of servitude or obligation towards his former owner.[177] Yet in 0722 Paul is clearly using the word ἀπελεύθερος to describe a continuing relationship: "A slave who has been called in the Lord is the Lord's freedman." The background for this phrase is to be found in Greek and Roman law, both of which required the freedman to live in a legal (and usually personal) relation to his former owner.[178] Such a freedman's obligations to his patron were often extensive.[179]

Urbach notes the influence of Greek law on Jewish manumission practices,[180] which means that Paul may have been acquainted with this aspect of Greek law before he left Jerusalem. In any case, ἀπελεύθερος (which appears in the New Testament only in 0722) is precisely the word that was used in Greek-speaking Roman provinces to describe the slaves who were manumitted by the local inhabitants in accord with their own usage.[181] The fact that this term does not appear in the Septuagint is an additional indication that in 0722 Paul is presupposing a Greek or Roman legal procedure.[182]

On the basis of Paul's residence among the Corinthians, his employment of Roman legal concepts which were commonly understood, and especially his use of ἀπελεύθερος in 1 Cor. 0722 to describe a definite, continuing relationship to Christ, I conclude that Paul was certainly familiar with the Greek and Roman legal situations in which the Corinthian Christians were living when he asked, "Were you a slave when you were called?". Beyond 1 Cor. 0721-22, then, what evidence does Paul give us that persons in slavery had become members of the congregation he gathered in Corinth?

---

[177] See Urbach, "The Laws Regarding Slavery," pp. 58-59.

[178] Lyall (pp. 78-79) argues for the primary influence of Roman law on Paul's expression in 0722 on the grounds that the relationship between a freedman and his patron under Roman law was lifelong, while under Greek law this relationship was regulated by a *paramonē*-contract which was valid for a limited period of time after which the former slave became completely free from his former owner.

[179] As has been noted above, pp. 48-49, the slave who was manumitted under Greek or Roman law remained, in a certain measure, subject to the authority of his former owner to whom he was obliged to render specified services. If the freedman viewed these duties with insufficient seriousness, he could expect to be punished, exiled or even re-enslaved.

[180] "The Laws Regarding Slavery," pp. 60-61.

[181] According to Urbach (p. 61), there are inscriptions which indicate that the freedmen of Romans who lived in Greek-speaking provinces were referred to as οὐινδικτάριοι (from the Latin *vindicta*--a form of Roman manumission).

[182] See Edwin Hatch and Henry A. Redpath, *A Concordance to the Septuagint and and Other Greek Versions of the Old Testament* (Oxford, 1897) ·I, 120. The verb form ἀπελευθεροῦν is used for שֻׁפְחָה ("to be freed") which appears only in Lev. 1920.

4. *Slaves in the Corinthian congregation.*

Although it is difficult to determine how many persons were in slavery in Greece during the early Empire,[183] it is safe to conclude that at least one-third of the urban Corinthian population in the first century A.D. were slaves.[184] Corinth's expanding economy (using industrial and maritime slavery) and a growing interest in a Roman "life-style" (which required a large number of household slaves) among the freedmen suggest a percentage at least this high.[185] An additional, large percentage of the people were freedmen; i.e., they had been in slavery at some point in their lives. Life as a slave was or had been the experience of as many as two-thirds of the

---

[183]Henri Wallon noted that Demetrius of Phalerum (born ca. 350 B.C.) reckoned 20,000 citizens, 10,000 metics and 400,000 slaves for Athens in his day, and 460,000 slaves for Corinth. Wallon commented that these figures were greatly exaggerated and then concluded that in Athens there were 19-21 thousand citizens, about as many metics and a total of 100,000 slaves. That is, two-thirds of the total population were in slavery. He assumes the same ratio for Corinth in that period. "Du nombre des esclavages en Grèce, et particulièrement en Attique," *Histoire de l'esclavage dans l'antiquité*, 3rd edn. (Paris, 1879), p. 224.

[184]In his review of Westermann's *Slave Systems* (*JRS* 48 [1958], 165), P.A. Brunt estimates that in the first century of the Empire, slaves made up more than one-third of the *total* population of Italy. Although Westermann holds that in many provinces slavery was less prevalent in the early Empire than in the late Republic, Brunt points to Galen's figures for Pergamum which strongly suggest that even under the *pax Augusta* slavery remained very important in prosperous Greek cities.

[185]During the first centuries B.C./A.D., Corinth may well have become the eastern "clearing house" for the slave-trade. Until the middle of the last century of the Republic, Delos had been the chief market for slaves. But after 48 B.C., the vast and picturesque activity of this market practically ceased to exist. The slave-dealers moved westward, and Rome became the new center of this business. But part of the slave-trade shifted only as far west as Corinth, as the slave name "Corinthus" seems to indicate. See M.L. Gordon, "The Nationality of Slaves under the Early Roman Empire," *JRS* 14 (1924), 94, 99 (also now found in *Slavery in Classical Antiquity*, ed. M.I. Finley [New York, 1968], pp. 172, 177). "Corinthus" is found in *CIL* v, 1305; vi, 11541, 3956 and 4454. Gordon (p. 99) notes that Varro (*De ling. lat.* viii. 21) "describes how a master might name his slave 'Ephesios' because he had bought him at Ephesus."

Corinthian population in the first century A.D.[186]

The best evidence we have that a number of these slaves were among the first members of the Christian congregation in Corinth is provided by Paul's reference in 1 Cor. 0116 to his baptizing the "household of Stephanas" (τὸν Στεφανᾶ οἶκον). In 1 Cor. 1615 Paul refers to these people as "the first converts in Achaia." Although it is not specifically stated that slaves were in this group, the terms translated "household" (οἶκος, οἰκία) in this context refer naturally not only to the immediate family but also to the other persons in the house, including the slaves.[187]

The first persons belonging to the Corinthian congregation whom Paul mentions by name are Κρίσπος and Γάϊος (0114). This Crispus is commonly identified with the ruler of the synagogue mentioned in Acts 1808.[188] This Gaius (as many as five distinct persons in the N.T. bear this name) is quite probably the man Paul mentions in R 1623, who not only was Paul's host but

---

[186]A substantial number of freedmen had lived in Corinth since its reestablishment in 44 B.C. Although most Roman colonies were founded as retirement towns for Roman veterans, Julius Caesar resettled Corinth with proletarian citizens of Rome, the majority of whom had been slaves. See Strabo, VII, 381, and Friedrich Vittinghoff, *Römische Kolonisation und Bürgerrechtspolitik unter Caesar und Augustus*, Abhandlungen der Geistes- und Sozialwissenschaftlichen Klasse 14 (Mainz, 1951), 87.

With regard to the persons in slavery in Corinth in Paul's time, note that Hans Conzelmann has recently shown that the often repeated supposition that there were many slaves owned by the Temple of Aphrodite who served as sacral prostitutes has no evidence to support it. "Korinth und die Mädchen der Aphrodite: zur Religionsgeschichte der Stadt Korinth," *Nachrichten der Akademie der Wissenschaften, Göttingen* I, Philologisch-Historische Klasse, 1967, Nr. 8, 247-261, esp. pp. 252-253. Conzelmann concludes (p. 260): "Strabos Behauptung über den Aphroditetempel in Korinth bezieht sich ausdrücklich auf die ferne Vergangenheit und schließt die Tempelprostitution für seine eigene Zeit aus....Belege ausser Strabo existieren nicht."

[187]See H. Gülzow who comments especially on the appearance of οἰκίαν Στεφανᾶ in 1 Cor. 1615, noting "daß οἰκία durchaus als Übersetzung des lateinischen *familia* gebräuchlich ist (z.B. Phil. 4,22) und damit erst recht auf die Sklaven deutet." *Christentum und Sklaverei*, p. 44. See also Heinz Kreissig, "Zur sozialen Zusammensetzung der frühchristlichen Gemeinden im ersten Jahrhundert u.Z.," *Eirene: Studia Graeca et Latina*, Československá Akademie Věd VI (1967), 99. (u.Z.=unserer Zeitrechnung). See also Walter Bauer, *A Greek-English Lexicon of the New Testament and Other Early Christian Literature*, trans. W.F. Arndt and F.W. Gingrich from the 4th German edn. 1952 (Chicago, 1957), p. 560. (Each citation from Bauer in this dissertation has been carefully compared with the 5th edn. of his *Griechisch-Deutsches Wörterbuch*, Berlin, 1963.)

[188]See H. Conzelmann, *Der erste Brief an die Korinther*, p. 43. (cited hereafter as *1. Korintherbrief.*)

who also hosted the "whole church in Corinth."[189] The "households" of such leading persons surely included a number of slaves,[190] and according to Acts 18 8 not only Crispus but "all his household" believed and were baptized.

Note also that it was "by Chloe's people" (ὑπο τῶν Χλόης) that Paul received the message that there was "quarreling" in the Corinthian congregation (1 Cor. 01 11). That is, some slaves belonging to a lady named Chloe brought Paul this message.[191] Whether or not Chloe herself was a Christian remains unclear. That her slaves were Christians seems certain, although it is difficult to determine whether they dwelled in Ephesus or in Corinth.[192] They may also count among the slaves in the Corinthian congregation.

A particularly interesting member of the Corinthian congregation mentioned by Paul is Ἔραστος ὁ οἰκονόμος τῆς πόλεως. "Erastus, the city treasurer."[193] He is assumed to be the treasurer of Corinth, and as such it is very probable that he was either a wealthy freedman or a slave with a large peculium.[194] Free men were willing to sell themselves into slavery in order

---

[189] E.J. Goodspeed suggested that this Gaius is the Titius Justus mentioned in Acts 18 7 (as a "worshipper of God" whose house stood next to the synagogue in Corinth). In this case, *Gaius* was his praenomen, *Titius* his nomen and *Justus* his cognomen. "Gaius Titius Justus," *JBL* 69 (1950), 382-383.

[190] See H. Kreissig, "Zur sozialen Zusammensetzung der frühchristlichen Gemeinden," pp. 98-100.

[191] See also "those who belong to the family of Aristobulus" (τοὺς ἐκ τῶν Ἀριστοβούλου) in R 16 10 and "those who belong to the family of Narcissus" (same Greek construction) in R 16 11. H. Kreissig (p. 99) is certain that these people were for the most part slaves.

[192] See H. Conzelmann, *1. Korintherbrief*, p. 46.

[193] Erastus was among those persons who were with Paul in Corinth when he wrote ch. 16 of "Romans" (whether or not this chapter was a part of the original letter to the Romans or was a separate letter to another congregation, such as Ephesus, is disputed) and who joined him in sending greetings to the congregation he addresses in that chapter (R 16 21-23).

[194] H.J. Cadbury has argued that in the Roman period οἰκονόμος in such a context as Corinth probably corresponded with *arcarius* (this is the Vulgate trans.). He adds that "the *arcarius* was invariably a slave or of servile origin though he may often have been wealthy." "Erastus of Corinth," *JBL* 50 (1931), 57.
   See also Cadbury, pp. 42-58, for an examination of the possibility of identifying the Erastus of R 16 23 with the Erastus mentioned in a Latin inscription from 50-100 A.D., found in Corinth in 1929. The inscription has been restored to read: *Erastus pro aedilitate sua pecunia stravit*, meaning that in return for his aedileship he paid for laying the pavement (in a plaza some sixty feet square). Cadbury concluded that this identification is possible but not probable. Oscar Broneer agrees with Cadbury, and observes that the offices are not the same, since *aedilis* in Greek is regularly ἀγορανόμος. *Biblical Archaeologist* 14 (1951), 94.

to secure such a desirable position.[195] Manumission with the opportunity to continue in this official position awaited a slave who did good work.

Unfortunately, no firm conclusions about social or legal status can be drawn on the basis of the names of the Christians in Corinth which are known to us from 1 Cor. and Romans 16. The rapid rate of manumission under Augustus Caesar had brought many names formerly used almost exclusively for slaves into the realm of freemen and citizens, with the result that in Greece in the first century A.D. there is hardly any name given to a slave which was not also worn by freemen and citizens.[196] Thus, contrary to the common assumption, no one in the early Christian congregations can be certainly identified as a slave on the basis of his or her name alone.[197]

Those Christians who were slave-members of urban households, such as those of Stephanas, Crispus and Gaius, were by no means the most debased section of Corinthian society. Rather, they usually enjoyed physical and psychological security and some even attained a certain prosperity.[198] Slaves who worked in the mines or on the large country-estates would have had no opportunity to share the life of the Corinthian congregation.[199] A slave's position depended largely on that of his owner; the only thing that slaves in the first century A.D. had completely in common was the fact of their enslavement. The slaves in the households which Paul mentions had, of course, Christian owners. Those to whom Paul speaks directly in 1 Cor. 0721cd may

---

[195]John Crook, *Law and Life of Rome*, pp. 187-188.

[196]M. Lambertz, *Die griechischen Sklavennamen* I (Vienna, 1907), II (Vienna, 1908), esp. II, 31. Lambertz derived his generalizations by comparing the names of more than 900 slaves and 8,000 freemen and citizens which he found principally in the Delphic manumission inscriptions which are dated between 200 B.C. and A.D. 75.

[197]Lambertz (II,24) observes, e.g., that Lucius is a Latin praenomen often borne by Greek slaves. But note also that this name was often borne by Roman freemen. So what can be said on this basis about the legal status of the Lucius whom Paul mentions in R 1621? The man called Φορτουνᾶτος whom Paul associates with Stephanas in 1 Cor. 1617 is most likely of all the persons known to us from Corinth to be identified as a slave (or freedman) on the basis of his name alone. The name *Fortunatus* is found in papyri and inscriptions in both Greek and Latin forms, and it is one of the most popular Roman slaves names. See M.L. Gordon, "The Nationality of Slaves," pp. 97, 106.

[198]See E.A. Judge, *The Social Pattern of Christian Groups in the First Century* (London, 1960), p. 60.

[199]C.F.D. Moule comments: "If the Christian Gospel had never reached down to the bottom, it is because the labour-gang type were incapable of being reached: who was there to preach to them, and how could he preach?" First, Christians themselves would have had to have been condemned to the mines. *The Birth of the New Testament* (London, 1966), p. 159.

have been from heathen households (note also Chloe's household).[200] In any case, there can be no doubt that a number of persons in the legal status of slavery were members of the Christian congregation in Corinth.[201]

How, then, are we to understand Paul's next phrase (0721b), when he advises: "Don't worry about it"? That is, what is the background which must be observed in order to "hear" these words as the Corinthian Christians may have heard them?

B. "Don't Worry About It."

In light of the conclusions that Paul had seen many Jews and Gentiles in slavery, that he was acquainted with Greek and Roman as well as Jewish laws and customs regarding slavery, and that a substantial number of slaves had become Christians at Corinth, the fact that he says very little about the institution of slavery in his letters may seem strange to the modern reader. What hindered Paul or Christian slaves and Christian owners from drawing the kind of social consequences from the Gospel which were drawn by the abolitionists in the nineteenth century? Paul's advice, "Don't worry about it," appears on the surface to be in tension with his own great concern for freedom.[202] In the case of a Christian who was enslaved to a human owner, was not "freedom" thought by Paul to be a positive good?

Paul's apparent indifference to the social and legal institution of slavery in the first century A.D. can be understood only in the broad context of the ways in which this institution was viewed during this period, the manner in which slaves were treated, the positions which slaves and freedmen

---

[200] If 1 Cor. 0721cd is read as a parallel to 0715 (where a Christian is married to an unbelieving spouse), the owners of these slaves may also be seen as nonbelievers.

[201] For discussion of 1 Cor. 0126-31 in light of the slaves in the congregation, see Josef Bohatec, "Inhalt und Reihenfolge der 'Schlagworte der Erlösungsreligion' in 1 Kor. 1,26-31," *Theologische Zeitschrift* 4 (1948), 252-257; and Ulrich Wilckens, *Weisheit und Torheit: Eine exegetische-religionsgeschichtliche Untersuchung zu 1 Kor. 1 und 2,* Beiträge zur historischen Theologie 26 (Tübingen, 1959), pp. 41-42.
For the suggestion that "those who have nothing" (1 Cor. 1122b) and who arrive late for the Lord's Supper at Corinth (1121,33) are slaves, see Günther Bornkamm, "Herrenmahl und Kirche bei Paulus," *Studien zu Antike und Urchristentum,* Gesammelte Aufsätze 2 (Munich, 1959), pp. 141-142; and Bo Reicke, *Diakonie, Festfreude und Zelos in Verbindung mit der altchristlichen Agapenfeier* (Wiesbaden, 1951), pp. 266-268. Bornkamm correctly rejects Reicke's assumption that a concern for "cultic purity" (i.e., that the Jewish Christians wanted to eat their meal before the Greek slaves arrived) explains 1 Cor. 1117-33. The contrast in this passage is not cultic but social. See also E. Schweizer, "The Service of Worship," *Neotestamentica* (Stuttgart, 1963), p. 334.

[202] See, e.g., 1 Cor. 0612b: "'All things are lawful for me,' but I will not be enslaved by anything." (*RSV*).

filled in society, and the attitudes toward slavery expressed by those men
and women who found themselves in slavery.

1. *First-century views of slavery.*

Owning and using men and women as slaves were such normal parts of
daily life in the ancient world, that the institution of slavery, as a social,
legal and economic phenomenon, seldom became an object of reflection.[203] No
ancient government ever sought to abolish slavery.[204] Furthermore, perhaps
the most striking sign that everyone in the Greco-Roman world thought that
slavery was an indispensable social institution is the fact that none of the
slave-rebellions in that world were caused by an intention to abolish the
institution of slavery as such.[205] All of the great slave-rebellions occurred
in the brief period between 140-70 B.C.; and in the cities where slaves came
to power, no revolutionary social programs were carried out in order to change
the legal or economic structures.[206] To the contrary, those who had been

---

[203] Will Richter, "Seneca und die Sklaven," *Gymnasium* 65 (1958), 198.

[204] Westermann, "Slavery and the Elements of Freedom," p. 347. M.I. Finley
comments: "To the ancient mind slavery was a fixed and accepted element of
life, and no moral problem was involved." *International Encyclopedia of the
Social Sciences,* XIV, 74.

[205] For example, the slave-wars in Sicily, the movement of Aristonicus in
Asia Minor, the revolt at the great slave-market on Delos, and the uprising
of Spartacus in Italy, all had as their goal the obtaining of personal freedom for the slaves involved. According to E.M. Štaerman, a Russian scholar
named Mušulins has argued that Spartacus wanted to abolish slavery. Štaerman,
who is also a Russian, comments that this author unfortunately gives no proof
from the primary sources for this opinion. In agreement with western scholarship, Štaerman concludes that no slave-rebellions tried to do away with slavery as such. *Die Blütezeit der Sklavenwirtschaft in der Römischen Republik,*
trans. Maria Bräuer-Pospelova from the Russian, Übersetzungen ausländischer
Arbeiten zur antiken Sklaverei 2 (Wiesbaden, 1969), pp. 214-16.
    Hermann Bengston summarizes very well the work of many scholars,
when he says: "Die Sklaven haben sich nie und nirgends erhoben, um die
Sklaverei als Institution abzuschaffen. Vielmehr wandten sie sich gegen die
teilweise unmenschliche Behandlung, sie erstrebten eine Verbesserung ihrer
Lage, zum mindesten aber Verständnis für ihre soziale Situation. Von der
Idee der Weltrevolution kann keine Rede sein." *Grundriss der Römischen
Geschichte mit Quellenkunde* I (Munich, 1967), 161.

[206] Joseph Vogt comments that it is always a little surprising to note that
the great slave-disturbances in the ancient world occurred in this comparatively short duration of seventy years. The reasons for these rebellions are
not altogether clear; bad treatment by their owners, especially in the mines
and on the great plantations (*latifundia*), appears to have been the primary
motive. "Zur Struktur der antiken Sklavenkriege," *Abhandlungen der Geistes-
und Sozialwissenschaftlichen Klasse,* Akademie der Wissenschaften und der
Literatur, Mainz, 1957, pp. 7-9 (also in his *Sklaverei und Humanität,* pp. 26-
28).

owners were forced into slavery; and the homes and workshops remained private property in the hands, then, of the former slaves.[207]

In addition, it is significant that none of the authors who had been in slavery, whose works are known to us, attacked the institution in which they had once lived.[208] They did write about the behavior (bad or good) of individual owners and slaves, but they never counseled the slaves to rebel. Indeed, no freedman-author comes near championing either slaves or freedmen as groups in themselves.[209]

For those writers who did reflect on slavery, the question was not whether slavery was essential to society but whether it was "natural" for those who were enslaved. For example, Alcidamas, a rhetorician of the fourth century B.C., expressed the "natural law" teaching of the Sophists when he wrote: "God has freed all men; nature has not made any man a slave."[210] But both Plato and Aristotle rejected this theory of natural law.[211] Aristotle, e.g., taught that δοῦλος had a double meaning: 1) the unfree position according to law; 2) the state of dependency of the "serving" man, who either has been created in his personal nature for serving or who stands in a "natural" position of dependency, such as a woman to a man or a son to a father.[212] These two conflicting opinions decisively determined the controversy over slavery until late antiquity. The sentiment of the Sophists was finally

---

[207] In an excellent article, S. Lauffer notes that the successful rebels took for themselves the titles of kings, bore Greco-Roman insignias of lordship, and began to build palaces, to mint coins and to organize armies. He concludes that it would be difficult to say that the slaves had any "revolutionary" goals when they in fact strove for personal, middle-class freedom and when they imitated the prevailing type of structure for state and society, including the institution of slavery. "Die Sklaverei in der griech.-röm. Welt," *Gymnasium* 68 (1961), 374-375.

[208] Susan Treggiari, *Roman Freedmen during the Late Republic* (Oxford, 1969), pp. 241-242.

[209] Treggiari, p. 243. She comments: "Most notable is Phaedrus' [a freedman] claim that slavery does not devalue a man's character or worth and that he and Aesop may occupy a high place in literature."

[210] Westermann suggests that this famous quotation from Alcidamas' *Messeniacus* came from the tradition of his teacher, Gorgias. For similar quotations from other Sophists, such as Antiphon and the comic poet Philemon, see the texts cited by Westermann, *Slave Systems*, pp. 24-25.

[211] For Plato, see G.R. Morrow, *Plato's Law of Slavery in its Relation to Greek Law* (University of Illinois Press, 1939).

[212] See the texts and discussion in S. Lauffer, "Die Sklaverei in der griech.-röm. Welt," pp. 391-392.

enshrined by the jurist Florentinus in the definition of slavery stated in Roman law: a slave is someone who is subject to the *dominium* of another person, contrary to nature.[213]

Whether or not the institution of slavery was regarded as "natural," there was no question among Greco-Roman writers that slavery was one of a number of relationships involving social and economic dependence which were essential to human society. It was the question of *personal* and *spiritual* independence, including the *inner freedom* of those persons who found themselves in slavery, which interested a variety of these thinkers.[214]

For example, the poet Sophocles, a contemporary of the Sophists, wrote: τὸ σῶμα δοῦλον· ἀλλ' ὁ νοῦς ἐλεύθερος ("the body a slave, but the mind free").[215] Socrates taught slaves as well as free men; he taught a free man that activities which the free man regarded as "slavish" were in reality "free."[216] W. Richter credits Menander with the phrase: ἐλευθέρως δούλευε· δοῦλος οὐκ ἔσει ("be a slave as though you were free--and you are not a slave!").[217] Bion, a freedman and a Cynic philosopher, called slaves who were morally good "free" and freemen who were morally bad "slaves."[218] Apparently lacking "inner freedom," King Antigonus Gonatas described the activity of governing as "honorable slavery."[219] Philo wrote a treatise

---

[213]*Digest* 1.5.4 ("servitus est constitutio iuris gentium, qua quis dominio alieno contra naturam subcitur") and *Digest* 21.1.23.3. Also see above, p. 39 n. 96.

[214]Lauffer (pp. 392-393) warns us that the legal standpoint has become so important to modern men that we have trouble taking seriously this "inner freedom." Such "freedom" appears to us rather to be spiritual resignation of a kind that covers over the "real problem." He suggests that a more appropriate historical perspective allows one to see that the more such "inner freedom" (which is irrelevant from the legal viewpoint) has been encouraged, the more often legal manumission has occurred as a by-product.

It is precisely this concept of "inner freedom" which was so noticeably lacking in the enslavement of men practiced in recent centuries. Those in "modern" slavery were taught to think of themselves as basically inferior to free men; and since they had no hope of ever being manumitted, they came to accept this judgment.

[215]*Fragment* 854 N². Will Richter notes: "Gerade diese Auffassung vom Problem des Sklaventums hat nun in der hellenistischen Welt ein lebhaftes Echo gefunden." "Seneca und die Sklaven," p. 209.

[216]Plato, *Meno*, 82b; Xenophon, *Memorabilia* II, 8.4.

[217]Richter comments that the idea of an ethical "inner freedom" existing at the same time as legal slavery began to be held by many thinkers at the time of the New Comedy poet Philemon (third century B.C.). "Seneca und die Sklaven," pp. 209-210.

[218]Bion, *Fragment* 2 = Stobaeus LXII, 42.

[219]Aelianus, *Varia Historia* II, 20.

entitled, "Every Good Man is Free," in which he argued as follows:[220]

> Slavery then is applied in one sense to bodies, in another to
> souls; bodies have men for their masters, souls their vices and
> passions. The same is true of freedom; one freedom produces
> security of the body from men of superior strength, the other
> sets the mind at liberty from the domination of the passions.[221]

Epictetus, freedman and philosopher, commented on a man just released from
slavery:[222]

> Has not the man to whom this had been done become free?--
> He has no more become free than he has acquired peace of mind.

Epictetus also traced the career of such a freedman who finally
became a senator by means of much flattery and many trials. When he entered
the senate, this former slave (in a legal sense), according to Epictetus,
entered "the handsomest and sleekest slavery."[223] For true slavery (as Arrian
reports Epictetus' words) is to live in deception, fear, grief, envy, pity,
unrestraint, with desire for unattainable things and with an abject spirit
(IV, 1, 1-5). True freedom, on the other hand, has nothing to do with legal
status but is the submission of one's freedom of choice to the will of God
(IV, 1, 89). That is, whatever external event happens is God's will; and true
happiness does not depend on external events but on an internal willingness to
yield to whatever happens. To possess such willingness is to possess "the
knowledge of how to live." How can such a one help but be the "master" (even
if he is legally a slave)? asks Epictetus (IV, 1, 118).

---

[220]Trans. F.H. Colson, Loeb edn., Philo IX, 17 (Cohn-Wendland VI, 5, 1-5).

[221]Philo continued: "No one makes the first kind [of slavery] the subject
of investigation. For the vicissitudes of men are numberless and in many
instances and at many times persons of the highest virtue have through adverse
blows of fortune lost the freedom to which they were born." Loeb IX, 18 (Cohn-
Wendland VI, 5, 5-8).

[222]Epictetus, II, 1, 27, tr. W.A. Oldfather, Loeb edn. (Cambridge, Mass.,
1925).

[223]Epictetus, IV, 1, 33-40. Regarding a Roman consul, Epictetus observed:
"If you hear him say 'Master,' in the centre of his being and with deep emo-
tion, call him a slave, even if twelve fasces [the number for a consul] pre-
cede him; and if you hear him say, 'Alas, What I must suffer!' call him a
slave; and, in short, if you see him wailing, complaining, in misery, call
him a slave in a *toga praetexta*" [the robe worn by high Roman officials].
IV, 1, 57, tr. Oldfather. Epictetus also called such a leader a μεγαλόδουλος
("a slave on a grand scale") IV, 1, 56.
See the discussion of Epictetus' concept of "freedom" by Dieter
Nestle, *Eleutheria: Teil I, Die Griechen* (Tübingen, 1967), pp. 120-135.

Because it comes from a former slave, this single-minded stress on the significance of "inner freedom" is particularly impressive. For although he uses the terms translated "free" (verb and adj.) and "freedom" more than one hundred and thirty times and seems to have set himself in principle against all restraints, at no time does Epictetus refer to legal freedom as a goal to be desired in itself.[224]

A similar lack of concern for the status of legal slavery can be found in the writings of the traveling Cynic preacher, Dio of Prusa (c. A.D. 40-c. 120?). After noting the variety of ways by which a person could become a slave and the variety in the behavior of persons irrespective of their legal status, Dio concluded that the social and legal status of slavery had nothing to do with the values which the philosophers held to be important.[225]

So, it was in a world in which everyone thought that legal slavery was an indispensable social institution ("natural" or not) and in which an increasing number of persons (including some who had been in slavery) believed that "inner freedom" was more important than legal freedom, that Paul asks: "Were you a slave when you were called?" and then advises: "Don't worry about it." To be sure, Paul's reasons for this advice are not the same as those of Epictetus or of Dio.[226] But what is important to notice at this point is that Paul's apparent lack of concern about legal slavery was by no means unique in the Greco-Roman world of the first century A.D.[227]

2. *The treatment of slaves.*

All this rhetoric about "inner freedom" could be understood as the paradoxical irony of free men or the resentful sarcasm of slaves if, in fact, those who were in slavery were not also increasingly recognized as human beings. It is indeed the case that the tendency of Roman legislation in the first and second centuries was to limit the power of the owner over his slaves

---

[224]Oldfather comments: "In youth he must have been almost consumed by a passion for freedom. I know no man upon whose lips the idea more frequently occurs." He notes that Epictetus uses the various terms for "freedom" with "a relative frequency about six times that of their occurrence in the New Testament and twice that of their occurrence in Marcus Aurelius." Epictetus, Loeb edn., I, xvii. For a good index of terms, see the standard edition of the Greek text by H. Schenkl, 2nd edn. (Leipzig, 1916).

[225]Dio Chrysostom 15, 29-32.

[226]See below, pp. 133-140, 151-154.

[227]Will Richter agrees with K.H. Rengstorf (*TDNT*, II, 272) against E. Lohmeyer (*Soziale Fragen im Urchristentum*, 1921), that Lohmeyer should not be surprised at the relative disinterest of New Testament writers in the social fact of slavery. "Seneca und die Sklaven," p. 211 n. 41.

and to guarantee more humane treatment to those in slavery.[228]

Joseph Vogt attributes the definite improvement in the lot of slaves in the first century to a combination of the teaching that ethical freedom could be enjoyed by those in legal bondage with a new social situation that strongly contributed to the credibility of this teaching.[229] This new social situation was the increasing number of slaves who were born in their owner's house.[230] These slaves were raised to serve in an increasing number of important and sensitive tasks. For slaves not only held high positions in the civil service and in the business world, they also attended their sick owners as doctors and nurses, their youthful owners as teachers and advisors, and their elderly owners as trusted companions and protectors.[231]

In slavery, as in marriage, the chief question remained: On whom was the slave or the wife or child dependent? For the only thing that slaves in the first century had completely in common was the fact that each of them had an owner.[232] A person's experience in slavery depended almost entirely upon the customs of the owner's family, the business and the particular class of society to which the owner belonged, and the character of the owner himself.[233]

---

[228] J.P.V.D. Balsdon states: "It is clear that from the first century A.D. onwards there was increasingly strong public disapproval both of the ruthlessness of the law and of the arbitrary power of masters." *Life and Leisure in Ancient Rome* (Toronto, 1969), p. 109. Administrative provision for both slaves and children, based on the feeling of *humanitas*, reached its peak in the second century A.D. See A.R. Hands, *Charities and Social Aid in Greece and Rome*, p. 87.

[229] "Wege zur Menschlichkeit in der antiken Sklaverei," Tübingen Rektoratsrede, 9 May 1958 (Tübingen, 1958), p. 38. This excellent article is made accessible in Finley's *Slavery in Classical Antiquity*, pp. 33-52.

[230] See above, p. 45 for the evidence that breeding became the principal source of slaves in the first century A.D.

[231] In contrast to the frequent assumption that it was principally the growing scarcity of slaves in the first century that led to improved conditions (see J. Balsdon, *Life and Leisure*, p. 109, for this "economic" explanation), J. Vogt has argued that this general amelioration was an effect of the wide variety of critical tasks performed by slaves. "Wege zur Menschlichkeit," p. 38 (Finley, p. 52).

[232] Note that the right of death which the owner had over his slaves was comparable in both Greek and Roman law to the power of death which a father had over his children. This power was gradually limited by protective clauses against its misuse. But it was not until Constantine that the killing of sons was in general something to be punished. Moreover, no law prevented a father from selling his son, even to a stranger. In the family of a master who treated people badly, being a slave was hardly worse than being a child. See Lauffer, "Die Sklaverei," p. 390.

[233] Crook summarizes the circumstances very well: "Every sort of treatment by masters ... and every sort of relationship between master and slave can be found in the sources, depending on what part of the labour force the slave belonged to, just as every condition of slave life can be met with from the treadmill to the boudoir--and to the office. And none is more typical than another." *Life and Law of Rome*, p. 57.

It is easy to view the treatment of slaves in the first century A.D. from a false perspective because of the outstanding cases of both kindness and cruelty known to us from ancient literature. For example, in his discussion of the futility of anger, Seneca reports that a very rich Roman freedman, Vedius Pollio, allowed his flesh-eating fish to dine on slaves.[234] One day, as a slave carelessly broke a crystal vase in the presence of some guests, including Augustus Caesar, Vedius commanded that the slave be thrown into the fishpond. In answer to the slave's cry for help, Augustus commanded that all the crystal owned by Vedius be brought before him, broken up and thrown into the grisly pond instead of the slave.[235]

On the other hand, when Zosimus, a highly accomplished slave of the younger Pliny, developed tuberculosis, Pliny sent him on a cruise to Egypt. The slave returned, seemingly cured, full of enthusiasm for his work as a reader and musician. He soon sickened again, however, and this time Pliny sent him to a friend's villa at Fréjus (*Forum Iulii*), whose climate and milk were recommended for victims of the disease.[236]

Ancient slavery has often been described on the basis of special cases like these, especially the cases of cruelty.[237] But these cases became noteworthy precisely because they were unusual. They should not be judged any differently than the special cases of strictness by fathers or cruelty by mothers reported in ancient literature. The punishment and reward of those in slavery in the first century were both so common that they are mentioned only incidentally.[238]

Owners of slaves (whether they were free men, freedmen or slaves)

---

[234]*De ira*, III, 40 (see also his *De clementia*, I, 18). Dio Cassius, LIV, 23 also reports this story. Westermann notes that "those of long established wealth customarily treated their slaves with greater kindness than the newly rich." *Slave Systems*, p. 22.

[235]Lauffer comments that this is an unusual story which shows not only the shocking and terrible side of slavery but also the official interest in overcoming it. "Die Sklaverei," p. 390.

[236]Pliny, *ep.* 5, 19. Balsdon notes that such great concern for the health of slaves as was exhibited by both Pliny and Cicero was unusual. *Life and Leisure in Ancient Rome*, p. 110.

[237]R.H. Barrow trenchantly comments: "Individual cases of cruelty must be left to the curious, and surely he will be satisfied." *Slavery in the Roman Empire*, p. 30.

[238]Lauffer observes: "Nach der guten wie nach der schlechten Seite der persönlichen Beziehungen zwischen Herr und Sklave war das Sklavenverhältnis völlig indifferent." "Die Sklaverei," p. 388.

usually regarded their slaves as investments which they hoped would pay for themselves.[239] Every injury or sickness suffered by a slave contributed to the owner's personal or financial disadvantage. The escape or death of a slave caused by inadequate nutrition, worn-out equipment or bad treatment was a direct loss to the owner.[240] It was especially mandatory for the relatively poor slave-owner that he maintain the working capacity of his slaves. For the replacement of one of them could cost as much as a wage-earner brought home in a year.[241] In Greece, slaves and freedmen in *paramoné*-contracts were often the means by which retirement became possible; many owners were motivated for this reason alone to treat their slaves well.[242]

The many expressions of gratitude and sorrow inscribed on the gravestones which owners erected for their slaves and freedmen stand as evidence that warm, friendly relationships often developed between those in slavery and their owners.[243] Under Roman law, manumitted slaves frequently continued to live with their former owners.[244] Under Greek law, many slaves were adopted into the family or were named as heirs of the family property.[245] From the general character of the slave/slave-owner relationship, then, a paradox developed in that it was not chiefly the slaves but the free workers who were exploited in Greco-Roman society; for the employer cared less about the welfare of his workers than the owner did about the welfare of his slaves.[246]

---

[239] As Balsdon writes: "The slave's interest and his master's were in this matter the same; at the crudest assessment, there was money in it for them both." *Life and Leisure*, p. 112. It was not uncommon for slaves to buy slaves, train them, and subsequently sell them at a profit.

[240] Seneca remarked that it was every owner's duty to feed and clothe his slaves. If he paid to have them learn a trade or to be educated, it was charity (*De beneficiis* 3, 21). This was "charity" which certainly benefited not only the slave and his owner but also Greco-Roman society at large.

[241] Lauffer, "Die Sklaverei," p. 388.

[242] Lauffer (pp. 388-389) traces this use of slaves and freedmen back to fifth-century Greece. These men and women usually led a life independent from their owners except for providing them certain goods and services.

[243] Rädle, *Freilassungswesen*, p. 173.

[244] See Alan Watson, *The Law of Persons in the Later Roman Republic* (Oxford, 1967), pp. 226-231. J. Vogt detects during the last half of the first century A.D. a tendency in the upper class of Roman society to hold slaves, freedmen and other clients more closely to the family than before. "Sklaventreue," p. 92.

[245] Rädle, *Freilassungswesen*, p. 149.

[246] Lauffer, "Die Sklaverei," p. 388. Jérôme Carcopino observes that "in Juvenal's day and after [i.e. after A.D. 50], it indeed seemed a happier fate to be a rich man's slave than a poor, freeborn citizen." *Daily Life in Ancient Rome* (New Haven, 1941), p. 64.

To be sure, the relationship of owner and slave must have continued
to be an invitation to exploitation and cruelty.[247] But it was to the owner's
self-interest to treat his slaves well, and most owners did so.[248] Epictetus,
who had been born in slavery, spoke of a freedman who even longed for his
previous slavery:[249]

> "Why, what was wrong with me? Someone else kept me in clothes,
> and shoes, and supplied me with food, and nursed me when I was
> sick; I served him in only a few matters. But now, miserable man
> that I am, what suffering is mine, who am a slave to several
> instead of one."[250]

The first century A.D., then, was a time in which the living conditions for those in slavery were improving. Legal action and public opinion
supported better treatment of slaves. The chief reason for this improvement
in slave-life was the fact that the principle source of slaves was no longer
war and piracy (with the hostility these acts involved) but breeding. That is,
most slaves in the first century were born in the households of their owners,
and they were given training for personal and public tasks of increasing importance and sensitivity. They were treated accordingly.

---

[247] See, e.g., the cases presupposed in 1 Pt. 0218-19: "House slaves (οἱ
οἰκέται) obey your masters with respect, not only when they are kind and considerate but also when they are unjust (σκολιός). For it is a favorable thing
when a man endures the pain of undeserved suffering because God is in his
thoughts." (Note that both the *RSV* and the *NEB* misleadingly translate οἰκέται
with "Servants.")
      Evidence that some owners continued to treat their slaves badly is
given by the edict of Claudius which condemned the exposure of sick slaves on
the island of Aesculapius and which gave such slaves their freedom upon their
recovery (Suetonius, *Claudius* 25). A few years later, the *Lex Petronia* (probably A.D. 61) prohibited owners from exposing their slaves to fight with wild
beasts without permission from the competent magistrate (approval was given
only when very bad conduct was proven). Antoninus Pius, Emperor during the
middle of the second century A.D., proclaimed that if a slave took refuge at
a statue of the Emperor, the provincial governor was to hold an enquiry; if he
was convinced of the owner's cruelty, the owner was to be forced to sell *all*
his slaves. (Gaius, *Inst.* I, 53).

[248] Balsdon concludes: "Whether considerate by nature or not, the Roman
appreciated that, except with the incorrigibly idle and vicious (who were best
taken to the market and sold), kindness to slaves paid rich dividends." *Life
and Leisure*, p. 110.

[249] Trans. Oldfather, Epictetus, IV, 1, 37.

[250] The "several" masters to whom Epictetus referred include the "chit of a
girl" who makes the freedman miserable, his dissatisfaction with life and his
self-pity. For a discussion of the advantages of being a slave (such as
social security, training and education), see Barrow, *Slavery in the Roman
Empire*, pp. 60-64.

Slave-owners generally viewed their slaves as investments to be protected and developed. We have evidence from both Greek and Roman sources that friendly relations developed between many slaves and their owners. Although both Greek and Roman law still permitted heads of households to treat both children and slaves with extreme cruelty, the stories of brutality from this period represent exceptional cases; most slaves were treated well. S. Lauffer concludes that the vast majority of slaves in the first century accepted their lot and were satisfied in it.[251]

In most cases, then, a slave did not spend much time worrying about his life as a slave, even though he probably was steadily preparing the way toward his manumission by doing well the tasks assigned to him. In light of this conclusion, it seems unlikely that Paul's advice in 1 Cor. 0721b ("Don't worry about it") was meant to encourage indifference to bad treatment.

About what, then, was a slave in first-century Corinth likely to be concerned? Before directly answering this question in terms of the slave's view of his situation, I turn to a description of the positions of the slave and freedman with respect to each other in order to clarify the actual differences which Paul may have had in mind when writing 1 Cor. 0721b.

3. *The positions of slaves and freedmen in society.*

It is not my intention in this section to describe the relations of the legal statuses of slaves and freedmen to the whole structure of Greco-Roman society.[252] Rather, with specific reference to 1 Cor. 0721cd, I seek to determine what was at stake in becoming a freedman; i.e., why would a person in slavery have preferred to be set free? Cruel treatment has been eliminated as a primary motive. What then are the factors that made manumission desirable and that could have encouraged a slave to be dissatisfied with his status?

In outward appearance it was usually impossible to distinguish a slave from a freedman or a free man. Neither his clothing nor his color nor

---

[251]"Die Sklaverei in der griech.-röm. Welt," p. 377.

[252]For a recent, excellent treatment of this question see J.-G. Gagé, *Les classes sociales dans l'empire romain* (Paris, 1964). He briefly offers a number of his conclusions in "Graeco-Roman Society and Culture, 31 B.C.-A.D. 235," *The Crucible of Christianity*, ed. Arnold Toynbee (London, 1969), pp. 161-170. Other useful literature includes M. Rostovtzeff, *The Social and Economic History of the Roman Empire*, 2nd edn. rev. P.M. Fraser (Oxford, 1957); A.M. Duff, *Freedmen in the Early Roman Empire*, 2nd edn. (New York, 1958); and S. Dill, *Roman Society from Nero to Marcus Aurelius* (1904; reprinted by Meridian Books, 1964).

his race revealed his legal status.[253] Neither his patterns of religious life
nor his friends nor his work separated him from freedmen or free workers.

The person in slavery in the first century worked, but his working
was not the specific way in which he could be distinguished from the rest of
his society. For only a very small part of the population did not work at
all, and the slave was involved in every kind of activity requiring work.[254]
That is, there seems to be no type of work in the first century which was considered exclusively the work of slaves.[255]

By no means was the slave's position always a "subordinate" one.
For in the household he served not only as cook, cleaner or personal attendant
but also as tutor of persons of all ages, doctor, nurse or close companion.
In business he was not only delivery-boy and janitor, he was also secretary
or manager of estates and shops and ships, contracting as an agent for his
owner. Often he joined in partnership with his owner or others on the basis
of his peculium. In the handcraft factories he was not only fuel-carrier and
artisan, he was also foreman and salesman. In the civil service he was not
only a part of the street-paving gang or the sewer-cleaning department, he was
also an administrator of funds and personnel and an executive with decision-
making power.[256] Indeed, during the first century, slaves and freedmen became
the most important part of the Roman administrative force.[257]

Thus, even though in Roman law the distinction between slave and
free was quite sharp, in daily life a continuum of statuses existed in terms

---

[253]Westermann remarks that "there are many indications that deeper racial
and class antipathies, such as those based upon differences of skin coloring,
were totally lacking in the Greek world." *Slave Systems*, p. 23.

[254]Lauffer, "Die Sklaverei," pp. 380-381. In his *Das Privatleben der Römer*
(2nd edn. Leipzig, 1886), J. Marquardt has compiled a list of more than 120
different duties and occupations in which slave labor was used. This great
variety has recently been examined again by M.N. Tod, "Epigraphical Notes on
Freedmen's Professions," *Epigraphica* 12 (1950), 3-25. Rädle says that without doubt these freedmen had the same jobs when they were slaves. *Freilassungswesen*, p. 132.

[255]It was not uncommon for freemen, freedmen and slaves to work together at
many tasks. Although many slaves were used for heavy manual labor such as
mining and rowing large ships, free workers were also used for the same work.
Lauffer, p. 382.

[256]Note that in Athens slaves were used not only in the bureaucratic services but also as a police force. They were armed and could arrest freemen!
See Westermann, "Slavery and the Elements of Freedom," p. 338.

[257]A.H.M. Jones notes that "while some public slaves got little more than
their keep, others ranked socially high enough to be elected to cult societies
and athletic clubs of citizens and were rich enough to buy deputies who did
their work for them while they enjoyed the emoluments." *The Greek City from
Alexander to Justinian* (Oxford, 1940), p. 242.

of social intercourse, culture and wealth.[258] Furthermore, under Greek law, special conditions blurred the distinction between slave and free even more. For example, because of the prevalent type of urban housing in first-century Greece, many of the slaves who worked in handcraft factories lived apart from their owners and enjoyed their own property and family life. Such a slave was employed by a person other than his owner and was paid a daily wage, part of which went directly to his owner.[259] He was free to use the remainder (one-third was not unusual) as he wished.[260] On the other hand, a slave could be manumitted and as a freedman still be bound by contract to a specific job in a specific place determined by his former owner; and he was subject to seizure if he did not fulfill this contract.[261] The difference, then, between the personal existence of a slave who worked as a "pay-earner" and that of a freedman who worked under a restrictive *paramoné*-contract was exceedingly small. For example, those slaves who worked to make possible the retirement of their owners differed little in their life-style from freedmen who had to render such support as a condition of their freedom.[262]

Of course, if the freedman did not enter a restrictive contract as the price of his freedom, he had an advantage over the slave in that he could give notice that he was quitting. Actually changing jobs, however, was as difficult for most freedmen as it is for many of the workers in today's

---

[258]See above, pp. 40-44.

[259]See above, p. 42 for a description of the "pay-earning slaves" and "those who live apart."

[260]As a general rule under Greek law, the slave received his "wages" in the form of board and room. But in those cases in which slaves worked for others in contracts arranged by their owners, it seems that the wages were the same for both freemen or freedmen and slaves. Contrary to the assumption that the slave "slowed down" in protest against his status as a slave, there is evidence that the slave, like the freedman in a *paramoné*-contract, had much to gain by improved performance, above all, manumission. Where the performance of ancient slaves can be measured, e.g., in the silver and lead mines at Larium in Attica, it seems to have been first class. See Lauffer, "Die Sklaverei," p. 382.

[261]Westermann has convincingly summarized the elements of freedom under Greek law as follows: The freedman is to be his own legal representative, he is not subject to seizure as property, he may do what he desires to do and he may go where he desires to go. But he stresses that "each of the three remaining freedoms, once the legal status was fixed, could be broken into or impinged upon." "Slavery and the Elements of Freedom," p. 343. M. Bloch observes that the conditions of a *paramoné*-contract were "manchmal nicht nur nicht besser, sondern sogar noch schlechter" than life as a slave. *Die Freilassungsbedingungen der delphischen Freilassungsurkunden* (Diss. Strassburg, 1914), p. 25. See above, pp. 42-44.

[262]Lauffer, "Die Sklaverei," p. 390.

industrial economies.[263] The chief advantage of his freedom was not having to share his "take-home pay" with anyone.

Many free workers (whether freemen or freedmen), however, did not have "job-security"; i.e., they worked on a day-to-day basis and had to suffer the anxiety of possible unemployment.[264] This possibility highlights the chief advantages of being a slave: personal and social security.[265]

Certainly, capable slaves had an advantage over their free counterparts in that they often were given excellent educations at the expense of their owners.[266] Famous philosophers, writers, artists, doctors, scholars and administrators were the result.[267] These slaves formed a major part of

---

[263]This situation leads Lauffer (p. 383) to the very interesting conclusion that a legal reform, such as the abolition of slavery, would not in itself have led to a change in the basic set of dependent relations which characterized the economy of the Greco-Roman world.

[264]A day-to-day worker in third-century Athens complained: "How much better it would be to be a slave of a comfortably situated owner than to live a lowly and poor life as a free man." (Philemon, *Fragment* 227, Kock edn.; also Menander, *Fragment* 1093, Kock edn.)

[265]The freedman Epictetus refers to the security and carefree life enjoyed by the slave as contrasted with the anxieties and trouble of independence (see the quotation, above, p. 66). Barrow quotes Martial on the same point as follows: (Martial is speaking to his slave Condylus) "You do not realize the cares of a master or the advantages of a slave's life. You sleep well on a rug, your master lies awake on a bed of down. You salute no one, not even your master-- he salutes in fear and trembling a number of patrons. You have no debts--he is burdened with them. Do you fear the torturer? He is martyr to gout" (*Epigrammaticus Latinus* ix. 93 -- 1st cen. A.D.). Barrow concludes: "Given a tolerable master, the slave could be sure of a living, enjoying the pleasures of the moment, careless of the future, leaving responsibility to others." *Slavery in the Roman Empire*, p. 171. Neither Martial nor Barrow seem to have noticed the "dehumanizing" aspects either of this kind of dependence or of the kind which could result from the parent-child relationship under Roman law.

[266]See C.A. Forbes, "The Education and Training of Slaves in Antiquity," *Transactions of the American Philological Assoc.* 86 (1955), 321ff.

[267]A few examples of famous first-century slaves: the philosopher Epictetus, who studied with Musonius Rufus while still a slave of the freedman Epaphroditus (who himself held the office of *a libellis* [legal secretary] under both Nero and Domitian); Verrius Flaccus, who was the most erudite of the Augustan scholars and the teacher of Augustus' grandsons; Marcus Antonius Felix, who served as procurator of Judea where he was Paul's judge; Phaedrus, the Roman fabulist, who came from Macedonia as a slave to Rome where he was educated and then freed by Augustus; Polybius, who was Claudius' *a studiis* (secretary for literary affairs) and who translated Homer into Latin and Virgil into Greek; Lucius Annaeus Cornutus, a philosopher who began his life as a slave of Seneca or of one of Seneca's relatives; Palaemon, who was the first Roman to write a really comprehensive grammatical treatise; Gaius Melissus, who was *grammaticus* in the household of Augustus' friend Maecenas and who invented a form of light drama. These are only a few examples from hundreds which could be listed.

the broad "class" of intellectuals in the first century.[268]

Once they were educated, of course, this advantage of status as a slave was no longer valid. Such slaves did not have to wait for manumission, however, before they established relationships with many persons who were not in slavery; they were capable of becoming friends of their owners *qua* men.[269] Even those who performed personal services which called for qualities of character rather than intellect were sometimes seen as "friends," such as the *"humiles amici"* noted by Seneca in one of his letters (47,1). A.R. Hands concludes that such slave/owner relationships confirm the classical estimate of the "worthiness" of a person, namely that what was important was not his legal status but his *disciplina et mores* ("education and character").[270]

Such friendships easily carried over into the religious life of the slave, for there was no cult preferred by slaves to which a freedman or a free man would not have wanted to belong.[271] In whatever cult he participated the slave usually found a social recognition and protection which he may have

---

[268]Lauffer, "Die Sklaverei," p. 394. Balsdon remarks: "A quick and bright young slave had the possibility of a really exciting future. The world was crying out for men of educated talent in fields in which the freeborn Roman would not (for social reasons) or could not (because he lacked the skill) engage." *Life and Leisure in Ancient Rome*, p. 112.

[269]Aristotle (*Nicomachean Ethics* VIII.12) stressed this *"qua* men" aspect of slave-relationships, even though his description of a slave *"qua* slave" ("a tool which has life") is more commonly remembered. See above, p. 38. The educated slave (or freedman) was normally regarded as more worthy of friendship (and its material expression) than the freeman who had always been poor.

[270]*Charities and Social Aid in Greece and Rome*, p. 86. Arnold A.T. Ehrhardt observes that for Seneca, Musonius Rufus and his student Epictetus, treating slaves as human beings was a religious affair. Seneca, e.g., advised: "Live with your subordinates just as you would like for a master to live with you" (*Ep.* 47,11). Ehrhardt notes, however, that other philosophical schools did not go as far; and he claims that the Academy expressed no kind feelings for men in slavery and that the Neopythagoreans had even less interest in them. *Politische Metaphysik von Solon bis Augustin II: Die Christliche Revolution* (Tübingen, 1959), p. 18. Note also that Zeno lived without slaves not because of his legal or human sensitivity but rather because of his conviction that the "wise" (σοφός) had no such needs. See Richter, "Seneca und die Sklaven," p. 211 n. 42. The Stoics taught nothing about the slave's position in society nor anything which dealt directly with the problem of slavery as such. Thus Seneca had no "Stoic foundation" for his own reflections on slavery. See Richter, p. 205.

[271]See Franz Bömer, *Untersuchungen über die Religion der Sklaven in Griechenland und Rom, Erster Teil: Die wichtigsten Kulte und Religionen in Rom und im lateinischen Westen*, Akademie der Wissenschaften und der Literatur in Mainz, Abhandlungen der Geistes- und Sozialwissenschaftlichen Klasse, Nr. 7 (1957), pp. 29-35, 46-47, 78-80, 105-111, and 180-185.

otherwise lacked. Wherever slaves are found in cult-fellowships with freedmen and freemen, they do not appear to have suffered any substantial disadvantages.[272] The freedman who had a Roman patron could, of course, participate in the official cults related to the Empire, because he normally received citizenship with his manumission. But in short, on the basis of very extensive research, Bömer concludes that little or no difference existed between the religious mentality of the average slave and that of the person who belonged to the lowest class of freemen.[273]

If the work that he did, the friends that he had, and the cult in which he participated did not separate the slave from the freedman, why did he prefer to become free? A chief reason was that nothing stood in the way of the social and civil ascent of men who had at one time been in slavery.[274] First in Greece and then in Rome, some slaves anticipated their manumission as the prelude to marrying into the families of their owners.[275] Such a marriage was advantageous because the security which typified the freedman's former status was not disturbed.[276]

On the other hand, manumission brought to most slaves a new life

---

[272] Bömer, I, 172-179.

[273] Bömer, IV (*Epilogomena*), 862.

[274] Although in comparison with the free-born (*ingenui*), freedmen lived under a number of legal disabilities (see the comprehensive description by A.M. Duff, *Freedmen in the Early Roman Empire*, 2nd edn., 1958, ch. 3), already by the time of Cicero's death they comprised a high proportion of all Roman citizens; and by the time of Claudius, freedmen had penetrated into many high positions, political and religious, and into every order of society (probably including the senatorial order--see Barrow, *Slavery in the Roman Empire*, p. 192). Duff (p. 187) speaks of "a rule of freedmen in the Roman Empire," a situation which was encouraged by the unwillingness of the senators to "serve" the Emperor by doing the work necessary to the administration of the Empire.

[275] This possibility existed from the time of the late Republic (Lauffer, p. 390). Paul was probably well-acquainted with this practice, for "in Biblical times and in recent Arab practice, slaves have been freed after seven or ten years and married to the owner's daughter!" (North, *Sociology of the Biblical Jubilee*, p. 138.)

[276] Barrow notes: "Marriage between slave and freed and even free was very common," and he points to the complicated relationships that often existed by describing the case of the slave, Oriens of Saepinum, whose wife was a slave, but whose father was a dignitary of the same town and whose brother was a magistrate (the father had been freed by the town; the brother was born after this manumission and was eligible as "free-born" for public office). *Slavery in the Roman Emprie*, pp. 170-171.

which in many respects was often more difficult and uncertain than their former one.[277] This independent life was attractive nevertheless because the freedman gained control of his person and his goods (including persons in slavery whom he already owned when he was in slavery). According to both Greek and Roman law, the freedman (ἀπελεύθερος, *libertus*) could not be sold (and was to that extent "free"), although he was still bound to his former master (προστάτης, *patronus*) in a variety of ways.

According to a very interesting peculiarity of Roman law, the person who was fortunate enough to have been a slave of a Roman citizen usually became a citizen himself by virtue of his manumission.[278] This citizenship granted the new freedman access to the courts, to public office and to the army.[279] As a freedman he could contract a legal marriage (*matrimonia*), and his children were born as freemen and citizens.[280]

In contrast, the slave who had a Greek owner became a member of a group of freemen who did not have citizenship (the metics) at his manumission. He gained access to the courts, but only through a representative, who often was his former owner.[281] In other matters, such as the exchange of property, the freedman was his own master. He could contract a legal marriage; his children were born in a legal status very similar to his own as a freedman. As a freedman the former slave was no longer subject to seizure, except by due process of the laws which applied to free men as well. The freedman could earn his living as he chose in the place where he chose.[282]

The anticipation of financial, civil and social success, therefore,

---

[277]Many of the persons in slavery in the first century A.D. enjoyed better living conditions than many of the poor people who were free. See above, pp. 44, 70-71. Especially striking are the many cases of persons who sold themselves into slavery in order to find a life that was easier than they had as freemen. See above, pp. 46-48.

[278]See above, p. 42 n. 110, for a description of the variety of statuses into which a slave with a Roman owner might be freed. See also F. de Visscher, "De l'acquisition du droit de cité romaine par l'affranchissement," *Studia et documenta historiae et iuris* 12 (1946), 69-85.

[279]See above, p. 40. The number of Roman citizens was constantly being increased by the former slave-membership of the Roman *familiae*.

[280]"How eagerly this privilege was accepted, how much affection and hope surrounded the children so born, and how tragic was their loss, is revealed even in the abbreviated and laconic grief of ancient grave-stones." M.L. Gordon, "The Nationality of Slaves under the Early Roman Empire," *JRS* 14 (1924), 111 (Finley, p. 189).

[281]Rädle, *Freilassungswesen*, p. 135.

[282]See above, pp. 42-44, for Westermann's clear analysis of the "four freedoms" of Greek freedmen (based on the manumission inscriptions from Delphi).

made the status of freedman attractive to most of the persons in slavery in the first century A.D. The achievements of a number of freedmen were out-standing enough to gain for freedmen in general a reputation for a spirit of initiative and of readiness to take risks.[283] Yet with reference to 1 Cor. 0721-22, it is especially important to notice that both Greek and Roman freed-men quite often remained very closely tied to their former owners in relation-ships resembling their former enslavement.[284]

For example, more than one-fourth of the manumission-inscriptions from Delphi fix limitations on at least two of the "four freedoms" (usually freedom of movement and freedom of employment) as conditions of the manumis-sions made public there.[285] The simplest and most frequent condition stipu-lated in these *paramoné*-contracts stated that the freedman had to remain with his former owner until one of them died (*GDI* 1752).[286] According to one in-scription (*GDI* 1801), the freedman had to obey all his patron's orders; accord-ing to another (*GDI* 1729), he had to be ready to serve his former owner at any time of the day or the night. According to *GDI* 1971, the freedman had to re-main with his patron until the freedman himself married. In many inscriptions the period of the *paramoné* is between two and ten years.[287] Rädle comments that the position of many slaves before and after manumission seems in most

---

[283]See J.-G. Gagé, "Graeco-Roman Society and Culture," p. 162.

[284]The modern assumption that manumission made it possible for the slave to make a clean break with his slave-status (in terms of work, religious recog-nition and relationship to his owner) has led not only to false interpreta-tions of 0721 but also to a great lack of appreciation of the force of the term "freedman" in 0722.

[285]See above, pp. 42-44 and 74.

[286]See Rädle, *Freilassungswesen*, p. 140. For a full description of *GDI* see above, p. 37 n. 90. The Delphic inscriptions indicate that citizens, non-citizens, metics, men, women, minors, individuals and groups were owners of slaves and then patrons in *paramoné*-contracts.

[287]Rädle, p. 143; also Westermann, "Between Slavery and Freedom," p. 217. The contract was sometimes continued to the son or daughter or to another per-son whom the manumittor wanted to favor with the freedman's services.

respects to have been the same.[288]

In contrast to those contracts in which slaves of Greek owners agreed to conditions which were often limited to periods of ten years or less,[289] Roman legislation demanded that the Roman freedman remain in a life-long relationship of duties and obligations to his patron.[290] The Roman freedman owed his patron *obsequium, operae, officium* and *bona*.

Under *obsequium* ("eagerness to serve") the freedman was obliged always to act for the good of his patron. He could bring civil suits against his patron only by permission of the civil authorities, and the only criminal proceedings he might initiate against him were for treason. The patron could apply "reasonable chastisement" to a freedman who was not "eager" enough.[291]

As a condition of manumission, a Roman slave was normally required to swear an oath that he would perform a certain number of *operae* (man-days of work) for his patron. The number of *operae* that could be required was not limited by law, but only tasks which could be performed without indignity or

---

[288] The nature of *paramoné*-contracts was not the same in all parts of the Greek-speaking world, and real differences can be detected between procedures in cities as close as Athens and Delphi. Rädle (p. 143) agrees with Westermann, in any case, that those persons serving in *paramoné*-contracts were legally freedmen even if they still appear to have been "enslaved" by the conditions of these contracts. The owner did not have the power of life and death over a freedman in *paramoné*; a large group of inscriptions indicate that the children of such a freedman were born free. A ceremony usually occurred at the end of the *paramoné*, which celebrated the transition from "freedom" to "complete freedom." C.B. Welles concludes: "Freedom was certainly divisible in the unsystematic Greek mind." "Manumission and Adoption," p. 515. Rädle refers to the summary article on this topic written by J. Herrmann, *Revue internationale des droits de l'antiquité*, 3rd ser. 10 (1963), 149ff.

[289] By paying a sum of money (called ἀπόλυσις), the freedman in *paramoné* could significantly shorten the period of his contract. See Rädle, p. 147.

[290] J. Crook concludes that the "freedman doing his obligatory work for a *patronus* was, in labour terms, just an extension of the slave in the less sordid levels of his activity." *Law and Life of Rome*, p. 191.

[291] Crook (p. 51) translates *Digest* 47.10.7.2: "The praetor is not obliged to put up with a man who was yesterday a slave and today is free, complaining that his master has been rude to him or mildly struck or corrected him."
There was no legal mechanism whereby a freedman could be reduced to slavery again for failing in his "dutifulness" (see the discussion of "ingratitude," above, p. 49); but just about the time Paul was writing to Corinth, many wealthy patrons were asking for such a mechanism (see Tacitus, *Annales* XIII, 26-27).

danger to life were permitted.[292] The extent to which the freedman still "belonged" in principle to his patron is seen in the patron's right to rent the *operae* of his freedmen to others.[293] *Officium* ("moral duty") made the freedman responsible for general services on behalf of his patron, such as accepting the guardianship of his children or supporting him if he fell into poverty.[294]

The Augustan legislation regarding the property (*bona*) of a Roman freedman is very complicated.[295] In short, a freedman's legitimate children could inherit from him; but any other heirs (by testament or not) received altogether only one-half of the remaining inheritance, for the other half belonged by law to the freedman's patron.[296]

Although these duties sound harsh to modern ears, the Romans liked to think that a freedman's relation to his patron had something personal and "filial" about it.[297] For example, the patron was obliged to support his freedman if impoverished, and a common kind of legacy was an annuity (*alimenta*) to freedmen.[298] Furthermore, Roman freedmen usually bore the name of their patron's family and were often buried in the family tomb.[299] The slave who

---

[292] For example, a freedwoman who had been a prostitute when a slave did not have to provide the same *operae* to her patron. *Digest* 38.1.38. Owners could insist that the price of freedom be an enormous sum of money or an unlimited number of *operae* on which the patron called when he wanted something done. In effect, such a freedman was always under the thumb of the patron through fear of his sudden demands. Efforts were made to repress this practice. See Crook, p. 54. Watson discusses a case in which a freedman was released from further duties after providing *operae* for a continuous period of seven years. *The Law of Persons in the Later Roman Republic*, p. 216.

[293] Such rentable *operae* included domestic and personal services and the work of skilled craftsmen. *Operae* were considered units of value convertible into cash, and sometimes the freedman could offer money in lieu (Crook, p. 52). Freedmen with two free children and freedwomen over 50 years of age became exempt from *operae*.

[294] Crook, p. 51. Watson observes: "Because of the rights which accrued to the patron, the question of who was patron had considerable significance." *The Law of Persons*, p. 234.

[295] See Watson, pp. 231-233.

[296] Crook (p. 54) suggests that these inheritance-laws should be viewed in the light of the fact that the foundation of a freedman's property was the slave-peculium which he had been allowed to keep at manumission.

[297] In light of all the circumstances, Crook insists that this was not wholly "doublethink" (p. 54). He points to the "faithful retainer" relationship of Tiro to the Cicero family (see Cicero, *Ad fam*. XVI) and suggests that it was a common situation.

[298] Crook, p. 55.

[299] Crook, pp. 136-137.

became a freedman, then, usually continued to live in circumstances similar to those of his enslavement. As a freedman he encountered many people who looked down on him as an "ex-slave."[300] Thus it should be noted that the sharp distinction between "slave" and "freedman" which has been regularly assumed by modern readers of 1 Cor. 0721 rarely existed in the Greco-Roman society of the first century A.D. Yet most of the persons in slavery did look forward to being set free for the reasons mentioned above. How, then, did slaves view their own enslavement and their future?

4. *The slave's view of his situation.*[301]

The probability that manumission would bring struggle as well as increased independence does not appear to have diminished the hope of the average person in slavery that he would be set free someday. How realistic was this hope, and how much did the slave "worry about it"? What evidence is there for "unrest" among the slaves in the first century A.D.?

Although those who were enslaved in the mines or on the *latifundia* (many of whom were criminals) had little hope of manumission, all other slaves in the first century A.D. had good reason to expect that they would be manumitted "someday."[302] Those who lived in fairly close contact with their owners, such as the slaves we know about in the Christian congregation in Corinth, had the best opportunities for impressing their owners with their diligent work; and "good service was the road to liberty."[303] Indeed, especially among the Greeks, it was recognized that the best way to secure efficient service from domestic slaves and skilled workmen was to make manumission the final reward for good work.[304]

---

[300] Balsdon speaks of the "cold draught of prejudice in the free society" that met many freedmen when they ventured beyond the circle of their friends. He writes that "Romans who were not conscious of having slave blood in their own veins were supremely contemptuous of these who had. Still there were those who overcame this prejudice." *Life and Leisure in Ancient Rome*, p. 114.

[301] S. Lauffer has urged that greater attention be paid to the mentality of the slave himself. He notes that there are numerous volumes written about religion, art, philosophy and literature of the ancient world in which the viewpoint of those in slavery or of freedmen never comes in question, as if they had had no viewpoint. It is as if slavery had only an economic or legal aspect and presented no "ideological" or personal perspectives. "Die Sklaverei," p. 378.

[302] Susan Treggiari, *Roman Freedmen during the Late Republic*, pp. 9 and 106-107.

[303] A.M. Duff, *Freedmen in the Early Roman Empire*, p. 14.

[304] Duff, p. 14.

Already in the first century B.C., Cicero had spoken of the situation of slaves as intolerable if some hope of liberty were not held out to them.[305] He implied, probably speaking rhetorically, that the average length of enslavement was seven years.[306] It appears as if a person in slavery could count on serving about ten to twenty years after his physical maturity before he would be set free.

The number of manumissions greatly increased during the last half of the first century B.C.; political opportunism and rewards for military service were among the many reasons for freeing slaves during this period.[307] By the beginning of the first century A.D., manumissions were being given at such a fast pace that Augustus put restrictions on the age of slaves who could be manumitted and the number who could be freed at one time.[308] Augustus seems to have been motivated both by his interest in protecting the heirs of manumittors and by his desire to slow down the number of slaves who were becoming Roman citizens when manumitted.[309] Yet Augustus himself established a precedent which worked contrary to this policy by employing a large number of slaves and freedmen in his own household. Most of the Caesars followed Augustus in this practice, and the position of slaves and freedmen improved

---

[305]*Pro C. Rabirio perduellionis reo* 15, (written in 63 B.C.).

[306]*Philippic* VIII. 32. (44 B.C.). Cicero made this statement in a comparison of the condition of the Roman Republic from 49-43 B.C. with slavery. It should not, therefore, be received as a definite statement on the length of time a slave had to work before he was set free.

[307]Public opinion in both Rome and Greece began to accept the freeing of slaves as normal and even desirable. (See Treggiari, p. 12). See the discussion under the heading, "The owners' reasons for manumission," in the next section, pp. 88-91.

[308]According to Augustus' *lex Fufia Caninia* of 2 B.C., the following limits were placed on the number of slaves who could be freed by testament: half in a household of 3 to 10 slaves; a third if there were more than 10 but not more than 30; a quarter if there were more than 30 but not more than 100; beyond 100 the limit was a fifth, with an absolute maximum of 100 who could be freed by these means. This law remained valid until it was abolished by Justinian. According to the *lex Aelia Sentia* of A.D. 4, the slave had to be at least 30 years old and the owner at least 20 years old in order for a manumission to be lawful. In addition an owner could not manumit his slaves to the detriment of his creditors. Exceptions were made when the reason for manumission was good enough to gain the approval of a special commission for extraordinary manumissions. A slave who was manumitted in violation of this law became free but did not receive Roman citizenship (i.e., he became *Latinus Iunianus*). See the definition of these terms in Berger, *Dictionary of Roman Law*.

[309]For the inheritance motive, see Buckland, *The Roman Law of Slavery*, pp. 546-547; for Augustus' "social improvement policy" (an attempt to restore those who were already citizens to a preferred position vis-à-vis freedmen and slaves), see Westermann, *Slave Systems*, pp. 89-90.

markedly during the first and second centuries.[310] During the first century, manumission became a very common occurrence both in Rome and in the provinces.[311]

Thus we can conclude that the slaves in Greek and Roman households, factories and businesses in the middle of the first century A.D. realistically anticipated the day when they would be set "free."[312]

In view of this hopeful future, how much did a person in slavery "worry" about his manumission? Lauffer claims that the vast majority of those in slavery were satisfied with their lot.[313] Certainly good treatment and personal security were big factors in this contentment.[314] Yet Epictetus was able to state in a general way:

---

[310] Gagé remarks that Claudius' practice of appointing freedmen to the highest posts in public administration angered many of the senators. He notes that most of these freedmen were of "Graeco-oriental origin" and he stresses that "it must be borne in mind that they were playing an active part in the Imperial administration long before the aristocrats of the same provinces were admitted into the senatorial order." "Graeco-Roman Society and Culture," p. 162.

[311] Westermann writes: "The change of legal status out of enslavement into liberty, by way of manumission, was as constant and as easy in Greco-Roman life as the reverse transition over the short passage from individual freedom of action into the constraints of non-freedom; and the methods employed for making either transition were many." "Between Slavery and Freedom," p. 215.

[312] Rädle (p. 173) states that a thrifty, hardworking slave who had good luck or who obtained a loan and thus was able to make an attractive offer to his Greek owner was practically certain of his manumission. He notes, however, that there was no legal way in which the slave could demand his freedom; to this extent the owner's higher legal status was an enormous advantage. Thus he could place hard conditions on manumission by means of a *paramoné*-contract.

[313] "Die Sklaverei," p. 377.

[314] In his article, "The Attitude of the Slave with Reference to His Manumission in Roman Comedy" (in Russian), J.N. Koržensky comments that during the Republic the slave's attitude toward his slavery depended entirely upon the treatment he received from his owner. Koržensky notes that according to Plautus (a freeman), the life of the slave was arduous and the enslaved tended toward running away. (Note, however, that Plautus has a master ask one of his slaves: "Am I your slave, or are you mine?" [*Bacchides* 25].) But according to Terence (who came to Rome as a slave and who was set free after receiving a fine education), the slave was generally content with his lot in life. *Vestnik Drevnij Istorii* ("Review of Ancient History") 61 (1957), 149-158.

The slave prays that he be set free immediately. Why? ... he
imagines that up till now he has been hindered and unlucky because
his manumission has not yet happened.[315]

Westermann translates a business letter written in 14 B.C. by a freedman to
his patron as follows:

> ... but you know in your soul that I, desiring your affection,
> have conducted myself blamelessly just as a slave wishes to be
> conciliatory in the interest of his freedom.[316]

These examples presuppose the fact that slaves generally looked forward to
their manumission and that they usually conducted themselves in a manner
which they hoped would bring nearer the day when they could call themselves
"freedmen."

This lively expectation of manumission must have been a major factor
in the relative "contentment" among those in slavery in the first century A.D.
Indeed, the ease and frequency of manumission during this period relieved any
pressures which might have led to slave-revolts, precisely because the most
capable and active slaves had the possibility of gaining a certain amount of
freedom by legal means.[317]

Without examining the evidence, some Biblical scholars have assumed
that a general climate of "unrest" within the slave population in the first

---

[315]My trans. from Epictetus IV.1.33: Ὁ δοῦλος εὐθὺς εὔχεται ἀφεθῆναι
ἐλεύθερος. διὰ τί; ... φαντάζεται μέχρι νῦν διὰ τὸ μὴ τετυχηκέναι τούτου
ἐμποδίζεσθαι καὶ δυσροεῖν.
    Epictetus has the slave continue: "When I am set free, immediately
life will be wonderful, I will not turn around for anyone, I will talk to
everyone as an equal, go where I please, and come when and where I please."
(IV.1.34). Epictetus goes on to expose the illusions of this slave who then
begins to wish he were still in slavery. See above, p. 71.

[316]*Slave Systems*, p. 106, from a papyrus included in the *Berliner Griechische
Urkunden (Ägyptische Urkunden aus den Königlichen Museen zu Berlin)* IV, 1141,
23-25.

[317]Westermann concludes that it was the "astonishing fluidity of status in
both directions, from slavery to freedom as from freedom to slavery ... which,
in large measure, explains the absence of slave revolts in the Greek classical
period." "Slavery and the Elements of Freedom," p. 346. The same conclusion
can be reached regarding the social situation in the first century A.D. See
also Lauffer, "Die Sklaverei," p. 390.

century A.D. was the background and occasion for 1 Cor. 0721.[318] Therefore, against this assumption, it must be stressed that the last serious slave-revolt in the Greco-Roman world occurred at least 120 years before Paul wrote to the Corinthian Christians.[319] By the first century A.D., "the days of serious slave or gladiator insurrections were over."[320]

The fact that no unrest or revolutionary impulses existed among those in slavery in the first century A.D. has been strikingly emphasized by the work of Russian historians.[321] These scholars have a strong, ideologically deter-mined interest in discovering slave-unrest in every corner of the Mediterranean basin at all times within the two thousand year era between primitive society

---

[318]For example, Rudolf Knopf grounded his interpretation of 1 Cor. 0721 ("stay a slave") on the assumption of a general "Emanzipationsgelüste der Sklaven" against which Paul is said to be fighting in this verse. *Das Nach-apostolische Zeitalter: Geschichte der Christlichen Gemeinden* (Tübingen, 1905), p. 69. J. Weiß made the same assumption, stressing that "der Freiheits-drang der Sklaven, der im Zusammenhang mit dem 4,8ff. geschilderten Hochgefühl erwartet sein mag, soll gedämpft werden." *Der erste Korintherbrief*, p. 191. More recently E. Käsemann has interpreted 1 Cor. 0721 against an assumed back-ground of slave-revolts and armies of runaway slaves. He writes: "Der Apostel nimmt das antike Sklavenwesen selbstverständlich hin und bejaht es gelegentlich sogar, obwohl es doch auch zu seiner Zeit schon Sklavenaufstände und, worauf der Philemonbrief hindeutet, Heere entlaufener Sklaven gab." *Exegetische Ver-suche* II, 215 (*New Testament Questions*, p. 208).

[319]All the great slave-rebellions in the Greco-Roman world occurred between 140-70 B.C. Earlier uprisings were limited to small areas and were put down with little trouble. After the middle of the second century B.C., a series of rebellions began which led to protracted wars, beginning with the first Sicilian uprising in 136-132 and ending with the fall of Spartacus in 71 B.C. See J. Vogt, "Zur Struktur der antiken Sklavenkriege," pp. 7-9. The increase in the number of "house-born" slaves, the general improvement in treatment, and the ease of manumission are the major factors behind the absence of "un-rest" in the first century A.D. See the discussion of slave rebellions, above, pp. 62-64.

[320]Ramsay MacMullen, *Enemies of the Roman Order: Treason, Unrest, and Alienation in the Empire* (Cambridge, Mass., 1966), p. 167. MacMullen (p. 242) concludes: "I can see no significant struggle of slave against free or poor against rich. Protest originated within whatever classes were dominant at different periods." He observes (p. 180) that the most common cause of urban unrest was hunger, which is attested in almost every period and province. Whatever was done, the poor suffered more than the rich; and they expressed their sense of wrong by rioting. Yet the return of abundance proved that their aims were linked to the amount of available food and not to the over-throw of "class-structures."

[321]The principal concern of Russian scholars working on ancient slavery has been focused on the slaves used in the production of goods; the slaves used in household services and the great variety in the forms of slavery have practically been ignored. Within the last fifteen years, these scholars have begun to compare Greco-Roman slaves with other economically dependent popula-tions; and the scientific quality of their work has markedly improved. See the review article by Friedrich Vittinghoff, "Die Sklavenfrage in der For-schung der Sowjetunion," *Gymnasium* 69 (1962), 269-286.

and the beginning of feudalism. Yet they have not been able to find in the
first century A.D. the "unrest" and the "class-war between masters and slaves"
which are required to support their theory of history.[322] Indeed, the liberty
of religious and fraternal association granted to slaves in the first century
A.D. by their owners and by the Roman government points to the degree of contentment which prevailed among those in slavery and to the absence of revolutionary impulses among them.[323] If someone in Greece or Rome in the middle
of the first century A.D. had cried, "Slaves of the world unite!" he would
have attracted only the curious. For neither the climate of unrest among
those in slavery nor the kind of class-consciousness presupposed by Marxist
theorists existed at that time.

The unquestioned acceptance of the institution of slavery in the
first century A.D., the improving conditions of slave-life during that period,
the respective places of slaves and freedmen in society, and the slave's view
of his own situation clearly indicate that the person in Greek or Roman slavery in the first century A.D. led an existence which differs in many significant ways from the slavery practiced in modern times. Perhaps the most
significant difference between that ancient slavery and modern slavery is the
manumission anticipated by first-century slaves.[324] In nineteenth-century
America, a slave had no hope of being set free; in first-century Greece, a
slave reasonably expected to be set free after a number of years of labor.
How, then, did manumission take place?

C. "But [Even] If You Are [Indeed] Able to Become Free ..."

The aspect of first-century slavery which has been least understood
by interpreters of 1 Cor. 0721 is the relation of the slave to his manumission.[325]

---

[322]Vittinghoff (p. 282) writes: "Die großen Sklavenaufstände am Ende der
römischen Republik, die ihre Stoßkraft aus der Zusammenpferchung von Sklaven-
massen auf den Latifundien gewannen, waren in Wahrheit so sehr Erscheinungen
einer Ausnahmesituation in der griechisch-römischen Welt, daß die sowjetische
Forschung sogar in Verlegenheit ist, auch nur einen dauernden Klassenkampf
zwischen Sklaven und Sklavenhaltern aufzudecken."

[323]Fraternal clubs (collegia) played a very important role in the private
lives of many slaves, combining the functions of a religious congregation, a
social club, a craft-guild and a funeral society. According to Digest 47.22.3,
a slave had to obtain his owner's permission to join a collegium, but this request seems to have been readily granted. See Barrow, Slavery in the Roman
Empire, pp. 161-168; and MacMullen, Enemies of the Roman Order, pp. 173-178.

[324]Other significant differences between first-century Greco-Roman slavery
and nineteenth-century American slavery are: Nineteenth-century owners were
forbidden by law to educate their slaves; thus slaves did not advance to
"responsible" positions; slaves were not able to own property; they had no
hope of ever having a "normal" family life.

[325]See above, pp. 11-13, 15, 18-19, 22 n. 54, 23 n. 59, 24-25.

To what possibilities might Paul have been referring when he wrote 0721c?
That is, how did manumissions take place and for what reasons? With specific
reference to 0721d, what could the person in slavery do either to obtain his
manumission ("take freedom") or to refuse it ("stay in slavery")?

1. *The owners' reasons for manumission.*

At the beginning of the first century A.D., owners were manumitting
their slaves with a frequency that provoked Augustus Caesar to introduce laws
which restricted the numbers and ages of those who could be lawfully manumitted.[326] As it is difficult for a person who is acquainted primarily with
modern slavery to conceive of slavery as a way of life which was preferred by
some persons in the first century, so it may seem strange to him that owners
of slaves often found it to their own advantage to manumit their slaves. Indeed, in many cases manumission brought greater benefits to the owner than to
the slave.

The most important general benefit which the institution of manumission brought to the owners of slaves was the increased efficiency of slaves
who anticipated their "freedom" as a reward for good work.[327] The slave who
wanted to be freed did his work well; the owner encouraged his slaves to work
well by regularly manumitting those who had given him a number of years of
faithful service.[328]

An owner often freed a slave because it was more economical to use
his services as a freedman than to support him as a slave.[329] That is, the
owner could bind his freedman to him by *operae*-obligations or by a *paramonē*-
contract (thereby continuing to benefit from the former slave's services),
while insisting that the freedman find his own food and lodging. It was relatively expensive to keep a slave, and when he grew old his upkeep could exceed
his value. He might be virtually unsalable, but he could be freed on terms
which gave his patron the benefit of his remaining strength.

Impoverished slave-owners, who found it difficult to provide both

---

[326]See above, p. 83. Augustus' attempt to deal with the rapid increase
of freedmen-citizens and the decrease of freemen in the upper classes was
spread over twenty-seven years of legislation; i.e., from the *Lex Iulia de
maritandis ordinibus* of 18 B.C. to the *Lex Papia Poppaea* of A.D. 9.

[327]See above, p. 82.

[328]See Duff, *Freedmen in the Early Roman Empire*, p. 14. Already in the
fourth century B.C., Aristotle and Xenophon advised owners to hold out the
prospect of liberty to their slaves as the best way of encouraging them to
diligence and loyalty. See Morrow, *Plato's Law of Slavery*, p. 97.

[329]See Treggiari, *Roman Freedmen during the Late Republic*, p. 16.

for their slaves and for themselves, could arrange a workable solution to their problem by means of such a condition-bound manumission. Urbach concisely remarks: "On the one hand a labour force remained at their disposal, while on the other they were exempt from all responsibility towards it."[330]

Even if the slave were relatively young and vital, his owner might free him in order that as a freedman he might function more effectively as a source of income.[331] The owner could benefit both from the manumission price which the slave paid from his *peculium* (in a Roman household) or his savings (in a Greek household) and from the financial arrangements of the promised *operae* or of the *paramoné*-contract.[332]

The owner could realize a financial gain by taking or accepting a part or the whole of a slave's *peculium* or property in exchange for the slave's manumission.[333] Greek slaves were allowed to own their own property, and some of them were even allowed to take a "second job" in order to increase their savings.[334] Roman slaves were usually permitted to acquire a *peculium* as a further stimulus to good behavior.[335] The amount of ready cash exchanged by a slave for his manumission was usually much higher than the price of slaves on the market, so that manumission could prove quite profitable for the owner.[336]

---

[330]Urbach notes that "the Jewish slave-owner might likewise regard this kind of manumission as a way of escape from the difficulties confronting him because of the halakhic considerations involved in the religious status of the slave. He would thus be discharging himself of all responsibilities." "The Laws Regarding Slavery," p. 59.

[331]This reason for manumission appears very frequently in *paramoné*-inscriptions in which the manumittors are women. In Greek practice, wives were commonly much younger than their husbands; and with the increase of childless marriages during the Empire, this kind of freedman became particularly important to a woman when her husband died. See Welles, "Manumission and Adoption," p. 516.

[332]P.A. Brunt observes that such an arrangement could benefit both slave and owner; the slave gained a higher status and the owner profited financially. *JRS* 48 (1958), 165.

[333]See Crook, *Law and Life of Rome*, p. 189.

[334]See above, p. 41.

[335]No Roman owner was required to give his slave a *peculium*, but no slave who was to have any independent role could manage without one. Technically it belonged to the owner, as did any additional funds which the slave might acquire; but the slave had day-to-day disposal of it. A *peculium* could consist not only of money received from the owner or earned in business but also land, inheritances and other slaves. Sons and daughters also held their possessions as *peculia*, and they held these possessions under the same rules which governed the *peculia* of the slaves. See Crook, pp. 110, 189.

[336]See Duff, *Freedmen in the Early Roman Empire*, pp. 16-18; also Urbach, "The Laws Regarding Slavery," p. 47.

In all these cases, the owner's appreciation for long service or for a specific achievement could play an important role. In some cases, gratitude was the sole reason for manumission.[337] Sometimes dying slaves were freed on this account; as freedmen they became legally capable of making a will benefitting their relatives.[338]

Sometimes an owner freed one of his slaves in order to marry her.[339] An owner who feared that his slaves might be forced under torture to reveal "too much" about the owner's activities could grant them freedom; for a freedman could be brought to court against his patron only in the case of treason.[340] A Roman owner sometimes freed a group of slaves in order that they might increase the number of his *clientes*.[341] A politically active freeman needed a coterie of citizens upon whom he could depend, and such freedmen could be obliged to appear in public as their patron's retainers and to remain under his jurisdiction.[342]

Another Roman practice was to free a large number of slaves by testament on the condition that the slaves in question would receive their

---

[337] See Duff, p. 17.

[338] See Barrow, *Slavery in the Roman Empire*, pp. 174-175.

[339] According to Augustus' *lex Aelia Sentia* (A.D. 4), a female slave freed by her owner "for the purpose of matrimony" had to marry in order to validate her manumission and her status as citizen. Barrow (p. 196) comments: "An awkward dilemma must often have arisen." Note that a woman might free a male slave "for the purpose of matrimony" only if she herself was a freed slave and he her fellow slave. See Crook, *Law and Life of Rome*, p. 52.

[340] Under Roman law torture was not a kind of punishment but a method of interrogation of witnesses. In the case of slaves, their testimony was only admissible when it was taken under torture. A *civis Romanus* was traditionally exempt from torture, but during the Empire at least a few citizens were tortured in connection with trials for treason. See Crook, pp. 274-275.

[341] Duff observes that while Roman political figures often freed a number of their slaves in order to gain additional free clients, the Greeks frowned upon such a show of "greatness" and "liberality." *Freedmen*, p. 15.

[342] See Berger, *Dictionary of Roman Law*, p. 391, for a description of the relations between clients and patrons.

freedom after a period of public mourning for their deceased owner.[343]

One striking feature, therefore, of manumission-practice in the first century A.D. is the variety of reasons an owner might have had for freeing his slaves, i.e., for changing their relationship to him from that of slave to freedman. Although a certain number of slaves were freed because of the gratitude of their owners or because of a vain owner's attempt to gain a reputation for his "liberality," the majority of slaves were manumitted because it was to the financial advantage of the owners to do so.[344] What methods, then, were available to owners at the time they decided to manumit one or more of their slaves?

2. *The owners' methods of manumission.*

In 1 Cor. 0721c Paul mentions the possibility of the slave's becoming free. If some slaves in the Corinthian congregation were, indeed, "able to become free," through what procedures did they pass on their way to becoming freedmen? Under Roman law, a variety of formal and informal methods were used; only the formal methods made the freedman also a citizen. Under Greek law, manumission was a private act of the owner which was not controlled by any public official and which never directly included citizenship in its benefits.[345] By the first century, religious sanctions had become the most important method of guaranteeing the Greek freedman's status.

---

[343]Manumission by testament was a very popular method for freeing slaves, since such generosity was gratuitous for the testator (i.e., his heirs had to pay the 5% manumission tax) and he gained an escort of new freedmen at his funeral (each of whom would wear a *pilleus*, a close-fitting cap signifying "freedom"). Note that Treggiari (*Roman Freedmen*, pp. 27-28) challenges the view of Buckland (*The Roman Law of Slavery*, p. 460) and Watson (*The Law of Persons*, p. 194) that manumission was given most often by testament (Buckland estimates 9/10). In any case, Augustus' restrictive legislation was provoked principally by the large numbers of slaves who had been manumitted by this method.

[344]See Treggiari, pp. 19-20. Many communities under Greek law used a statute according to which a slave who performed the service of an informer (against one who endangered the community) was purchased from his owner by the community and set free. See Taubenschlag, *The Law of Graeco-Roman Egypt*, p. 98.

[345]While manumission in Greece could be effected by the action of a private citizen (or any other slave-owner), admission to citizenship required a special (and unusual) act of the sovereign body in the city. See Morrow, *Plato's Law of Slavery in its Relation to Greek Law*, p. 100.

From its beginnings, Roman law dealt with the question of the manumission of persons in slavery.[346] Three formal methods were described: *manumissio censu*, *manumissio vindicta*, and *manumissio testamento*. All three modes conferred both *libertas* and *civitas*.[347]

By the first century A.D., the census was no longer used as a means of freeing slaves.[348] Manumission by testament, however, remained a popular method of emancipation because of the many advantages it offered the owner.[349] In contrast to the other two formal methods, *manumissio testamento* could be conditional; i.e., a slave could be required to pay a fixed sum to an heir or to another party or to perform certain services either before or after the death of his owner, in order for his manumission to become effective.[350] On the other hand, slaves were often given a bequest or even made the sole heir in addition to being manumitted.[351]

---

[346]The *Twelve Tables*, Rome's earliest code of laws, was drawn up in the fifth century B.C. and was still being memorized by schoolboys in Cicero's time. As the laws developed, the exact nature of manumission was clarified. "It was not transfer of *dominium*, for a man has no *dominium* in himself (*Dig.* 9.2.13); nor was it mere release from a *dominus*, which was *derelictio* (*Dig.* 41.7.2), because some rights are left to the owner after manumission (*Dig.* 41.7.3). It is, instead, a negative thing, the destruction of the possibility of being owned." A.A. Rupprecht, "A Study of Slavery in the Late Roman Republic from the Works of Cicero" (unpubl. diss., U. of Penn., 1960), p. 46.

[347]See Treggiari, *Roman Freedmen during the Late Republic*, p. 21.

[348]*Manumissio censu* involved three steps: the slave's claim that he was a citizen, the assent of the owner, and the inscription on the census list. While it was in effect, this opportunity came every five years for an eighteen month period. The method fell out of use and was a rare event by the time of Cicero. See Treggiari, p. 27 and Rupprecht, pp. 46-47.

[349]See above, p. 91 n. 343. Manumission by will was a very easy procedure. The master needed only to name or describe the slave and to assert in some such formulas as *liber esto*, *liber sit* or *liberum esse iubeo* that this slave should be freed. Persons freed by this method became *liberti orcini*, the freedmen of the dead man. See Barrow, *Slavery in the Roman Empire*, p. 177; and Rupprecht, "A Study of Slavery," p. 48.

[350]Slaves who were freed conditionally by will were called *statuliberi* until the condition was fulfilled. Augustus made it obligatory for the heirs to honor the testator's request (called *fideicommissum*) upon the fulfillment of the prescribed conditions. Watson discusses a case in which the slave was to go free when he had given *operae* to the heir for a continuous period of seven years. *The Law of Persons*, p. 216.

[351]Barrow (p. 179) remarks that "in days when family unity counted less than hitherto, the heir often found himself with little of the family property left to him, and the next of kin saw faithful slaves inheriting what he had deemed to be his."

Manumissio vindicta, which took its name from the rod (*vindicta*) used in the manumission ceremony, may have been the most commonly used method of formal emancipation.[352] The owner and the slave who was to be freed appeared before a competent magistrate along with a third person who was called an *adsertor libertatis*.[353] This person asserted that the slave was free and touched him with the *vindicta*. The manumittor allowed this claim to go unanswered, whereupon the magistrate pronounced the slave free (probably using the words: *"Eum liberum addico"*).[354] In first-century Corinth the "competent magistrate" was the provincial governor.[355]

Treggiari suggests that *manumissio vindicta* was preferred by owners for slaves of particular merit or for those who were supposed to become more useful to their owners as freedmen. This method was also preferred by those owners who freed their slaves in order to be relieved of the trouble of supporting them.[356]

If no magistrate were available or if the slave were dying, none of the formal methods of manumission would have been possible. Thus, by the end of the Republic an informal method had been developed called *manumissio inter amicos*, meaning that the ceremony was an informal one, as between friends.[357] This kind of manumission could occur in a number of ways. For example, the owner could invite the slave to his table and simply declare that he was free (*manumissio per mensam*); or he could announce the manumission at a banquet before guests (*manumissio in convivio*); or the emancipation could be declared in a letter to the slave (*manumissio per epistulam*).

However it was administered, *manumissio inter amicos* allowed the owner to retain full control of the freedman's *peculium* and to keep the

---

[352]Treggiari, *Roman Freedmen*, p. 31.

[353]See Berger, *Dictionary of Roman Law*, for definitions of these legal terms.

[354]The exact procedure followed in *manu.vindicta* has caused considerable discussion. For the traditional view that it was a judicial process, see Buckland, *Roman Law of Slavery*, p. 441. Recent discussion of the problems has been summarized by Treggiari (pp. 21-23), who concludes that the *manu.vindicta* did retain "all the characteristics of *in iure cessio*" (i.e., a fictitious trial the purpose of which was transfer of ownership).

[355]Treggiari, p. 21. The governor could ratify such manumissions *in transitu* (e.g., when at the theater or in a bathing establishment) or in a private home (*Digest* 40.2.7.8).

[356]See Treggiari, p. 31.

[357]Note that the *"inter amicos"* referred not to the presence of friends of the manumittor but to the informal character of the procedure. In some cases, it seems that no witness was present; in such cases some evidence of the manumission, presumably written, was needed. See Treggiari, p. 29.

freedman's children as his slaves. The chief benefit of this act for the slave seems to have been that he could no longer be compelled by his owner to work for him full-time.[358]

Although some of the slaves who were manumitted by Greek owners at Corinth received their freedom by testament,[359] the chief method of Greek manumission was similar to the Roman *manumissio inter amicos*. Most frequently, owners used *manumissio per epistulam*.[360]

The history of manumission procedures in Greece is the history of the gradual growth of this private act into a public form with legal witnesses.[361] This development had its dynamic in the need to give greater security (i.e., publicity) to the liberty of the freedmen.[362] The state as such did not trouble itself with the manumission of slaves or the protection of freedmen. In this legal "vacuum" arose the custom of making a public announcement of the manumission through a herald (διὰ κήρυκος) before an assembly--in a theater, in a law-court (ἐν δικαστηρίῳ) or near an altar

---

[358] Before the *lex Iunia Norbana* of A.D. 19, the liberty enjoyed by informally manumitted slaves was conditional; they were said to enjoy liberty by their owners' consent, although the praetor (in Corinth, the governor) might intervene to protect them. After A.D. 19, these slaves enjoyed the status of *Latini Iuniani* (see above, p. 42 n. 110); i.e., they could not make a testament and they were not citizens. They did have access to the courts and could also later receive citizenship by means of a formal manumission. See Berger, *Dictionary of Roman Law*, pp. 537, 555. Treggiari (p. 30) suggests that informal manumission did not become common until after the *lex Junia Norbana*. For details regarding all aspects of Roman manumission-practice, see Buckland, *Roman Law of Slavery*, pp. 449-551.

[359] In Greek practice the heirs had to agree to the manumission of the slaves named by the testator. See Mitteis, *Reichsrecht und Volksrecht*, pp. 372-373.

[360] Mitteis, p. 376. Both Mitteis and Rädle (*Freilassungswesen*) use Latin legal terminology for many Greek procedures.

[361] Research on Greek manumission-practice followed closely the work on Greek epigraphy in the first half of the nineteenth century. The findings in the second half of that century clearly established redemption from slavery as one of the most important institutions of social and legal life in Greece. In his recent dissertation, Herbert Rädle has traced the development of manumission-procedures in Greece from their beginnings at the end of the fifth century B.C. to the end of the first century A.D. Rädle's discussion of "Delphi und Mittelgriechenland" (pp. 56-88) and "Peloponnes" (pp. 111-123) in his chapter on "Die Freilassung in der Jüngeren Zeit (um 200 v. Chr.-100 n. Chr.)" has been very helpful in confirming judgments I had already made as well as in calling to my attention additional evidence and insights. *Untersuchungen zum griechischen Freilassungswesen* (Munich, 1969).

[362] This conclusion is one of Rädle's major contributions to our understanding of manumission in Greece. His argument runs throughout his dissertation.

(ἐπὶ βωμόν).[363]

Private acts of manumission (*inter amicos*) continued to be quite frequent in Corinth during the first century A.D.[364] There is evidence, however, that during this period public manumission-procedures were preferred in Corinth and many parts of Greece, especially those emancipations which were carried out under the auspices of a temple.[365] The bulk of this evidence comes from the retaining walls along the left side of the street leading to the famous Temple of Apollo at Delphi.[366] The inscriptions engraved on the polygonal stones out of which these walls were built indicate that the manumission-procedures used at Delphi offered two advantages not found in most "secular" manumission-methods.[367]

The most important advantage was the practice of the temple authorities of including the witnesses' names and the financial terms in these inscriptions, which functioned as permanent records of the manumission-arrangements.[368] The second advantage was the function of Apollo (through his priestly representatives) as the "middleman" through whom the person in slavery was able to offer money to his owner in exchange for freedman-status.

---

[363]Mitteis, *Reichsrecht und Volksrecht*, p. 376. See also Urbach, "The Laws Regarding Slavery," pp. 60-61. Urbach (p. 61) detects the influence of this type of public announcement of manumission on Jewish practice during the early Empire. In any case, Jewish law put special emphasis on the importance of a written document of manumission signed by witnesses. The slave of a Jew also received his freedom if his owner left his entire estate to him by testament or if his owner gave him permission to marry an Israelite. See Zeitlin, "Slavery during the Second Commonwealth," pp. 216-217.

[364]Rädle, p. 168.

[365]See Rädle, pp. 4, 56-58, 68 and 144.

[366]For the full references to the published collections of these inscriptions, see above, p. 37 n. 90.

[367]In 1954, F. Sokolowski proposed the theory that the religious sanctions supporting manumission-procedures at Delphi originated in the ancient right of protection granted to slaves who took asylum in Greek temples. "The Real Meaning of Sacral Manumission," *HThR* 47 (1954), 178. His theory was a refinement of the recurrent view that manumission of slaves was originally a sacred act which became increasingly secularized. F. Bömer has convincingly shown, however, that Sokolowski is wrong and that he constructed the details necessary for his thesis. After a very thorough review of all the pertinent evidence, Bömer concludes that "die sakrale Form der Freilassung nicht älter ist als die Überlieferung und nichts anderes darstellt als eine zusätzliche sakrale Sanktion eines älteren profanen Vorgangs." *Untersuchungen über die Religion der Sklaven in Griechenland und Rom II: Die sogenannte sakrale Freilassung in Griechenland*, pp. 10-11. Rädle (pp. 5-6) notes that recent finds in Macedonia support this conclusion.

[368]Rädle, pp. 60-64. See Rädle, pp. 65-68, for the text and a translation of a typical, Delphic manumission-inscription.

Such a middleman was necessary because the slave was not legally capable of entering into a contract with his owner.[369] Apollo acted on the slave's behalf; the owner received the amount he had stipulated and the slave gained his manumission. The actions of the priests facilitated the manumission and the inscription of the contract on walls leading to the temple gave the manumission a high religious sanction.[370]

Thus, owners of slaves in first-century Corinth could manumit their slaves by means of a variety of procedures--formal or informal, public or private, religious or secular. In 1 Cor. 0721c, Paul could be referring to *any* of the manumission-procedures described above. In view of these methods and the various reasons which owners of slaves had for using them, to what extent could a person in slavery influence his owner to grant him freedman-status? With specific reference to 1 Cor. 0721d, what could the slave in Corinth do either to "strive" after his manumission ("take freedom") or to reject the possibility of manumission ("stay in slavery")?

3. *The options open to the slaves.*

The entire history of the interpretation of 1 Cor. 0721 has been dominated by the fundamental assumption that a person in slavery in first-century Corinth enjoyed the possibility of deciding for himself whether or not he would accept manumission when that possibility was presented to him.[371] That is, the exegetes of this text have argued either that Paul is urging Christians in slavery to "take freedom" when the possibility of manumission

---

[369]The legal significance of the manumission-procedure followed at Delphi has been sharply debated. Rädle agrees with the conclusion of the French legal scholars, R. Dareste, B. Hausoullier and Th. Reinach, *Recueil des inscriptions juridiques grecques* II (Paris, 1898), 233ff, namely, that the activity of the god was used in this form because the slave was not capable before the law. That is, the god rather than some other third party paid for the manumission. Usually the money was first entrusted to the god by the slave himself. Thus Rädle (p. 65) writes: "Der Sklave, der aufgrund seiner Rechtsstellung nicht in der Lage war, mit seinem Herrn einen rechtsgültigen Vertrag abzuschliessen, hatte dem Gott die für den Freikauf erforderliche Summe übergeben, und der Gott schloss für ihn mit dem Herrn den Kaufvertrag ab."
    Rädle notes that according to the Greek law practiced in Egypt (as known from the papyri) the necessary middlemen were often bankers. He concludes (p. 66) that a person in slavery could conduct business with a "third person" but that he could enter no legal contract with his owner.

[370]For an evaluation of the influence of this "sacral manumission" on Paul's expression, "freedman of the Lord" in 1 Cor. 0722, see the excursus below, pp. 121-125.

[371]The only interpreters of 1 Cor. 0721 known to me who have not made this assumption are those who have allegorically interpreted the "slavery" in this passage as the "state of marriage," namely, Origin, Jerome, Haimo of Auxerre and Sedulius Scotus.

mentioned in 0721c comes to them or that Paul is urging them to "use slavery" (i.e., remain in slavery) by refusing manumission.

The interpreters who supply τῇ ἐλευθερίᾳ after μᾶλλον χρῆσαι in 0721d have assumed that the matter of manumission was sufficiently within the control of the slave that Paul's encouragement to "take freedom" could have made a real difference in the Christian slave's decision. On the other hand, the interpreters who supply τῇ δουλείᾳ in 0721d have assumed that the slave who wanted to stay in slavery could simply inform his owner of this decision and that the owner would quickly agree.[372]

It is characteristic of both of these interpretations that neither the interests of the owner nor his function as manumittor are ever brought into consideration. Is it not evident, then, especially in view of what has already been observed about the relations between slaves and their owners in the first century A.D., that this assumption regarding the decision-making capability of the person in slavery must be examined carefully in order to achieve a clear understanding of 1 Cor. 0721?

Under both Greek and Roman law, a person in slavery could seek to bring nearer the day of his manumission by working hard and by conducting himself in a manner which pleased his owner.[373] Furthermore, a slave could offer his owner an attractive sum of money in exchange for manumission; or he could encourage a third party to purchase him in order to manumit him. In the face of bad treatment a slave might decide to run away from his owner. Such a slave could take refuge in one of the temples where the priests concerned themselves with improving the relations between slaves and their owners. In short, a person in slavery was able to choose from a number of ways by which he could encourage his owner to manumit him. Or if for some reason he had little hope of being manumitted he might attempt to run away.[374] Strikingly,

---

[372]This assumption appears to be based on the further assumption that every owner wanted to keep as many slaves as possible. Exegetes who argue in this manner seem to be completely unaware of the many reasons a slave-owner in the first century might have had for not wanting to keep his slaves in slavery. See above, pp. 88-91.

[373]See above, p. 74 n. 260 and pp. 82-84.

[374]Slaves with cruel owners (see above, pp. 68-70) might try to solve their problems by running away; also those who had somehow earned their master's disfavor might therefore have had their expected date of manumission pushed into an uncertain future. In addition, those persons who had been enslaved as the result of condemnation to eventual capital punishment (e.g., fighting with wild beasts or forced labor in the mines) could not be legally manumitted. In certain other cases, a person condemned to slavery (servus poenae) might also be given the additional penalty called "ne manumittatur," which meant that he could not be manumitted and had to remain a slave for life. See Berger, Dictionary of Roman Law, pp. 705-706.

however, there was no way that a slave could refuse freedman-status, if his owner decided to manumit him.

As one example of the legal helplessness of a person in Roman slavery, H. Jolowicz notes that even though owners usually allowed their slaves to accumulate money in their *peculia*, an owner could not be forced by law to accept a slave's *peculium* in exchange for manumission.[375] Nevertheless, most owners must have been trustworthy with regard to the agreements which they made with their slaves, for the hope of becoming a freedman after a number of years of hard and productive work encouraged a high level of performance among the slaves in the first century.[376] In order to make the arrangement sufficiently attractive to his owner, a slave might have to give up his entire *peculium*; on the other hand an owner could simply tell his slave that he was going to manumit him and going to take a part or all of the slave's *peculium* as well.[377]

In contrast, a slave under Greek law had the right of private ownership, and he could sometimes obtain his owner's permission to take a "second job" as a means of increasing his property.[378] He could obtain a loan from a third party as well as save his earnings in order to make an attractive offer to his owner.[379] Yet also under Greek law there was no legal way in which a

---

[375]*Historical Introduction to the Study of Roman Law*, p. 80. For the legal aspects of *peculium*, see A. Watson, *The Law of Persons*, pp. 178-181.

[376]A.M. Duff observes that some slaves went to great lengths to increase their *peculia*, even going hungry in order to sell their food ration. Other slaves had the opportunity to sell the remains of banquets at which they had served. Some slaves were tempted to steal from their owners. Of course, those slaves who administered businesses or factories or government offices had many opportunities to increase their wealth. *Freedmen in the Early Roman Empire*, pp. 16-17.

[377]Note that the *peculium* technically belonged to the slave's owner in any case. See Buckland, *The Roman Law of Slavery*, pp. 187-238. Also see above, p. 89.
    A.H.M. Jones comments: "It is not improbable also that manumission prices were higher than the market rate; for masters were in a strong bargaining position and slaves might have been willing to pay more for their freedom than they would fetch on the open market." "Slavery in the Ancient World," p. 191 (Finley, p. 7).

[378]See above, pp. 40-41 and 89.

[379]H. Rädle writes: "Jeder Sklave, der in den Besitz eines genügend hohen Kapitals zu gelangen vermochte, sei es durch Ersparnisse aus eigener Arbeit, sei es auch durch eine Anleihe von dritter Seite, und der somit in der Lage war, seinem Herrn als Anreiz zur Freilassung ein attraktives Geldangebot zu machen, konnte seiner Freilassung so gut wie sicher sein." *Freilassungswesen*, p. 173.

slave could demand his freedom.[380]

The slave of a Roman owner might turn to a third party to help him obtain manumission, but since his *peculium* actually belonged to his owner, he did not need a third person in order to effect the "exchange" of that *peculium* for freedman-status.[381] On the other hand, the slave of a Greek owner required some kind of middleman in order to exchange his property for manumission, because his legal position made it impossible for him to deal directly with his owner with respect to his own emancipation.[382]

Because of his helplessness before Greek law, a slave would choose a person to serve as middleman whom he was certain he could trust to free him without the protection of legal recourse. For example, the priests of Apollo at Delphi functioned as trustworthy middlemen.[383] A slave and his owner could travel to such a temple; the slave would hand over the agreed-upon amount to the priests who could then purchase him from his owner and vouchsafe his freedman-status.[384]

In many cases the "third party" involved in purchasing a slave's

---

[380]R.H. Barrow observes that a "slave could buy his freedom, though the master was not obliged to accept the ransom offered." "Freedmen," *The Oxford Classical Dictionary* (Oxford, 1949), p. 371. Rädle (p. 173) is more forceful in his expression: "Natürlich gab es für den Sklaven nie ein Rechtsmittel, die Freilassung auch gegen den Willen seines Herrn zu erzwingen. Insofern bleibt die höhere Rechtsstellung ein enormer Vorteil."

[381]The slave who was redeemed by a third person (a fiduciary) was called *"redemptus suis nummis."* (See Berger, *Dictionary of Roman Law*, p. 670.) In this case the money could come either from the slave's *peculium* or from the fiduciary, who might have been motivated by a promise from the slave to perform certain duties or to repay the money by a certain date. Such a "redeemer" was morally obliged to free the slave (the transaction took the form of a direct purchase); only after a rescript of Marcus Aurelius and Verus could the slave seek a remedy in court if his fiduciary failed to grant him freedman-status. See Lothar von Seuffert, "Der Loskauf von Sklaven mit ihrem Geld," *Festschrift für die Juristische Fakultät Giessen zum Universitäts-Jubiläum* (Giessen, 1907), pp. 1-20.

[382]See above, p. 96.

[383]Seuffert, "Der Loskauf von Sklaven mit ihrem Geld," pp. 19-20. For a typical inscription describing this procedure, see Collitz-Baunack-Bechtel, *GDI*, 1738.

[384]See above, pp. 95-96. The great advantage of the Delphic form of manumission was that the financial arrangements were included in the inscribed text. Apart from this feature and the function of Apollo as the "redeemer," the manumission-procedures at Delphi followed the form that was usual in the rest of Greece. See the excursus on sacral manumission below, pp. 121-125.
For a discussion of the influence of Greek law on Roman law with regard to the function of the "middleman," see H.F. Hitzig, "Zum griechisch-attischen Rechte," *Zeitschrift der Savigny-Stiftung für Rechtsgeschichte* (Romanistische Abteilung) 18 (1897), 167-171.

freedom was a free relative of the slave, a club (*collegium*) to which the slave belonged or an ad hoc group gathered specifically in order to loan the slave the money which his owner required for manumission. This kind of redemption from slavery was also practiced by first-century Christians as individuals and as congregations.

The fact that individual Christians and congregations did purchase the freedom of slaves who were sisters and brothers "in Christ" is verified by three early Christian writings: 1 Clement 5502, Ignatius to Polycarp 0403 and Hermas, Mandates 0810 and Similitudes 0108.[385]

In his letter to Corinth, Clement wrote:

> We know that many among ourselves have given themselves to bondage (δεσμά) that they might ransom others (ἑτέρους λυτρώσονται).[386]

The context makes clear that this "ransoming of others" refers to purchase from legal slavery. In his letter to Polycarp (0403), Ignatius urged those in slavery not to be puffed up and he admonished:

> Let them not desire to be set free (ἐλευθεροῦσθαι) at the church's expense, that they not be found the slaves of lust.

From this exhortation we can infer that there were slaves, at least in Smyrna, who knew that some congregations had indeed bought the freedman-status of some Christians who were in slavery.[387]

Hermas (Mandates 0810) recommended buying a person out of slavery as an act appropriate to a Christian:

---

[385]For the Greek text of 1 Clement and Ignatius see Karl Bihlmeyer, ed., *Die Apostolischen Väter*, Zweite Auflage, Erster Teil (Tübingen, 1956). For the Greek text of Hermas see Molly Whittaker, *Die apostolischen Väter* I: *Der Hirt des Hermas* (Berlin, 1956). The English translations quoted below are by Kirsopp Lake, ed., *The Apostolic Fathers* (Cambridge, Mass., 1913), 2 vols.

[386]This self-sale into slavery is important to notice for the exegesis of 1 Cor. 0723. The text continues: "Many have delivered themselves to slavery and provided food for others with the price they received for themselves." It is the *ransoming* of others, however, that is of chief interest here.

[387]A. Harnack comments: "From the epistle of Ign. to Polycarp (iv.) two inferences may be drawn: 1) that slaves were ransomed with money taken from the church collections; 2) that no claim to this favour was admitted." *The Mission and Expansion of Christianity in the First Three Centuries*, tr. J. Moffatt (New York, Harper edn., 1962), p. 170 n. 4 (*Mission und Ausbreitung des Christentums* I, 3rd edn. [Leipzig, 1915], 177 n. 4).

Next hear the things which follow: to minister to widows, to look after orphans and the destitute, to redeem from distress the servants of God (ἐξ ἀναγκῶν λυτροῦσθαι τοὺς δούλους τοῦ θεοῦ), to be hospitable ... to resist none, to be gentle, to be poorer than all men ... to practice justice, to preserve brotherhood ... not to oppress poor debtors, and whatever is like to these things."

And in the Similitudes (0108) the Shepherd says:

Therefore instead of lands, purchase afflicted souls (ἀντὶ ἀγρῶν οὖν ἀγοράζετε ψυχὰς θλιβομένας) as each one is able, and look after widows and orphans, and do not despise them, and spend your wealth and all your possessions for such fields and houses as you have received from God.

It would be strained in these contexts to suggest that Hermas spoke of a "spiritual purchasing," i.e., evangelism. On the contrary, Hermas recommended that Christians who could afford it should ransom slaves from their slavery, just as they should care for widows and orphans.[388]

Rudolf Knopf is probably correct in observing that primitive Christianity was very attractive to many persons in slavery, not only because they could find comfort for their hearts in this faith, but also because they could find real help among the Christians. Their brothers "in Christ" could assist them in many ways; e.g., a free Christian could take a mistreated slave into his own home, after having bought him from his unsympathetic, heathen owner. Or, as the letter from Ignatius to Polycarp indicates, a congregation might take money from its collection in order to purchase and manumit such a slave.

But it would be wrong to think that slaves were attracted to these congregations because Christians were unique in purchasing the freedom of slaves who became members of their fellowships. For when first or second century Christian individuals or congregations raised money with which to manumit one of their "brothers" who was in slavery, they may well have been encouraged by the manumission-practices of Jewish families, of the *collegia* or of the ἔρανος groups.

Jewish Christians in the early congregations may have felt a special urgency to set Christian brothers free from slavery because of the practice of slave-redemption by Jewish families whose members had been made slaves in the Diaspora. According to Salo Baron, such slaves were quickly ransomed by their family or by friends. He writes:

---

[388]See R. Knopf, *Das nachapostolische Zeitalter*, p. 69. Also Günther Harder, "Miszelle zu 1 Kor. 7.17," *ThLZ* 79 (1954), 372.

The families of Jewish prisoners, as well as the Jewish communities already established in the vicinity of their new places
of settlement, left no stone unturned until they secured their
freedom, since the commandment to "ransom captives" ranked among
the highest in the Jewish religious law (M. Giṭṭin IV, 6.9).[389]

Perhaps Jewish Christians in Corinth followed this practice by purchasing the
freedman-status of slaves in the congregation there.

Another possible model for the congregations in Greece and Italy
was provided by various *collegia*, some of which, at least sometimes, purchased the freedom of their members who were in slavery.[390] These clubs played a very important role in the private lives of many slaves.[391] It seems
clear that in many respects, such as regular meetings, common treasury, religious worship, festive meals, administrative officers, and perhaps a common
cemetery, most early Christian congregations did appear, at least to outsiders,
to be very similar to the *collegia funeraticia*.[392] These clubs were certainly
very popular and included men from every social class.[393]

Marcus Aurelius may have been the first emperor to give to the
collegia the right to manumit slaves, but Barrow believes that "all colleges
undoubtedly manumitted long before this date."[394] In view of the many similarities between the early Christian congregations and these *collegia*, it is
quite probable that both slaves and free men in these congregations found it

---

[389]Baron asserts that the paucity of Jewish slaves found in the papyri and
inscriptions of the ancient world "is understandable only as the result of
concerted communal resistance." *A Social and Religious History of the Jews* I,
260.

[390]Although the evidence for regarding Christian congregations as *collegia*
is very ambiguous and quite difficult to evaluate, it is still possible to
suppose that the activities of the *collegia* presented models for some aspects
of the conduct of these congregations.
  Theodor Mommsen, a commanding expert on ancient law and society, was
the first to suggest that the Christian congregations gained legal recognition by the Roman Empire as *collegia tenuiorum* or *collegia funeraticia*, in his
doctoral dissertation: *De collegiis et sodaliciis Romanorum*, 1843. For a
recent survey of the seemingly endless literature see Francesco de Robertis,
Il fenomeno associativo nel mondo romano (Rome, 1955).

[391]See above, p. 87 n. 323.

[392]See Jean Gagé, *Les classes sociales dans l'empire romain*, p. 308.

[393]R. MacMullen estimates that by the second century A.D., about one-third
of the urban male population belonged to these fraternal groups. He judges
that the average size of such a group was 150 men. *Enemies of the Roman
Order*, p. 174.

[394]*Slavery in the Roman Empire*, p. 189.

most appropriate for the group to purchase the freedom of members who were in slavery.   Another model of manumission-practice existed in the first century A.D. which may have influenced early Christian congregations in Greece, namely, the ἔρανος group. The term ἔρανος originally referred to a "banquet of friends," the cost of which was shared by the participants.[395] Beginning in the fifth century B.C. it was used for the contributions brought together by a group under a leader (ἀρχερανιστής or προστάτης ἐράνων) who paid out the loan and received it in repayment. Such a group often came together solely to accomplish a specific purpose, such as payment of a fine, ransom out of imprisonment or ransom out of slavery.[396] Already in the fourth century B.C. such groups were helping slaves to purchase their freedom. Beginning in the second century B.C., slaves as well as freedmen began to serve as leaders of such "eranos" groups which they organized for mutual assistance.[397]

It is reasonable to suggest that groups of Christians, perhaps even an entire congregation, raised an "eranos" in order to advance to a brother in slavery the money which his owner would accept as the price for his manumission. In any case, long before the ransoming of slaves by Christians mentioned by Clement, Ignatius and Hermas, various social groups were assisting slaves in moving from slavery to freedman-status. Many early Christian congregations may have been influenced by their practices, and the congregation in Corinth may have acted in some cases as an "eranos" group already in the first few years of its existence. An "eranos" or gift of money from this congregation might have been one way in which Christian slaves in Corinth secured enough money to interest their masters in manumitting them.

In addition to calling upon a "third party" for financial assistance, a slave who believed himself to be illegally enslaved might ask a freedman or a freeman to act as his *adsertor libertatis* in a court

---

[395]H.D. Liddell, R. Scott and H.S. Jones, *A Greek-English Lexicon* (Oxford, 1940), p. 680.

[396]Herbert Rädle, "Selbsthilfe-organisationen der Sklaven und Freigelassenen in Delphi," *Gymnasium* 77 (1970), 2-3. The loan seems to have been made without interest. F.M. Heichelheim observes that "papyri from Alexandria suggest that this type of loan was often used by Hellenistic Jews to evade the biblical prohibition of interest." *Oxford Classical Dictionary*, p. 366.

[397]Rädle, p. 4.

investigation of his status.[398] If no one submitted a counterclaim (e.g.,
that the person in question had been born a slave and not a freeman) the
slave was declared a free man.[399]

How often those in slavery took the initiative with regard to their
manumission is not clear.[400] The most direct way in which a slave could encourage his owner to manumit him was to do his work well and to save his money
(or increase his *peculium*). He might then ask a third party to help him carry
out the proper legal procedures for manumission. Whether or not a slave was
manumitted, however, remained entirely a decision of his owner. This decision
usually served the master's own advantage and was not based on any particular
concern for the interests of the person in slavery.[401] As has been suggested
above (pp. 75-76), there were cases in which the slave had little or no interest in being manumitted. But if his owner decided to manumit him, the slave
had no recourse apart from informally entreating his owner to allow him to
remain in slavery. That is, neither Greek nor Roman law viewed the slave as
a "legal person," and thus he had no legal means by which he could refuse
manumission. On the other hand, if a slave found his particular situation
increasingly intolerable, he could take the initiative by fleeing to an asylum
(with the hope of being sold to a new owner) or by running away (with the hope
of not being caught).[402]

---

[398] See Berger, *Dictionary of Roman Law*, p. 351; and Watson, "The *Liber Homo*
Treated as Slave," *The Law of Persons*, pp. 218-225. Watson (p. 218) remarks:
"It seems not infrequently to have happened that, unknowingly or even know-
ingly, a free man would serve as a slave." Note, e.g., the case of Melissus,
a slave of Maecenas, who rejected the assistance of his mother when she wanted
to assert in court that her son had been born a free man (Suetonius, *De grammaticis* 21). This case is discussed below, pp. 107-109.

[399] Although this action, called *vindicatio in libertatem*, was very similar
in form to *manumissio vindicta*, the slave did not become a freedman (as by
manumission), but a free man. See Berger, p. 766.

[400] See S. Treggiari, *Roman Freedmen*, p. 17.

[401] See the discussion of the owners' reasons for manumission above, pp. 88-
91.

[402] S. Lauffer states that when individual slaves "freed" themselves from
their owners by running away, it was not at all a question of a consciousness
of rank or class based on a general legal or economic situation of the slave.
Rather, it happened on the basis of personal impulse, because they could not
bear their individual situation and treatment. "Die Sklaverei in der griech.-
röm. Welt," p. 377.

According to Greek law, a slave could flee to an altar or temple and request asylum.[403] The slave was at least temporarily protected from his owner until the priests decided if he should be reconciled to his owner or should be sold to a new one.[404] Although Roman imperial law did not grant the right of temple asylum to slaves, slaves of Roman owners were permitted to flee for refuge to statues of the Emperor, where their grievances were heard.[405]

Some slaves were willing to take the risk of trying to escape completely from their owners. They sought some means of securing their freedom or of passing as free.[406] If caught, the runaway slave (*servus fugitivus*)

[403]An asylum (ἄσυλος τόπος) was a place from which a person could not be forcibly removed, i.e., a place where every συλᾶν ("right of seizure") was forbidden. (See Polybius 4,18,10 and Livy 1,35,51). The general Hellenistic restrictions upon temple asylum for slaves are reflected clearly by Philo (*De virtutibus* 124) in his interpretation of Deut. 2315-16. See the discussion by Colson, "Appendix to 'On the Virtues'," Philo (Loeb edn.) VIII, 447.

[404]In his book on Greek holy law published in 1920, Kurt Latte sought to describe an historical progression in the benefits which became available to a slave who sought asylum: 1) Originally the rights of the owner were not really affected by the asylum; they were only temporarily suspended. 2) The slave could demand better treatment and obtain an oath to support the owner's promise of such treatment. 3) At least at Athens, the slave could ask to be sold to a different owner. 4) Finally, according to Latte, the slave could ask to be declared the property of the god and in this way be manumitted by the priests. *Heiliges Recht: Untersuchungen zur Geschichte der sakralen Rechtsformen in Griechenland* (1964; reprint of 1920 Tübingen edn.), pp. 106-108. L. Wenger ("Asylrecht," *RAC* I, 838) completely accepts Latte's conclusions. In contrast, however, both Bömer (*Untersuchungen* II, 152-154) and Rädle (*Freilassungswesen*, p. 42 n. 3) assert that Latte has misread the evidence on which he based his judgment that priests had the power to manumit a slave against the will of his owner. That is, contrary to Latte's interpretation, the persons mentioned in the pertinent inscriptions had never been in slavery; and the dedications described in these inscriptions have nothing to do with manumission. In a later article entitled "ΣΥΛΑΝ," Latte does not mention anything about priests manumitting slaves. *Kleine Schriften*, eds. Gigon, Buchwald and Kunkel (1968), pp. 416-419.

[405]Seneca, *De beneficiis* 3, 21 and *De clementia* 1, 18,1-3; also *Digest* 1.12.1 and 8. See also Westermann, *Slave Systems*, p. 108.

[406]Waiting for the fugitive slave, to assist or betray him, was the *fugitivarius*, the "runaway man," whose activities are described by David Daube, *Juridical Review* 64 (1952), 12-14. This fellow could try to convince the owner of a runaway slave to sell him the slave at a reduced price (by arguing that the slave would never be found by the owner). The "runaway man" (who probably knew where to find the slave) could then buy the slave and later sell him for his market price to an owner whom the slave preferred. Or the slave could be manumitted if he could pay what the "runaway man" demanded. J.A. Crook refers to a law promulgated early in the Empire which stipulated that a slave bought by a *fugitivarius* could not be freed for ten years after his escape without the consent of his former owner. Crook concludes that this rule "made the game not worth the candle for the slave who hoped for freedom." *Law and Life of Rome*, p. 187. It is not clear if this law was already in effect in A.D. 50.

might be imprisoned by the local magistrate or subjected to hard labor in the mines, awaiting return to his owner.[407] The slave-owner could enter other municipalities and provinces than his own and call upon the local authorities for help in locating his *fugitivus*. He sometimes offered a reward for information leading to the return of the slave.[408] In any case, the fugitive slave was the exception.[409] S. Lauffer states that the usual situation was one in which the slave accepted his slavery and worked steadily, usually looking forward to his future manumission.[410]

It has been stated above (p. 104) that a person in slavery was completely dependent on the wishes of his owner as to whether or not he was given freedman-status. According to both Greek and Roman legal practice, the slave could neither force his owner to manumit him nor could he resist manumission when his owner decided to make him a freedman. This observation is particularly significant because it calls into question all interpretations of 1 Cor. 0721 which seem to presuppose that manumission (as Paul refers to it in 0721c) was a possibility which the slave was able to accept or reject.

To be sure, there was no Greek or Roman law that expressly declared that it was illegal for a slave to refuse to be manumitted (or to be sold,

---

[407]Westermann, *Slave Systems*, p. 77.

[408]Westermann (p. 77) comments that the amount of assistance a slave-owner could expect depended on his personal influence. When he caught the runaway slave, the owner could severely punish him. Petronius (*Satyricon* 103,4) describes one of the punishments which was often used, namely branding on the forehead, which he calls the *notum fugitivorum epigramma*. Coleman-Norton suggests that this was either the single letter *"F"* or *"FVG"* (for *"FVGITIVVS"*). He also notes that Galen (who was born about two generations after Paul's death) reports that it was customary for runaway slaves to be punished by the application of hot metal plates (καίειν) to their legs. F. Dölger observes that burning plates were also used to punish slaves who were thieves (applied to their hands) or who were gossips (applied to their tongues). See P.R. Coleman-Norton, "The Apostle Paul and the Roman Law of Slavery," *Studies in Roman Economic and Social History* (Princeton, 1951), pp. 175-177; and F.J. Dölger, "Der Feuertod ohne Liebe. Antike selbstverbrennung und christlicher Martyrium-Enthusiasmus: Ein Beitrag zu 1 Kor. 13,3," *Antike und Christentum* I (Münster, 1929), 255-257.

[409]Note that in Roman law it was not considered running away (*fuga*) to run to a friend of the owner to secure intercession, and in this case mere failing to return was also not considered *fuga*. There had to be some definite act of flight (see Buckland, *The Roman Law of Slavery*, p. 268).

For a good discussion of other Roman laws which have been cited in connection with the case of Philemon and Onesimus see Coleman-Norton, "The Apostle Paul and the Roman Law of Slavery," pp. 172-177. Note also, however, that contrary to the common assumption that Roman law helps explain Paul's return of Onesimus to Philemon, it is highly probable that Philemon was a provincial who did not enjoy the privileges of Roman law (see above, p. 15 n. 31).

[410]"Die Sklaverei in der griech.-röm. Welt," p. 377.

rented, loaned or given as a gift).[411] No such law was needed, however, for the slave was not a "legal person," and thus he had no means of resisting such actions by his owner, except by pleading with him privately. Since the owner's financial gain was usually at stake, such pleading may not have been very effective. This inability of the slave to refuse manumission is illustrated by a case in which a slave who tried to remain in slavery because he liked his position was nevertheless manumitted by his owner and sent as a freedman into another household.

This case is described by Suetonius, *De grammaticis et rhetoribus* 21, as follows:[412]

C. Melissus Spoleti natus, ingenuus sed ob discordiam parentum expositus, cura et industria educatoris sui altiora studia percepit ac Maecenati pro grammatico muneri datus est. cui cum se gratum et acceptum in modum amici videret, quamquam adserente matre permansit tamen in statu servitutis praesentemque condicionem verae origini anteposuit, quare cito manumissus Augusto etiam insinuatus est. quo delegante, curam ordinandarum bibliothecarum in Octaviae porticu suscepit....[413]

---

[411]Note that although the Jewish slave of a Jewish owner could elect to stay in slavery longer than his "normal" enslavement of six years (see above, p. 53), he could do so only if his owner wanted to keep him. Salo Baron (*A Social and Religious History of the Jews* I, 269) observes that manumission was by no means always a desirable prospect for the unskilled, the aged or the sick slave, or for the Gentile slave who in contrast to the Jewish slave did not receive any money with his manumission with which he could "get started" again. It is clear from b. Giṭṭin 40b that the Rabbis discussed the case of the slave who tried to refuse manumission by claiming that he had not really been manumitted. The testimony of the owner in this case was preferred to that of one hundred witnesses. Maurice Simon translates this text as follows: "Our Rabbis have taught: If a man says, 'I have made my slave So-and-so free,' and the slave says, 'You have not freed me,' we take into account the possibility that he has presented him a deed of emancipation through a third party [without the slave's knowledge]. If, however, the master says, 'I have written and given to him,' and he says, 'He has not written for me nor given to me,' this is a case where the admission of the litigant is worth the evidence of a hundred witnesses." *The Babylonian Talmud*, ed. I. Epstein (London, 1936).

[412]This book formed a part of a larger work by Suetonius entitled *De viris illustribus*, which treated the lives of Romans who were eminent in literature. It appears to have been written between A.D. 106-113. See J.C. Rolfe, *OCD*, p. 865.

[413]The text continues: "atque, ut ipse tradit, sexagesimum aetatis annum agens libellos Ineptiarum qui nunc Iocorum scribuntur componere instituit absolvitque centum et quinquaginta quibus et alios diversi operis postea addidit. fecit et novum genus togatarum inscripsitque trabeatas." The critical text is *C. SUETONI TRANQUILLI, PRAETER CAESARUM LIBROS RELIGUIAE*, collegit Giorgio Brugnoli, pars prior *De Grammaticis et Rhetoribus*, Editio Altera, Bibliotheca Scriptorum Graecorum et Romanorum Teubneriana (MCMLXIII), pp. 23-24.

Here we are told about a certain Gaius Melissus from Spoletium who became the
slave and grammarian of Gaius Maecenas who was a scion of the ancient Etruscan
aristocracy and a trusted friend, counselor and diplomatic agent of Augustus
Caesar.[414] Melissus was born as a free man, but was taken into slavery as a
child after his parents had "exposed" him (see above, p. 48) following a
family quarrel. The man who reared him as a slave gave him an excellent education (see above, pp. 75-76) and he became a grammarian, i.e. a tutor, in
the household of a very interesting owner, Maecenas of Rome. Melissus made a
good impression on Maecenas, who treated him as a friend (see above, p. 76).

At one point, Melissus' mother tried to act as her son's *adsertor
libertatis* (see above, pp. 103-104) in order to free him from slavery. But
Melissus was quite pleased with his work and position, and he rejected his
mother's efforts on his behalf. Whereupon (*quare*)[415] Maecenas, without any
apparent regard for Melissus' expressed interest in remaining his slave, manumitted Melissus, who as a freedman won the favor of Augustus. It appears as
if Augustus became Melissus' patron, for he appointed him to the task of
arranging a library in the "Colonnade of Octavia." According to a writing by
Melissus known to Suetonius, when Melissus was in his sixtieth year he began
to compile a number of volumes, including one containing one hundred and fifty
jokes. He also created a new kind of drama in which the principal characters
were Roman knights.

Suetonius, of course, did not write with a lawyer's interests or
precision. What should be clear, however, is that Suetonius believed that
Melissus could have been recognized as a free man when his mother initiated
the *vindicatio in libertatem* on his behalf. It should also be clear that
although Melissus was able to refuse freedom by ignoring his mother's claim,
he was not able to refuse manumission and his subsequent separation from

---

[414] Maecenas was also a great patron of literature. "He was the friend and
benefactor of Horace, and Virgil wrote the *Georgics* at his suggestion." G.W.
Richardson, *OCD*, pp. 527-528.

[415] The precise force of *quare* ("therefore, for that reason") at the beginning of this sentence is not clear. If Melissus' refusal to claim his true
status as *ingenuus* was regarded by Maecenas as a praiseworthy act which should
be rewarded by manumission, then the manumission itself was somewhat ironic.
For Melissus obviously wanted to remain a slave of Maecenas rather than be set
free. Suetonius makes clear, however, that even as a freedman Melissus lost
his direct contact to Maecenas and came under the patronage of Augustus. Note
that Barrow saw a contrast between Melissus' desire and Maecenas's action; in
his summary of Melissus' career, Barrow (*Slavery in the Roman Empire*, p. 10)
wrote: "He remained in slavery, preferring his present status to that given
him by birth. Soon, however, he was freed, and passed into the service of
Augustus." It is this "however" which indicates that Barrow saw the same
tension between Melissus' own interests and Maecenas's decision that I am
stressing here.

Maecenas.[416]

It is important to remember that Suetonius's account of Melissus' experience does not *prove* anything about the options of a person in Greek or Roman slavery. Rather it simply *illustrates* the situation which is already clear from Roman (and Greek) law itself, namely that a person in slavery could do nothing to remain a slave if his owner decided to manumit him.[417]

The options open to those in slavery in first-century Corinth, therefore, were such that the slave could encourage his owner by various means to manumit him. If the owner decided that it was to his advantage to grant freedman-status to the slave, he did so. If, on the other hand, the slave wanted to remain in slavery for any reason, he could make certain that his owner was aware of this desire; but the slave's "security" in slavery was continually subject to change according to the will of his owner. The slave could remain in slavery only as long as the owner wanted to keep him as a slave. When the owner decided to manumit him, he became a freedman whether or not he had been looking forward to his manumission.

What, then, does this discussion of the range of action open to a slave in the first century with respect to his manumission mean for the interpretation of 1 Cor. 0721? First of all, this discussion shows that Paul's words in 0721c (ἀλλ' εἰ καὶ δύνασαι ἐλεύθερος γενέσθαι) could not have referred to flight to an asylum, since it was not possible to become free by such a flight. Secondly, this discussion shows that it is very unlikely that Paul was trying to persuade Christian slaves not to run away from their owners. For while it is true that some slaves in the first century A.D. did try to escape from their owners (e.g., Onesimus), the fugitive slave was an exception in this period because conditions of slave-life were improving and because

---

[416]As I have mentioned above (pp. 47-48), Roman lawyers argued about the precise legal status of a person who was born a free man but who became a slave by self-sale, by being sold as a child or by "exposure." To be sure, these people were in slavery, but it was debated if their legal status were that of a slave. For example, Alan Watson (*The Law of Persons*, p. 171) observes that Melissus' state of slavery was *de facto* rather than *de iure* and that technically speaking no manumission was necessary or possible in Melissus' case. Despite the technical question, however, it is clear that from Suetonius's viewpoint Melissus was made a freedman by *manumission*.

This case is all the more interesting and persuasive precisely because Melissus' birth as a free man gave him the possibility of later claiming his status as a free man through an *adsertor libertatis* and because he so clearly rejected this possibility and chose to stay in slavery. His own interests are thus unmistakably clear, perhaps clearer than if he had been a house-born slave who simply told his master that he did not want to be manumitted.

[417]Indeed, even as a freedman the former slave of a Roman owner could not sell himself to another owner without his patron's permission. The freedman who had been manumitted under Greek law could try to sell himself back into slavery if he were not bound in a *paramoné*-contract of some kind.

almost every urban slave could expect to be manumitted.[418]

Thus, I conclude that when Paul said "if you are able to become free" he meant "if you are able to be manumitted."

The third and most important conclusion which can be drawn from the discussion of the slave's options is that all interpretations of 1 Cor. 0721 which are based on the presupposition that a person in slavery could determine whether or not he would accept manumission are false because this presupposition is false. For neither Greek, Roman nor Jewish law made it possible for a person in slavery to refuse or forego manumission. Since a slave could not choose not to be manumitted, it would have been rather pointless for anyone to have advised him to choose to be manumitted (i.e., "take freedom").

Notice again that *both* alternatives which have been suggested for completing 1 Cor. 0721 are based on the assumption that the slave who is addressed in 0721c had to make a choice about his future. That is, both the scholars who have completed 0721d with "take freedom" and those who have completed this phrase with "use slavery" seem to have assumed that in 0721c Paul was addressing a situation which might be described as follows:

Before the slave heard Paul's words in 0721, his owner had said to him: "If you are interested, I'm willing to manumit you (and you will become my freedman); but if you are not interested, I'm willing to keep you (as a slave)." When the slave then heard Paul's words in 0721d, he heard advice from Paul (according to these scholars) to say either yes or no to this friendly or disinterested offer of manumission by his owner.

So, e.g., A.P. Stanley wrote that the Christian slave was to remain in slavery even when the "offer of freedom is made."[419] Frederick Godet wrote that the question in 1 Cor. 0721 is whether or not a Christian slave was "to profit by an offer of emancipation."[420] Robertson and Plummer concluded that Paul was speaking of "an opportunity for emancipation" and that 0721c could be

---

[418] For these reasons there was no general climate of unrest among the slaves to whom Paul was speaking. Nor is there any indication that the slaves who became Christians at Corinth also became restless in their slavery because of their new faith. The "enthusiasm" in the Corinthian congregation did have social consequences in that it affected male and female relationships, but it does not seem to have affected the slaves as such (see below, ch. 3).

[419] Stanley further suggests that the "prospect of liberty" probably resulted "from the fact of the master's being a Christian." *The Epistles of St. Paul to the Corinthians* (London, 1855), p. 132.

[420] Godet speaks of "an opportunity providentially offered of becoming free" and of "the liberation which was offered him." *Commentary on St. Paul's First Epistle to the Corinthians*, trans. A. Casin (Edinburgh, 1886), I, 360.

paraphrased: "if the one course is as possible as the other."[421] A. Schlatter
observed that although he preferred the interpretation "take freedom," most of
the scholars who were his contemporaries concluded that the Christian slave
was to remain in slavery "wenn ihm sein Herr die Freilassung anbiete."[422]

Notice that all these interpretations understand the manumission in
question as something which was "offered" to a slave. Thus, quite naturally,
0721d is interpreted as advice to accept or reject this offer. On the basis
of the evidence discussed above, however, especially under the topic "The
owners' reasons for manumission," it must be clear that such a friendly or
disinterested offer of manumission rarely, if ever, occurred. For an owner
decided to manumit one or more of his slaves in order to serve his own advantage, not that of a slave. Manumission, therefore, was not an act which was
"accepted" or "refused" by the slave. It happened to him. And while some
slaves were undoubtedly glad that it did, others would have preferred to remain in slavery.

In the fourth place, the discussion of slavery in this chapter leads
me to challenge the interpretations of 1 Cor. 0721 given by those scholars who
conclude that Paul was urging Christian slaves not to strive after manumission
or to do anything which might encourage their owners to manumit them.

We have seen that there were a number of ways by which the person
in slavery could try to increase his chances of being manumitted, i.e., a number of ways by which he could encourage his owner to manumit him. In short,
he could do his work faithfully and well in the hope of receiving manumission
as his reward or he might offer his owner a sum of money in the hope of buying
himself out of slavery. Such "striving" to be manumitted has been seen by a
number of interpreters as an action which presupposed an attitude to which Paul
objected and which he thus sought to change in 0721d (understood as "rather
use slavery").

The situation which is assumed in this case may be described as
follows: In 1 Cor. 0721c Paul was addressing those Christians in slavery who
knew that if they would fulfill certain conditions, such as working hard or
obtaining a certain amount of money, their owners would most probably manumit
them. When these slaves heard Paul's words in 0721d, they heard advice either
to fulfill such conditions (presumably because "freedom" was a desirable thing)
or not to fulfill them (presumably because this would demonstrate the slave's
lack of concern about his status).

[421]On this basis, Robertson and Plummer paraphrased 1 Cor. 0721: "Slavery
is not intolerable for a Christian, but an opportunity for emancipation need
not be refused." *I Corinthians*, pp. 147-148.

[422]*Paulus der Bote Jesu* (1934), pp. 231-232.

So, e.g., J. Weiß claims that Paul was referring exclusively to the possibility of self-purchase in 0721c: he expressly eliminates from consideration any manumission which might take place for any other reason.[423] J. Héring also says that "to become free" (0721c) means to have "the possibility of liberating yourself from slavery."[424] H. Gülzow accepts Weiß's argument and extends the possibilities in question to include those slaves who would have to endure some post-manumission obligations as part of the price of manumission.[425]

H. Bellen must have presupposed the specific situation described by Weiß when he stated that Paul saw two possibilities for the slave with respect to the manumission mentioned in 0721c: "das Streben nach ihr und der Verzicht auf sie."[426] Bellen puts great weight on the decision-making power of the slave and stresses the "Selbstüberwindung des Sklaven angesichts der möglichen Freilassung."[427]

By his stress on "striving" Bellen introduces the claim that Paul was referring not only to money which the slave already had at his disposal for purchase of freedman-status (as is assumed by Weiß and others) but also

---

[423]Thus, Weiß (*Der erste Korintherbrief*, p. 188) paraphrased 0721c: "Selbst in dem besonderen Falle, daß du die Mittel hast, dich frei zu kaufen, selbst in diesem Falle, der ja sehr verlockend wäre." He expressed his limitation of 0721c to "self-purchase" as follows: "Voraussetzung ist hierbei natürlich, daß die Freiheit dem Betr. nicht etwa geschenkt wird, sondern daß er nur die Möglichkeit hätte sich selbst loszukaufen." Weiß thought that Paul was referring especially to those manumission-transactions which took place at Delphi. It is most unlikely, however, that the particular circumstances of Delphic sacral manumission played any role in Paul's thinking. See the excursus on sacral manumission, below, pp. 121-125.

[424]*The First Epistle of Saint Paul to the Corinthians*, p. 55.

[425]Gülzow writes: "Seit Weiß wird auch mit Recht hervorgehoben, daß bei diesen möglichen Freilassungen nicht an ein Geschenk zu denken ist, sondern Belastungen durch einen Loskauf oder nachträgliche Verpflichtungen vorausgesetzt sind." *Christentum und Sklaverei*, p. 178.
H. Conzelmann also agrees with Weiß, but he concludes his discussion of 0721 with the somewhat astounding note: "Es wäre natürlich absurd, auf den problematischen Charakter mancher Freilassungen hinzuweisen." *1. Korintherbrief*, pp. 152-153.
C.K. Barrett, who also appears to assume that the slave was in complete control of his manumission in that he had the means to purchase his freedom, but who at least notes that "emancipation could take place in a variety of ways and was not infrequent," paraphrases 0721cd as follows: "But even though you should be able to become free, put up rather with your present status." *First Epistle to the Corinthians*, p. 170.

[426]"Μᾶλλον χρῆσαι: Verzicht auf Freilassung als asketische Leistung?" *Jahrbuch für Antike und Christentum* 6 (Münster, 1963), 178.

[427]Note that if Bellen was thinking of manumission in general, his argument is wrong because of the impossibility of "renouncing" manumission.

to one or more of those ways noted above by which a person in slavery might yet obtain the necessary money. Whether or not the Christian slaves at Corinth needed to be persuaded not to pester the congregation (or some other person or group) for money cannot be decided apart from the exegesis of 1 Cor. 7. Whether or not Paul in 0721c was interested in commenting on such practices as "working faithfully and well" or taking a second job also cannot be decided apart from exegetical considerations.[428] On the basis of this chapter alone, however, it can be shown that the view represented by Weiß, Bellen and others is very questionable because none of these exegetes have presented any reasons for limiting the means of the manumission from slavery which is mentioned in 0721c to "self-purchase."

Furthermore, these exegetes seem to have assumed that manumission was an exceptional event in the social life of the first century A.D. and that Paul in 0721cd was extending his general advice in 0721b ("Don't worry about it.") to cover this special case.[429]

In striking contrast to this view we have seen that at least a very large majority of those persons who were in urban slavery in first-century Corinth could reasonably expect to be manumitted after a number of years of labor.[430] The percentage of these manumissions which resulted from the direct initiative of those in slavery (i.e., "self-purchase") is not clear. Both Buckland and Watson have claimed that most of the slaves during this period were set free by means of the testaments of their owners.[431] It is clear that owners who manumitted their slaves had many different motives for doing so, e.g., the need to reward good work and to encourage good work by those yet in

---

[428]At this point it may simply be observed that such "striving" by those in slavery is certainly not clearly evident from the text of 0721c itself.

[429]This assumption, which perhaps has been encouraged by translating the words εἰ καί as if they meant "even if," seems to be the primary reason these scholars have effectively ignored the usually strong adversative force of the particle ἀλλά which begins 0721c. That is, instead of allowing 0721c to express something in contrast to 0721a or 0721b, they have read 0721c as a description of one specific way by which a Christian slave could demonstrate his lack of concern about his social status, namely by ignoring an opportunity to purchase his freedom from his owner. They have interpreted 1 Cor. 0721 as if it had been written: "Were you a slave when you were called? Don't worry about it. *And even if* you are able to become free (i.e., purchase your freedom), rather stay in slavery (i.e., don't give the money to your owner)." For the grammatical arguments against this view see below, pp. 176-178.

[430]See above, pp. 83-84.

[431]See above, p. 91 n. 343. Buckland (*The Roman Law of Slavery*, p. 460) estimated that 90% of all manumissions happened by testament. Treggiari (*Roman Freedmen*, pp. 27-28) has recently challenged this high figure. In any case, a large number of slaves were freed by this method during the first century A.D.

slavery, the interest in using a person as a freedman rather than as a slave, the intention to marry a woman in slavery or to prevent a person from having to testify in court as a slave, the desire to increase the number of one's political supporters, as well as the financial benefit which might be gained by accepting the savings or *peculium* of a slave who wanted to be manumitted. Thus, to accept the limited understanding of motives for manumission advocated by Weiß and others would necessitate restricting Paul's words in 0721cd solely to those Christian slaves who knew how to persuade their owners to manumit them but who had not yet used this knowledge. Yet it is not possible to find in 0721c or its context any clear indication that Paul was concerned in any way about how the manumission might take place or what reasons there might be for such an action.[432]

Therefore, in light of the wide variety of motives and methods for manumission to be found in the first century A.D. and in light of the frequency of its use by owners as an instrument for regulating their households, I strongly suggest that Paul intended his words in 0721c to take account of any reason and any method according to which manumission might happen to any of the Christian slaves in Corinth. Thus in contrast to the restricted view of Weiß and others I conclude that in 1 Cor. 0721c Paul intended to refer to those persons in Corinth who had been in slavery when they were called to become Christians but who later were set free by their owners for any of the reasons noted above, including that of making a profit by a slave's "self-purchase."[433]

In short, I conclude that in 0721ab Paul had in mind those Christians who were in slavery and in 0721cd he was giving advice to those Christians whose owners set them free.

Conclusion and Summary

I. "Were you a slave when you were called?" Among the ideas which have distorted both the modern comprehension of slavery in the Greek and Roman world and the meaning of 1 Cor. 0721 are the assumptions that there was a wide separation between slave and freedman-status, that slaves in general were

---

[432] It is very unlikely that Paul in 0721c referred only to those Christian slaves who had control of a large sum of money and whose owners were interested in manumitting them. The fact that neither the owner nor his reason(s) for manumission are mentioned in 1 Cor. 7 has unfortunately allowed the attention of the interpreters of this text to be focused exclusively on the activity of the slave with regard to his manumission.

[433] This understanding of 0721c leads me to the conclusion that in 0721d Paul was giving advice to a Christian who had been in slavery but who now had to face life as a freedman.

badly treated, and that everyone who was enslaved was trying to free himself from this bondage. None of these assumptions are true for first-century Corinth.

It is true that the slave of a Roman owner in the first century was separated from freedmen and free men by the totality of his powerlessness in principle. Yet the step from slave-status to freedman-status was often a relatively small one. Although Roman law distinguished sharply between the status of slave and free (or freedman), there was a broad continuum of statuses between slave and free in Roman society, business and culture. This continuum also existed in Greek culture where, in addition, it was expressed in the Greek legal system. For example, the slave of a Greek owner could own property and might even obtain permission to take employment beyond his duties as a slave. He might even live in separate quarters from his owner and lead a fairly "independent" life.

Under Greek law, "freedom" consisted of four parts: freedom to act as one's own legal person, freedom from seizure as property, freedom to earn one's living as one might choose and freedom to dwell where one wished. The granting of the "first part" of freedom was enough to establish freedman-status under this law, and the other three parts of freedom were often severely limited in favor of the former owner. The *paramonē*-contract in which the freedman's duties were specified also usually included a clause which limited the duration of his obligations.

Slaves of Roman owners also continued to have both general and specific obligations to their patrons after manumission (in this case, throughout the patron's life-time). So the step from slave-status to freedman-status was often a small one. Furthermore, many of the slaves who lived under either Greek or Roman law enjoyed more favorable living conditions than many free laborers. No color line between slave and free existed in Corinth and no single race or caste was identified exclusively with slavery.

A person's experience as a slave depended primarily upon the character, customs, business and social class of his owner. Most slaves were treated well. An owner's control over his slaves was very similar to his control over his children, and the owner who treated his children well usually gave the same treatment to his slaves. Warm, friendly relationships often developed between slaves and their owners; these relationships sometimes resulted in adoption or marriage into the family.

Whereas in former centuries most persons in slavery had been enslaved by means of capture in war or kidnapping by pirates, during the first century A.D. the chief way persons entered slavery was by being born to a woman in slavery. In addition, some people sold themselves into slavery; under Greek law such a self-sale could be arranged for a limited period of enslavement. Other people sold their children into slavery. Some persons "exposed" their infants, who when found were raised as slaves. Some persons were enslaved as punishment for breaking the law.

Contrary to the supposition that first-century slavery was a way of life which was to be avoided if possible, many persons sold themselves into slavery in order to climb socially, to secure a specific job open only to slaves, and to find greater security than they had experienced as free men. The chief advantage of living as a slave was personal and social security.

Thus, when Paul asked, "Were you a slave when you were called?" he was referring to a legal and social status which was very complex and diversified. How much did he know about slavery, especially slavery in Corinth?

As a first-century Jew from Tarsus who had spent much time in Jerusalem, Paul was well-acquainted with the enslavement of both Jews and Gentiles, and he knew that people were enslaved for a variety of reasons and in a variety of circumstances. He even saw slaves serving as helpers in the Temple. As a Pharisee he was aware of the attempt in Jewish law to consider the slave as a person rather than a thing. It is highly probable that he knew that the Essenes had rejected slavery and that they challenged this institution on the grounds that it tempted men to act unjustly.

Certain aspects of Paul's use of language are best explained by the assumption that he was familiar with Greek and Roman law. In particular, the way in which he uses the term *apeleútheros* in 1 Cor. 0722 to describe a definite, continuing relationship of the Christian with Christ indicates that Paul was familiar with the Greek and Roman understanding of the status of freedmen.

The closer Paul came to Rome, the more he found the institution of slavery to be an essential part of the economy and a normal part of the life of most families. In Corinth, persons in slavery were among the first to become Christians in response to Paul's preaching. During his period of ministry there, he became closely acquainted with the daily lives of those in the congregation, including the circumstances of those in slavery.

Thus, when Paul asked, "Were you a slave when you were called?" he was quite familiar with slavery as a legal and social status and with the circumstances of the Christian slaves in Corinth. How, then, are we to view his advice to such a slave: "Don't worry about it"?

Paul's apparent indifference to the social and legal institution of slavery as he knew it can only be understood in the context of the general attitude toward slavery in the first century A.D. Owning and using men and women as slaves were such normal parts of daily life in the ancient Mediterranean world that the institution of slavery, as a social, legal and economic phenomenon, seldom became an object of reflection. No ancient government ever thought of abolishing the institution, and none of the slave-rebellions in that world were caused by any intention to abolish the institution of slavery as such. None of the authors who had been in slavery attacked the institution in which they had once lived. No freedman-author ever championed slaves or freedmen as groups in themselves.

The opinion of many Greeks became enshrined in Roman law which defined a slave as someone who is subject to the *dominium* of another person, contrary to nature. But whether or not slavery was "natural," there was no question among Greco-Roman writers that slavery was one of a number of relationships involving social and economic dependence which were essential to human society.

The question which did interest some writers was that of the "inner freedom" of those who were in slavery. Indeed, they were concerned about the personal and spiritual independence of all persons. True freedom and real slavery, according to writers such as Philo and Epictetus, had nothing to do with legal status but rather had everything to do with matters such as virtue and obedience to God's will. Although Epictetus was greatly concerned about freedom, at no time did he refer to legal freedom as a goal which was to be desired in itself.

Thus Paul lived in a world in which everyone except the Essenes thought that legal slavery was an indispensable social institution ("natural" or not); it was a world in which an increasing number of persons (including some who had been in legal slavery) believed that "inner freedom" was more important than legal freedom. Paul's apparent lack of concern about legal slavery ("Don't worry about it"), therefore, was by no means unique in the Greco-Roman world of the first century A.D.

The fact that the chief source of slaves in the first century A.D. was no longer war or piracy (with the hostility these acts involved) but rather birth in the home of the slave-owner created a new social situation in which the teaching of "inner freedom" could find a receptive audience among those in slavery. These house-born slaves were given training for a wide variety of domestic, industrial and public tasks of increasing importance and sensitivity. Roman legal practice kept pace with this development by guaranteeing to those in slavery more humane treatment.

Indeed, in the work that he did, the friends that he had, and the cult in which he participated, the person in slavery was not separated from freedmen or even from free men. Most slaves looked forward to their manumission, however, because a freedman generally had a greater amount of control of his person and goods than a slave did. In addition, slaves of Roman owners usually received Roman citizenship with their manumission. The anticipation of financial, civil and social success (especially for their children) made freedman-status attractive to most of those who were in slavery in the first century. Yet both Greek and Roman freedmen quite often remained very closely tied to their former owners in relationships similar to those of their former enslavement. The sharp distinction between "slave" and "freedman" commonly assumed by modern readers of 1 Cor. 0721 rarely existed in Greco-Roman society during the first century A.D.

II. Other uncritical assumptions which have distorted both the modern understanding of ancient slavery and the interpretation of 1 Cor. 0721 run as follows: "Unrest" among the slaves was a major problem in the first century A.D., and there were a large number of runaway slaves during this period. The owner of a slave would be glad to keep any slave who wanted to remain in slavery. Manumission was a comparatively rare event which a slave-owner would usually try to prevent. With particular respect to 1 Cor. 0721, it seems to have been further assumed that the owner did not play a very significant role in the situation to which Paul refers in 0721c. That is, it seems to have been assumed that the slave in question had to decide between two alternatives ("stay in slavery" or "take freedom") and that either decision would have been acceptable to his owner. These assumptions have also been shown to be false.

All slaves who were involved in domestic and urban slavery in the first century could reasonably expect that they would be manumitted after serving their owners for ten to twenty years beyond physical maturity. The rate of manumission had increased greatly during the last half of the first century B.C., and during the first century A.D. manumission was a very common occurrence both in Rome and in the Roman provinces.

Owners of slaves in the first century A.D. appear to have followed a regular policy of manumitting slaves as a reward for hard work. Manumission was used as a means for increasing the efficiency of those yet in slavery. Contrary to modern assumptions, these owners served their own interests when they manumitted their slaves. For example, a man's labor might be more economically obtained if he were a freedman than if he were a slave. In any case, the majority of slaves were manumitted because it was to the financial advantage of the owner to do so.

Slaves in the first century A.D., therefore, enjoyed a lively expectation of being manumitted. Indeed, the ease and frequency of manumission during this period relieved any of the pressures which might have led to slave-revolts, precisely because the most capable and active slaves had the possibility of gaining a certain amount of freedom by legal means. The general climate of "unrest" among the slaves which has been assumed by some Biblical scholars simply did not exist in the first century. Indeed, the liberty of religious and fraternal association granted to slaves by their owners and by the Roman government during this period points to the comparative contentment

felt by those in slavery and to the absence of revolutionary impulses among
them.

Owners manumitted their slaves by means of a variety of procedures--
formal or informal, public or private, religious or secular. Paul's general
statement in 1 Cor. 0721c ("If you are able to become free") could be referring to any of these manumission-procedures.

1 Cor. 0721c raises the question of how much control a person in
slavery had over his social and legal future. There were cases in which the
slave had little or no interest in being manumitted. Most slaves, however,
do seem to have been interested in becoming freedmen. The most direct way in
which a slave could encourage his owner to manumit him was by doing his work
faithfully and well. He could also save his money with the hope that his
owner would be willing to take it in exchange for manumission.

A slave might also try to interest some third party in loaning him
money or in purchasing him in order to grant him manumission. In most cases
this third party was a free relative of the slave, a club (collegium) to which
the slave belonged or an ad hoc (ἔρανος) group whose specific purpose was
loaning the slave the money which his owner required for manumission. This
kind of redemption of slaves was practiced also by first-century Christians
both as individuals and as congregations.

In short, a person in slavery was able to choose from a number of
ways by which he could encourage his owner to manumit him. Strikingly, however, there was no way that a slave could refuse freedman-status, if his
owner decided to manumit him. Neither Greek nor Roman law viewed the slave
as a "legal person," and thus he had no legal means by which he could refuse
manumission. If an owner decided that it was to his advantage to grant a
slave freedman-status, he did so. If, on the other hand, the slave wanted to
remain in slavery for some reason, he could make certain that his owner was
aware of this desire and he could entreat him not to manumit him. But the
slave's security in slavery was continually subject to change according to
the will of his owner. When the owner decided to manumit him, he became a
freedman whether or not he had been looking forward to that event.

This detailed investigation of the legal and social nature of slavery and manumission in the first century has led to the following conclusions with respect to 1 Cor. 0721cd:

1)   Paul could not have been referring to flight to an asylum.

2)   It is very unlikely that Paul was trying to persuade Christian
slaves not to run away from their owners.

3)   Since manumission was not a possibility which a slave could reject
or accept, 0721c cannot be rightly understood as a reference to an offer of

freedom with regard to which Paul was giving advice in 0721d.

4)   Since manumission occurred frequently and was the result of a wide
variety of motives and methods, and since Paul in 0721c does not mention any
particular reason or procedure, 0721c is best understood as Paul's general
reference to the manumission of any Christian slave in Corinth without respect
to the motive or the method.

On this basis I conclude that Paul in 0721c was speaking of *any*
situation in which a Christian slave became a freedman. Thus his advice in
0721d presupposes that the person addressed is a slave who has been set free
by his owner. What, then, is such a Christian freedman to "use"?

In the following chapters I argue that Paul was urging any person
in the Corinthian congregation who had received the call (κλῆσις) of God in
Christ when he was in legal and social slavery to continue to "use" (in the
sense of "live in" or "obey") this *call* after his manumission, i.e., in his
new status as a freedman.[434]   In these chapters I demonstrate that this interpretation of 1 Cor. 0721 helps to clarify both the structure of Paul's
argumentation in 1 Cor. 7 and the cutting edge of his "theology of calling."

Before turning to chapter three dealing with Paul's "opponents" in
the Corinthian congregation and his response to them in 1 Cor. 7, I discuss
in a brief excursus the topic: sacral manumission.

---

[434]This proposal calls to mind the suggestion made in 1953 by F.W. Grosheide
(*Commentary of the First Epistle to the Corinthians*) that 1 Cor. 0721cd means:
"If you can be free, make a better use of your vocation" (see above, p. 5 n.
12). On the basis of my own study of the social and legal situation in first-
century Corinth as well as of the text of 1 Corinthians, I had formulated my
own argument in full before discovering this suggestion by Grosheide. Grosheide bases his suggestion on the general importance of κλῆσις for 0717-24.
My work confirms his suggestion and gives it a firm anchor in the larger context of ch. 7, in Paul's response to the theology of many of the Christians
at Corinth and in the social and legal situation in which they lived.

EXCURSUS

SACRAL MANUMISSION

Sacral manumission must be discussed here because of its possible relevance to 1 Cor. 0722 (ὁ γὰρ ἐν κυρίῳ κληθεὶς δοῦλος ἀπελεύθερος κυρίου ἐστιν·) and to 0723 (τιμῆς ἠγοράσθητε· μὴ γίνεσθε δοῦλοι ἀνθρώπων). Adolf Deissmann was the first scholar to suggest that Greek sacral manumission, especially the manumission-procedure followed by the priests of Apollo at Delphi, strongly influenced Paul's expression of his doctrine of redemption.[435] The manumission-practices at Delphi have, indeed, become exceedingly important for our understanding of Greek sacral manumission both because we have more than 1,000 manumission-inscriptions from Delphi and because slaves from all parts of the Greek-speaking world were manumitted there between 200 B.C. and A.D. 74.[436]

These inscriptions are written in the form of a sales contract which has as its expressed purpose the manumission of the slave named in the contract. This contract is a πρᾶσις ἐπ' ἐλευθερίᾳ ("purchase for freedom"), which was the usual form used throughout Greece for recording the redemption of persons from slavery.[437] Named in the contract were the slave who was "purchased for freedom," his owner who was "selling" him, the third party who was "purchasing the freedom" of the slave and the witnesses to this transaction. Since according to Greek law the person in slavery was not a "legal person" in relation to his owner, he needed a trustworthy intermediary who could effect the legal transfer of money to his owner in exchange for manumission.[438]

---

[435]On the basis of the Delphic inscriptions, Deissmann sought to clarify not only 1 Cor. 0722f. and other similar sounding passages (1 Cor. 0619, Gal. 0313, 0405) but also the full range of Paul's understanding of freedom and redemption. He wrote: "An den auf diesen Urkunden zum Ausdruck kommenden Brauch knüpft Paulus an, wenn er von unserer Befreiung durch Christus redet." *Licht vom Osten*, 4th edn., p. 275 (*Light from the Ancient East*, p. 323).

[436]Franz Bömer remarks: "Delphi ist mit weitem Abstand der Ort, der für die sakrale Freilassung die grösste Bedeutung besitzt." *Untersuchungen* II, 13. For bibliographical data see above, p. 76 n. 271.

[437]See Rädle, *Freilassungswesen*, p. 64, and his sections on "Delphi und Mittelgriechenland" (pp. 56-88) and on "Peloponnes" (pp. 111-123).

[438]It appears that a slave could do business with a "third person" who acted as a middleman in the manumission-transaction but that he could conduct no legal business with his owner. This procedure is also known from the papyri, where the middlemen are bankers. See Rädle, p. 66.

The special feature of the manumission-procedure at Delphi is the fact that it was Apollo who bought the slave from his owner; i.e., Apollo redeemed the slave from slavery.[439] His function is described either as follows: ἐπρίατο ὁ Ἀπόλλων ὁ Πύθιος τὸν δεῖνα ἐπ' ἐλευθερίᾳ (GDI 2116) or as follows: ἀπέδοτο ὁ δεῖνα τῷ Ἀπόλλωνι τὸν δεῖνα ἐπ' ἐλευθερίᾳ (GDI 1738).[440] Thus the manumission-money came formally from the hand of Apollo, i.e., from his priests at Delphi. In practice, however, the money usually came from the pocket of the slave himself.[441] That is, the slave, who was not able to deal directly with his owner in legal matters, entrusted the money which his owner required in exchange for manumission to the priests of Apollo, who executed the legal exchange and who prepared the inscription which publicized the manumission and gave it a strong religious sanction.[442]

How, then, is the relationship between the manumitted slave and Apollo to be understood? Paul Foucart was the first scholar (1867) to suggest that from the legal viewpoint this manumission-procedure was a "fictitious sale" by which the slave became the property of the god.[443] According to this view, Apollo did not make any use of his formal property rights in the slave, for real manumission was the goal of the procedure. But because the former slave now belonged to Apollo, he enjoyed divine protection: to touch the new freedman would be to injure the god himself. This explanation has been adopted by many scholars during the past one hundred years, including A. Deissmann and Franz Bömer.[444]

---

[439] The only other sacred aspects of the inscriptions are the clauses which indicate that the transaction had taken place at the Temple of Apollo and that certain of his priests were witnesses to the act.

[440] In English: "The Phythian Apollo purchased 'John Doe' for freedom" or "Mr. 'So-and-So' sold 'John Doe' to Apollo for freedom." Bömer (Untersuchungen II, 140) thinks that the form which states that the god himself purchased the slave betrays the influence of oriental practice on Greek conceptions. This form is not found in the inscriptions from the first century A.D.

[441] According to Greek law and custom, the person in slavery could own property and save the money which he earned or borrowed. In some cases, the money came from the owner himself, who came to Delphi in order to dignify the manumission of his slave by the action of Apollo's priests. In any case, the children who were manumitted must have had some third person who gave them the necessary money. See Rädle, p. 73.

[442] See above, pp. 94-96 and 98-99.

[443] Mémoire sur l'affranchisement des esclaves par forme de vente à une divinité (Paris, 1867).

[444] See Deissmann, Licht vom Osten, p. 274 (Light from the Ancient East, p. 322); and Bömer, Untersuchungen I, 72, 123; II, 138-139.

In his very interesting article, "The Freedmen and the Slaves of God," W.L. Westermann highly praised Deissmann for explaining the meaning of 1 Cor. 0722-23 with the help of the Delphic inscriptions.[445] At the same time, however, Westermann correctly observed that the transaction "was not a 'fictitious sale' as Deissmann thought. It was clearly an entrustment sale."[446] Nevertheless, Westermann's great interest in using his understanding of the *paramoné*-contracts from Delphi to explain 1 Cor. 0722, 24 apparently caused him to overlook the fact that an entrustment sale did *not* relate the slave to the god in the manner necessary to Deissmann's theory. For by an entrustment sale (in which the slave entrusted his money to the god, as described above) the slave did not become in any way the formal property of Apollo. The slave who was set free at Delphi became neither a "slave of Apollo" nor a "freedman of Apollo."

Although Bömer's understanding of the legal nature of the Delphic manumission-procedure also is not correct,[447] this mistake did not prevent him from completely demolishing all the other arguments necessary to Deissmann's conclusions.[448] On the basis of a very thorough investigation of all the manumission-inscriptions cited by Deissmann, Bömer has shown that *Licht vom Osten*[4] is riddled by seriously mistaken interpretations and harmonizations of these inscriptions. One important result of Bömer's work is his conclusion that there is no evidence that the inscriptions from Delphi had *any* influence on either Paul's language in 1 Cor. 7 or his doctrine of redemption. Paul was certainly aware of Greek manumission-practices, but the procedures of sacral

---

[445]*Proceedings of the American Philosophical Society* 92 (1948), 55, 61-63.

[446]Westermann, p. 55. Rädle's dissertation has given decisive support to the view that the Delphic manumission-procedure was an entrustment sale. He bases his conclusion on three points (pp. 60-65): 1) He agrees with the French legal scholars, R. Dareste, B. Hausoullier and Th. Reinach (*Recueil des inscriptions juridiques grecques* II [Paris, 1898] 233ff.), who argued that the act of dedication was preferred in this form at Delphi because the slave was not a "legal person" and needed a middleman; 2) Because the sale was often accompanied by certain conditions (the *paramoné*-contract) and because the person was no longer a slave but a freedman, Rädle concludes that the slave as slave cannot have become the property of a god; 3) His basic thesis is that the need for publicly announcing and securing the act of manumission led to the practice of dedicatory manumission as well as to the development of most of the other specific forms for manumission used in Greece.

[447]Bömer (*Untersuchungen* I, 72, 123-124) holds the opinion that there was a very close legal connection between the act of manumission and the sacred procedure at Delphi, which leads him to agree with the view that the slave became the formal property of Apollo (II, 138-139).

[448]See his section called "Die Bibel" in II, 133-141.

124

manumission at Delphi played no role in his thinking.[449]

For example, the Delphic term πρίασθαι ("to buy") is never used in the New Testament, whereas the Pauline (1 Cor. 0620, 0723) term ἀγοράζω ("to buy from the market") never appears in connection with sacral manumission.[450] At Delphi the term σῶμα is always used in its special meaning, "a person in slavery"; Paul never uses the word in this way.[451]

Furthermore, the phrase ἐπ' ἐλευθερίᾳ, which at Delphi (with πρίασθαι) meant "purchased for freedom," is never used by Paul in connection with his terms for "to buy" or "to redeem."[452] To be sure, the Christian is redeemed "from the curse of the law" (Gal. 0313) and from slavery to the στοιχεῖα τοῦ κόσμου (Gal. 0403-10). But he is *called* for freedom," i.e., ἐπ' ἐλευθερίᾳ ἐκλήθετε (Gal. 0513).[453]

On the other hand, Paul's phrase δοῦλος Χριστοῦ has no counterpart

[449]Bömer (II, 138) concludes: "Es ist sogar wahrscheinlich, daß gerade die delphischen ihm *nicht* bekannt waren." He stresses that eastern concepts and practices were the background for Paul's expression.

[450]Bömer (II, 134 n. 9) states that Deissmann (*Licht vom Osten*, p. 275 n. 9) misunderstood the use of ἀγοράζω in Dittenberger, *Orientis Graeci Inscriptiones Selectae* 338, 23: it does not mean "to purchase freedom" in this context. Note, then, that Bömer's conclusion justifies the earlier claim by Werner Elert ("Redemptio ab hostibus," *ThLZ* 72 [1947], 267) that ἀγοράζω could be used only for a sales transaction by which the slave was sold by one owner to another owner. This means that the second meaning which W. Bauer (depending on Deissmann) gives for ἀγοράζω, namely, "fig., based on the analogy of religious law which in reality bestowed freedom on a slave purchased by a divinity (*A Greek-English Lexicon*, p. 12; 5th ed., col. 24), is wrong and should be changed to a phrase expressing the following: "fig., based on the actual sale of a slave by one owner to another owner." Note also that although the term ἐξαγοράζω (Gal. 0313, 0405) sometimes has the meaning "to redeem from slavery," it never bears this meaning in the LXX or in cult-language outside of Christianity. Thus, there is no relation between this term and sacral manumission. See Friedrich Büchsel, *TDNT* I, 126-128.

[451]See Bömer, II, 31 n. 1 and 137 n. 2.

[452]Note that ἐπ' ἐλευθερίᾳ appears in other Greek inscriptions from the first century A.D. which report dedications (ἀνατιθέναι) of slaves by owners who expected that the slaves would receive legal freedom as one result of the dedication. See G. Klaffenbach, *Griechische Epigraphik*, Studien zur Altert. Wiss. 6, 2nd ed. (Göttingen, 1966), p. 84. Bömer (I, 117-119) thinks that the lack of any mention of an exchange of money in these inscriptions, means that the manumissions were gifts from the owners. Rädle (*Freilassungswesen*, pp. 28-33, 62) strongly objects to this view because it overlooks the evidence he has found that often financial arrangements had been made by these slaves and their owners.

[453]See Darrell Doughty, *Heiligkeit und Freiheit: Eine exegetische Untersuchung der Anwendung des paulinischen Freiheitsgedankens in I Kor. 7* (diss. Göttingen, 1965), pp. 73-74. (See above, pp. 11-13.)

at Delphi. Indeed, Bömer observes that no Greek would ever ask another Greek to become a "slave of a god"; to describe "freedom" in such terms would have been unthinkable for a Greek.[454]

Thus, the only term which is common to Paul (1 Cor. 0620, 0723) and the Delphic inscriptions is τιμή, a general word for "price" which tells us nothing about sacral manumission.[455] In short, against Deissmann's conclusions it must be said that Paul in no way relied on Delphic manumission-customs in giving expression to his doctrine of redemption or in 1 Cor. 0722-23. In fact, had he attempted to do so, "er wäre da wirklich schlecht beraten gewesen."[456]

---

[454]Bömer, II, 136; he relies heavily on the work of K.H. Rengstorf, *TDNT* II, 261-265.

[455]See J.H. Moulton and G. Milligan, *The Vocabulary of the Greek Testament* (London, 1930), p. 635.

[456]Bömer, II, 139.

CHAPTER III

I CORINTHIANS 7 AND THE ΠΝΕΥΜΑΤΙΚΟΙ AT CORINTH

There can be no doubt that many persons in the legal status of slavery were members of the Christian congregation in Corinth.[457] What, then, can be discerned about the new self-understanding which these persons received when they became Christians, especially with regard to their social status? Is there any evidence that the Corinthian Christians who were in slavery needed any special admonition from Paul for the purpose of correcting their attitudes toward their owners or their status as slaves?[458]

In my attempt to answer these questions, I first describe the theological-ethical situation in the Corinthian congregation which Paul was trying to correct by his writing of 1 Corinthians. I seek especially to clarify the background of those social problems which did arise in the congregation. Then, I sketch Paul's response in 1 Cor. 7 to this pneumatic view of Christian faith and life, giving special attention to his "theology of calling" in 0717-24 and the decisive interrelationship of 0720 and 0721.

---

[457]The texts which mention the baptizing of the "households" of Stephanas, Crispus and Gaius make it clear that slaves were among the first Corinthians to become Christians. See above, pp. 59-62.

[458]Among those who have claimed that 1 Cor. 0721 is such an admonition are the following: Shailer Matthews ("The Social Teaching of Paul, Part V,1: The Opposition of Apostolic Christianity to Social Revolution," *Biblical World* 19 [1902], 437) spoke of the "restless Corinthians" and argued that "Paul knew only too well the danger which lay in any social extravagances.... Above all, he tried to keep his converts free from even an appearance of social unrest-- 1 Cor. 7:20f."

According to Rudolf Knopf (*Das Nachapostolische Zeitalter*, 1905, p. 69), "der Anspruch der Sklaven, als Christen frei zu werden, ist übrigens von Beginn an in der Christenheit vorhanden gewesen, da bereits der Apostel Paulus dagegen ankämpft (I Kor 7,21-24)."

J. Weiß (*Der Erste Korintherbrief*, 1910, p. 191) asserted that it was the purpose of 1 Cor. 0721cd and 0723 ("don't become slaves of men") to dampen the "Freiheitsdrang der Sklaven, der im Zusammenhang mit dem 4,8ff. geschilderten Hochgefühl erwartet sein mag...."

Hans von Campenhausen (*Die Begründung kirchlicher Entscheidungen beim Apostel Paulus* [Heidelberg, 1957], p. 20) has also stated that Paul needed to calm down slaves who were trying to carry over into the "world" their new freedom in Christ. He concluded: "Paulus scheint es als eine Missachtung der göttlichen Erlösung anzusehen, wenn jemand seine neuen Erkenntnisse dazu benützen möchte, sich irdische, 'menschliche' Vorteile zu erringen."

H. Gülzow (*Christentum und Sklaverei*, 1969, p. 180) interprets 0721 with reference to a "starken Freiheitsdrang der Sklaven" in the Corinthian congregation.

A. *The Theology and Ethics of the Corinthian Pneumatikoí.*

According to Paul's references to the Corinthian Christians in
1 Corinthians, their theological-ethical self-understanding could be described
as follows:

They are Christians who did not lack any spiritual gift (0107) and
who thought of themselves religiously as "wise," "powerful" and "wellborn"
(0126), as "*téleioi*" (0206), as "*pneumatikoí*" (0301), as "wise in this age"
(0318), as ones who could "boast of men" (0321 and 0406-07) and who could
judge Paul (0402), as ones who were already "filled," "rich" and "kings"
(0408), as "wise in Christ" (0410), as ones who boasted that one of their
members was "living with his father's wife" (0501-02, 0406), as ones who could
take Christian brothers to court before unbelieving judges (0601-06), as ones
who could live according to the slogan: "All things are lawful for me" (0612),
as ones who were free to have sexual intercourse with prostitutes (0615-16),
as ones who could live successfully in "spiritual marriages" (0701-05, see
0736-38), as ones who should separate themselves from unbelievers (0712-16,
see 0509-13), as ones who believed that "all of us possess *gnosis*" (0801),
i.e., that "an idol has no real existence" and that "there is no God but one"
(0804), as "weak" ones who were defiled by food offered to idols (0807) and
as "strong" ones with *gnosis* who "destroyed" their Christian brothers by eat-
ing such meat (0811), as those "upon whom the end of the ages has come"
(1011), as women who could pray and prophesy with "unveiled heads" (1105-16),
as ones who ate the "Lord's Supper" without waiting for each other (1133),
i.e., "without discerning the body" (1129), as ones who had received ecstatic
"spiritual gifts" (1201, 1229-30), as ones who were "eager for manifestations
of the Spirit" (1412), as ones who spoke in tongues and received revelations
(1426-30), as women whose boldness prompted Paul's rebuke (1434-35), as ones
who said "there is no resurrection of the dead" (1512), as ones who were
"baptized on behalf of the dead" (1529), and as ones who already bore "the
image of the man of heaven" (1549).

No obvious, unified picture arises immediately from these descriptive and critical phrases which Paul used in this letter.[459] But a consensus
is developing within recent scholarship in which pneumatic enthusiasm, sacra-
mental realism and present (heavenly) exaltation in identification with the
exalted Christ are stressed as the most significant factors in the

---

[459]Note that this list specifically excludes at least one characteristic
which has been attributed to the Corinthians, namely that they cursed the
earthly Jesus (1203). With this exclusion I follow H. Conzelmann (*1. Korintherbrief* pp. 241-242) and Birger Pearson ("Did the Gnostics Curse Jesus,"
JBL 86 [1967], 301-305) and reject the proposals of Walter Schmithals (*Die
Gnosis in Korinth*, 3rd ed. [Göttingen, 1969], pp. 117-121) and Robin Scroggs
("The Exaltation of the Spirit by Some Early Christians," *JBL* 84 [1965], 366-
370.

self-understanding of these Corinthians.[460]

A particularly outstanding ethical correlate of this viewpoint appears in the bold activity of the women and the curious sexual practices in the congregation.[461] With specific regard to the concerns of this investigation of slavery in Corinth, however, it is quite striking that Paul's description of the Corinthians in no way indicates that relationships between Christian slaves and their owners were at all disturbed by the Corinthians' pneumatic Christianity. Indeed, we have evidence in 1 Cor. 1213 which strongly suggests that no "unrest" was caused among those in legal slavery by their conversion to Christ. The verse is translated as follows: "For by one Spirit we were all baptized into one body--Jews or Greeks, slaves or free-- and all were made to drink of one Spirit" (RSV).[462]

The fact that slaves are mentioned in 1 Cor. 1213 may not seem at first glance to be "evidence" for the absence of unrest among the Christian slaves in the Corinthian congregation. In light of the "unrest" among the Christian women in Corinth, however, a comparison of 1213 with Gal. 0328 leads me to this conclusion.

Observe, first of all, that only one of the three contrasting pairs which Paul mentioned in Gal. 0328 is directly relevant to his argument in Galatians: "There is neither Jew nor Greek, there is neither slave nor free, there is no male and female (οὐκ ἔνι ἄρσεν καὶ θῆλυ); for you are all one in Christ Jesus." That is, nothing in the Galatian letter can account for the phrase "no male and female" in 0328 (we know of no "woman problem" in the Galatian congregations); and the metaphorical usages of "slave" and "free" in chaps. 4 and 5 have no relation to these terms in 0328. The single contrast "neither Jew nor Greek," which Paul used in many other contexts, would have been adequate to climax the development of his thought in chap. 3.[463] This observation gives strong support to the conclusion that 0328 is not an ad hoc listing of contrasts which were overcome in Christ at baptism, but rather

---

[460]See, e.g., Helmut Köster, "Häretiker im Urchristentum," *RGG*[3] III, 19, and Ernst Käsemann, "Primitive Christian Apocalyptic" in *New Testament Questions of Today* (London, 1969), pp. 124-137 (*Exegetische Versuche* II, 120-131). For useful summaries of the history of research on the views of the Corinthians, see Dieter Georgi, *Die Gegner des Paulus im 2. Korintherbrief* (Neukirchen-Vluyn, 1964), pp. 7-16 and Jack H. Wilson, "The Corinthians Who Say There Is No Resurrection of the Dead," *ZNW* 59 (1968), 90-107.

[461]See specifically 1 Cor. 0501-02, 0615-16, 0701-05, 0736-38, 1105-16, and 1434-35.

[462]Cf. Gal. 0328 and Col. 0311.

[463]See R 0116, 0209-10, 0309, 1012 and 1 Cor. 0122, 0124, 1032.

is a baptismal formula which was part of Paul's vocabulary prior to his composition of Galatians.[464]

Next, notice that Paul did not use the phrase "no male and female"
in 1 Cor. 1213, even though 1213 appears to be a baptismal formula or a statement based on such a formula. The absence of this phrase is striking, and I
argue that Paul intentionally omitted it because he had just finished (1102-
16) speaking to problems caused by women in the congregation who most probably
understood themselves to be acting in full accord with such equality in
Christ, an equality which must have been taught by Paul himself when he lived
among them.[465]

On the basis of these observations, I further conclude that Paul
would not have written "slaves or free" in 1 Cor. 1213 if there had been any
unrest among the slaves in the congregation which was caused by their conversion to Christ. We have seen above (pp. 85-87) that contrary to the conditions which are often assumed to have existed in the first century A.D., no
basic unrest or revolutionary impulses can be found among those persons who
were in slavery at Corinth during this period. Beyond this, it is now possible to conclude that the evidence available to us does *not* indicate that
the pneumatic enthusiasm of the Corinthian congregation affected the behavior
or attitudes of the slaves in the congregation with respect to their slave-
status.[466]

This means that it is quite unlikely that Paul's expression in
1 Cor. 0721 was provoked by any "social unrest" or demands to be set free,
such as have often been attributed to the Christian slaves at Corinth.[467]
Both the social situation in Corinth and the evidence from 1 Corinthians

---

[464] Krister Stendahl (*The Bible and the Role of Women, A Case Study in Hermeneutics* [Philadelphia, 1966], p. 32) has pointed to the fact that οὐκ ἔνι
ἄρσεν καὶ θῆλυ is not strictly parallel to οὐκ ἔνι δοῦλος οὐδὲ ἐλεύθερος and
οὐκ ἔνι Ἰουδαῖος οὐδὲ Ἕλλην, and that this distinction between the use of
"and" and "neither/nor" is ignored in the AV, RSV and NEB. He notes that
the terms ἄρσεν καὶ θῆλυ "are the technical terms from Genesis 1:27 ('male
and female created he them'; cf. Mark 10:6, Matt. 19:4), and their technical
character is clear as they are not the ordinary words for 'man' and 'woman'
but actually mean 'male and female.'"
See below, ch. 4, for further discussion of the Jewish background
of Gal. 0328 and the way this formula functioned in suggesting the topics
Paul used in 1 Cor. 0717-24 to illustrate his theology of "male and female."

[465] Stendahl (p. 35) states that in 1 Cor. 1213 the male/female phrase "is
conspicuous by its absence. This is understandable when we consider the concrete situation in Corinth..."

[466] On the basis of 1 Cor. 7 alone (i.e., without reference to Gal. 0328),
Darrell Doughty (*Heiligkeit und Freiheit*, p. 67) also concludes that there is
no evidence that the pneumatic enthusiasm in the Corinthian congregation led
to a desire among the Christian slaves to be freed from their worldly status.

[467] See above, p. 127 n. 458.

support the conclusion that 1 Cor. 0721 was *not* written to keep restless
Christian slaves "in their place."[468]

Since there is also no evidence that the Corinthians in their
letter to Paul asked him anything about Christians in slavery, it must be
asked: What prompted Paul to mention the topic of slavery in 1 Cor. 7?
In the next chapter, I answer this question by showing that Paul used the
cases of "circumcision" and "uncircumcision" (0718-19, i.e., Jew/Greek) and
"slave" and "free" (0721-22) first of all as illustrations of his "theology
of calling," which functions as one of his principle theological arguments
in ch. 7 against the Corinthians' pneumatic view of male/female relationships.
I argue that Paul was prompted to use these particular illustrations by the
threefold thought-pattern which he expressed also in Gal. 0328.

The specific problem, then, which Paul addressed in 1 Cor. 7 was
the Corinthian Christians' pneumatic understanding and practice of male/female
relationships. It is clear that the Corinthians' conviction that "there is no
male and female in Christ" expressed itself in two contrasting kinds of sexual
behavior (chs. 5 and 6 versus ch. 7) and in the bold activity of the women in

---

[468] In light of the actual conditions in the first century A.D., the admonitions given to Christian slaves in the *Haustafeln* should also be checked
again. R. Knopf (*Das Nachapostolische Zeitalter*, p. 69) suggested that "die
Emanzipationsgelüste der Sklaven sind eine Voraussetzung, von der aus die
Mahnungen der 'Haustafeln' an die Sklaven zu verstehen sind." But such an
explanation is in no way needed.

In Col. 0322-25, e.g., nothing is said to the slaves which indicates
that they needed to be admonished because of any "striving" to become manumitted. Rather they are addressed with regard to their role in the family
structure, as are the wives, the husbands, the children, and the masters:
"Slaves, obey in everything those who are your earthly masters, not with eyeservice, as men-pleasers, but in singleness of heart, fearing the Lord. Whatever your task, work heartily, as serving the Lord and not men, knowing that
from the Lord you will receive the inheritance as your reward; you are serving the Lord Christ. For the wrongdoer will be paid back for the wrong he has
done, and there is no partiality" (RSV).

Likewise, the slave who followed the admonition given in Eph. 0605-
08 could expect to be manumitted more quickly than one who did not: "Slaves,
be obedient to those who are your earthly masters, with fear and trembling,
in singleness of heart, as to Christ; not in the way of eyeservice, as men-
pleasers, but as slaves of Christ, doing the will of God from the heart, ren-
dering service with a good will as to the Lord and not to men, knowing that
whatever good any one does, he will receive the same again from the Lord,
whether he is a slave or free" (RSV). The admonition in Tit. 0209 sounds
very similar; those Christian slaves who gave "satisfaction in every respect"
were on the shortest route to manumission. 1 Tim. 0601-02 indicates that some
Christian slaves were not being respectful to their owners who were also
Christians: "Let all who are under the yoke of slavery regard their masters
as worthy of all honor, so that the name of God and the teaching may not be
defamed. Those who have believing masters must not be disrespectful on the
ground that they are brethren; rather they must serve all the better since
those who benefit by their service are believers and beloved" (RSV). Certainly any disobedience to one's owner on the basis of "equality in Christ"
would have been counter-productive behavior, if one was interested in receiving legal freedom.

their worship services (chs. 11 and 14). From a social viewpoint these women (and the men who encouraged them) were among the avant-garde in the first century, for during this period a "women's liberation movement" was gaining ground.[469] From a theological perspective, they must have claimed that their sexual freedom and their freedom from sexuality, as well as their public prophecies and their ecstatic spiritual gifts, were all signs and confirmations that they had already been called by God to an exalted and perfected existence. These Christians must have claimed that precisely these actions were important indications that they were "leading lives worthy of the calling to which they had been called" (see Eph. 0401).

For this reason, Paul supports his discussion of the Corinthians' questions about marriage and celibacy with a brief exhortation (0717-24) which specifically emphasizes the relation of God's call to Christian existence in the world. By means of a careful analysis of Paul's use of κλῆσις ("call, calling, invitation") in this pericope and in 1 Cor. 0126, I seek to clarify his seemingly complex answers in ch. 7, his basic theological argument with the Corinthians, and particularly his admonition in 0721d.

B. *Paul's "Theology of Calling" as a Response to the Corinthian Pneumatikoí*.

In 1 Cor. 0701-16, Paul began to respond to the questions which had been sent to him by the Corinthian congregation about the effect of the new life in Christ on sexual relations.[470] As part of his advice to those

---

[469] Samuel Dill (*Roman Society from Nero to Marcus Aurelius*, 1904 [New York, 1964], p. 88) called "the movement of female emancipation, which was to culminate in the legislation of the Antonine age," one of "the great facts in the social history of the first century." He observed (p. 81) that "for good or evil, women in the first and second centuries were making themselves a power." For additional literature, see Joseph Vogt, *Von der Gleichwertigkeit der Geschlechter in der bürgerlichen Gesellschaft der Griechen* (Akademie der Wissenschaften und der Literatur in Mainz, Abhandlungen der Geistes- und Sozialwissenschaftlichen Klasse 1960, Nr. 2). Vogt (p. 40) notes that in the writings of the Peripatetics, the Pythagoreans and the Stoics, the differing positions of the sexes was still presupposed, but that there is evidence from the first century that women in both Greece and Rome were breaking out of their traditional self-understanding. Vogt (p. 47) especially praises the women in Greece, because they accomplished more than the Roman women, even though they did not have as strong a position in society as the women in Italy.
Thus, while the social position of the persons in slavery in first-century Corinth has been falsely understood with regard to 1 Cor. 0721, the social situation of women during this period seems to have been overlooked as background for the activity of the women in the Corinthian congregation. Unfortunately, a detailed investigation of this background and a more exact evaluation of its importance for the Christian congregation in Corinth lie beyond the scope of this book.

[470] Ch. 7 begins: Περὶ δὲ ὧν ἐγράψατε ... ("Now concerning the matters about which you wrote..."). See below, p. 163 n. 560.

Christians who were married to non-Christians, Paul reasoned: "But God has called (κέκληκεν) you to peace" (0715). With this phrase he introduced the motif of God's calling which he then developed in 0717-24 in order to clarify the theological basis of his ad hoc argumentation in the previous verses.[471]

Paul's exhortations and illustrations in 0717-24 indicate that the primary problem which he judged to be at the root of the specific cases which he discussed in chapter 7 may be expressed as follows: How was the Christian to understand the relation between his calling from God and the circumstances of his life? For example, were changes in his social circumstances, such as renunciation of sexuality or dissolution of marriage, implied or demanded by this calling? Or were all such changes specifically to be resisted in order to demonstrate that the calling had made all earthly circumstances completely irrelevant to salvation.[472] Or were changes in a Christian's social circumstances, such as marriage and manumission, understood by Paul to be events which were neither encouraged nor forbidden by this calling? How, indeed,

---

[471]To be sure, Paul also used this motif at the beginning of this letter. In 0101 and 0102 he employed the verbal adjective κλητός in a technical way to refer to himself ("called by the will of God to be an apostle of Christ Jesus") and to the Corinthian Christians ("called to be saints"). The same usage appears in 1024: "to those who are called, both Jews and Greeks." In 0109 Paul used the verb καλέω in the same way with reference to the Corinthians: "God is faithful, by whom you were called into the fellowship of his son, Jesus Christ our Lord." Then in 0126 Paul used the verbal noun κλῆσις in a very interesting manner which requires further comment below: "For consider your calling, my brothers, not many of you are wise according to human standards..." Outside of 0717-24 the only other usages of these three terms in 1 Cor. are 1027 ("If one of the unbelievers invites [καλεῖ] you to dinner") where the verb bears one of its common meanings, "to invite" and 1509 ("For I am the least of the apostles, unfit to be called [καλεῖσθαι] an apostle") where the verb may bear its other common meaning, "to name."

[472]Perhaps the clearest defender of this understanding of "calling" was Albert Schweitzer who found in 0717-24 Paul's "theory of the *status quo*." According to Schweitzer, the natural condition of the Christian's existence has "become of no importance, not in the general sense that it does not matter what is done to it, but in the special sense that henceforth nothing must be done to it." "If, therefore, a slave became a believer he should not, on this theory, if he were afterwards offered freedom, accept it." Note also that Schweitzer claimed that the "take freedom" interpretation of 1 Cor. 0721 "is both grammatically and logically impossible." *The Mysticism of Paul the Apostle*, 2nd ed. (New York, 1968), pp. 194-195 (trans. W. Montgomery, *Die Mystik des Apostels Paulus*, 1929).

was a Christian to lead a life worthy of the calling with which he was called?[473]

Paul strikingly emphasized the chief point in his "theology of calling" by repeating it three times within the brief space of eight verses: 0717, 0720 and 0724.[474] Notice the very interesting parallelism in these three exhortations:

17) ἑκάστῳ ὡς μεμέρικεν ὁ κύριος	ἕκαστον	ὡς κέκληκεν ὁ θεός	οὕτως	περιπατείτω.
20) ἕκαστος ἐν τῇ κλήσει		ᾗ ἐκλήθη	ἐν ταύτῃ	μενέτω.
24) ἕκαστος ἐν ᾧ		ἐκλήθη	ἐν τούτῳ	μενέτω παρὰ θεῷ.

A close comparison of these three admonitions with each other yields some suggestions which help solve a number of problems which have troubled exegetes

---

[473]See Eph. 0401: "Therefore I, a prisoner in the Lord, entreat you to live your life in a manner worthy of (ἀξίως περιπατῆσαι) the calling with which you were called (τῆς κλήσεως ἧς ἐκλήθητε)." Both Paul and the Corinthians he addressed in ch. 7 believed themselves to be leading lives "worthy of the calling." The fact that they drew contradictory conclusions from this kind of ethical description is one indication among many that often Paul was not understood by the Corinthians on his own terms.

It seems clear that Paul and the Corinthians represent two very different ways of apprehending reality, which allowed the same words to carry two different sets of meanings. They had shared the beginning of a common language during Paul's ministry there. A field of language had been laid down on which they could meet each other. But their "meetings" often seem to have been superficial, most probably because the Corinthians perceived reality in terms which were fundamentally spatial (they were exalted and bore "the image of the man of heaven," especially in the ecstatic worship services), whereas Paul perceived reality in terms which were basically temporal (thus his great concern for an eschatological timetable). To Paul the Corinthians appeared to be living as if they believed that they were already resurrected; his constant attempts to place them in this timetable at a point *before* the general resurrection make this clear. But it may well be that the category of resurrection, at least in any sense which was related to a temporal frame of reference, was simply not very important to the Corinthians. For a useful description of the "spatial pattern" and the "temporal pattern" see Eduard Schweizer, "Two New Testament Creeds Compared. 1 Corinthians 15,3-5 and 1 Timothy 3,16," *Neotestamentica* (Stuttgart, 1963), pp. 124-126. For possible variety in the meaning of "resurrection" see J.H. Wilson, "The Corinthians Who Say There Is No Resurrection of the Dead," pp. 99-107.

Although it is not the proper task of this investigation to treat in detail the theology of the Corinthians or the extensive secondary literature on that topic, my discussion of Paul's "theology of calling" seeks to indicate the importance of 0717-24 for such a treatment.

[474]The verb καλέω dominates the eight verses in this pericope (0717-24); it is used eight times--once with the verbal noun κλῆσις (0720). The threefold repetition of the principal exhortation in this passage clearly defines its limits and forcefully underlines its purpose.

of 0717-24, such as the meaning of κλῆσις in 0720,[475] the specific action indicated by the term μένω in 0720 and 0724, and the purpose of the phrase παρὰ θεῷ in 0724.[476] The many obvious similarities between these three verses lead me to suggest that the few obvious differences are merely different ways of saying the same thing.[477] For example, I suggest that περιπατεύτω in 0717 and μενέτω in 0720 and 0724 refer to the same activity, i.e., that "walking according to God's calling" is the same as "remaining in the calling" (0720) and "remaining in the calling in the sight of God" (0724). In 0724 the phrase ἐν ᾧ does not require an antecedent; it is often used in a vague manner, and I suggest that here it is equal to the use of ὡς in 0717.[478] Then the masculine gender of ἐν τούτῳ (which I translate as referring to τῇ κλήσει in 0720) can be accounted for on the basis of attraction to ἐν ᾧ. The discussion which follows assumes these suggestions and increases their persuasiveness.

The chief theological problem in 0717-24 is the meaning of κλῆσις in 0720. In two of the other three non-disputed Pauline usages of this term, namely Phil. 0314 ("the upward *call* of God in Christ Jesus") and R 1129 ("the gifts and the *call* of God are irrevocable"), there is no doubt that Paul meant God's call to salvation.[479] It has been argued, however, that in 1 Cor. 0126

---

[475]For example, Hans Lietzmann concluded that κλῆσις in 0720 means *Stand* or *Beruf*; but W.G. Kümmel disagreed, claiming that it means (*Zustand der*) *Berufung*. Lietzmann-Kümmel, *An die Korinther I-II*, Handbuch zum Neuen Testament (Tübingen, 1949), pp. 32 and 177. Martin Luther seems to be the first translator to have given this term the meaning "status/occupation" (*Beruf*). For a good, brief summary of the German debate about this term's meaning, see K.L. Schmidt, *TDNT* III, 491-492. Schmidt (p. 493) strongly argues for translating the term in 0720 (as elsewhere in the N.T.) with *Berufung*, i.e., "God's call in Christ."

[476]For example, J. Weiß (*Der erste Korintherbrief*, pp. 191-192) had difficulty explaining the presence of παρὰ θεῷ in 0724. He concluded: "Wir haben also die Wahl, hierin entweder eine rein phraseologische Wendung des P. zu sehen oder eine Zutat von späterer Hand, die vielleicht an falschem Platze steht."

[477]None of the textual variants in these verses, namely ἐμέρισεν (ACDG) vs. μεμέρικεν (B ℵ* pc) in 0717 and the absence of παρὰ θεῷ in 309 and Chrysostom (0724) are significant for this comparison.

[478]See C.F.D. Moule, *An Idiom-Book of New Testament Greek* (Cambridge, 1960), p. 131.

[479]In all other usages of this term attributed to Paul, namely 2 Th. 0111 ("To this end we always pray for you, that our God may make you worthy of his *call*"), Eph. 0118 ("that you may know what the hope of your *calling* is"), Eph. 0401 ("lead a life worthy of the *calling* with which you were called"), Eph. 0404 ("you were called to the one hope that belongs to your *call*"), and 2 Tim. 0109 ("God, who saved us and called us with a holy *calling*"), there is also no trace of any meaning except God's call in Christ.

136

and 0720 Paul has given this term the special connotation "position, vocation, station in life."[480] This interpretation is said to be supported by the context, namely Paul's advice to the virgins in 0726b-27 ("It is good, I think, for a person to be what he already is. Are you bound to a wife? Do not seek to become free. Are you free from a wife? Do not seek to become married.") and Paul's interest in hindering divorce, which is expressed in 0710-16.[481] But such an interpretation makes it necessary to postulate a completely unique significance of κλῆσις;[482] it also obscures the full force of Paul's argument

---

[480] Walter Bauer (*A Greek-English Lexicon*, p. 437; 5th edn., col. 862) is a very important representative of this view of 0720. C.K. Barrett (*First Epistle to the Corinthians*, pp. 169-170) reads both 0720 and 0126 in this way. H. Conzelmann (*1. Korintherbrief*, p. 152) finds the usual meaning of κλῆσις in 0126, but he favors this special connotation in 0720. See below, note 482.

[481] See H. Bellen, "Μᾶλλον χρῆσαι: Verzicht auf Freilassung als asketische Leistung?", pp. 178-180.

[482] Neither Liddell-Scott-Jones, *A Greek-English Lexicon*, p. 960, nor G.W.H. Lampe, *A Patristic Greek Lexicon* (Oxford, 1968), pp. 757-758, indicates that κλῆσις can bear such a meaning. (Note that there is no entry for this term in L. Mitteis and U. Wilcken, *Grundzüge und Chrestomathie der Papyruskunde*, Leipzig, 1912.)
In F. Preisigke, *Wörterbuch der griechischen Papyrusurkunden* (Berlin, 1925-31), the only meanings given for κλῆσις are *Vorladung* and *Namensnennung*. Moulton and Milligan, *The Vocabulary of the Greek New Testament*, also report only these two meanings. (Note also their comment: "...as always in the NT, κλῆσις is the divine call to salvation.")
In the 5th edn. of his *Wörterbuch*, Bauer claims that Philo, *Legatio ad Gaium* 163, and Libanius (iv A.D.), *Progymnasmata* 9,2,1, used κλῆσις in a way that supports his translation of this term with *Stand*. But in both instances the term clearly refers to a "naming." Dietrich Wiederkehr, *Die Theologie der Berufung in den Paulusbriefen* (Freiburg, 1963), p. 134, has also noted that Bauer's claim is not justified in these two cases.
In the only other text cited by Bauer, namely Libanius, *Argumenta Orationum Demosthenicarum* 2, κλῆσις is used in a way that may introduce the connotation *Stand*: τὴν τοῦ μαχαιροποιοῦ κλῆσιν ἔλαβεν = "he took up the call of a cutlery-maker." But this text was written 400 years after 1 Cor. Even Lietzmann (see above, p. 135 n. 475) concluded that there were no parallels to support his interpretation of κλῆσις in 0720.
As K.L. Schmidt (*TDNT* III, 492, n. 1) correctly stressed, Karl Holl was not justified in crediting Paul with a "kühne Wortumprägung" in 1 Cor. 0720 (in his famous essay "Die Geschichte des Worts Beruf," *Gesammelte Aufsätze zur Kirchengeschichte* [Tübingen, 1928], p. 190). Max Weber's judgment ("Die protestantische Ethik und der Geist des Kapitalismus," *Gesammelte Aufsätze zur Religionssoziologie* I [Tübingen, 1920], 63 n. 1), still stands: "Im Griechischen fehlt eine dem deutschen Wort (sc: 'Beruf') in der ethischen Färbung entsprechende Bezeichnung überhaupt."
In short, there is no convincing evidence to support Bauer's "2nd meaning" for κλῆσις in 1 Cor. 0720.

in 0717-24.[483] For in 0717 he strongly stressed that each Christian should act in accordance with the fact that he had been called by God.[484] And in 0724 he concluded that each Christian should continue to live in God's sight in accordance with this calling.

If, as I argue, Paul expressed in 0717, 0720 and 0724 the same, basic admonition: "live according to your calling from God in Christ," what were the Corinthians doing to make such an admonition necessary from Paul's perspective? That is, in light of my conclusion that κλῆσις refers to God's call and not to status in society, what could they have been doing *not* to live or remain in this calling?

At first glance, Paul's explication of 0717 in 0718 sheds no light

---

[483]Note also that the assumption that Paul in 0721d was urging the Corinthians to stay in a particular social status, namely slavery, has been an important factor encouraging the translation of κλῆσις in 0720 with *Stand* or "status." Now that this assumption has been shown to be false (see above, pp. 109-114), there is no longer any pressure from 0721 to invent a special meaning for κλῆσις in 0720. Likewise, when this term is given its usual meaning "call," there is no longer any pressure from 0720 to translate 0721d "rather stay in slavery."

[484]This statement is based on my conclusion that μερίζω and καλέω in 0717 are synonyms and that both parts of this verse carry the same meaning (so also Conzelmann, *1. Kor.*, p. 151). Against J. Weiß (*Der Erste Korintherbrief*, p. 184) and Günther Harder ("Miszelle zu 1 Kor. 7.17," *ThLZ* 79 [1954], 371), I conclude that καλέω is not limited by μερίζω but rather μερίζω is clarified by καλέω. In R 1203c we find Paul's only other use of μερίζω with God as subject: ἑκάστῳ ὡς ὁ θεὸς ἐμέρισεν μέτρον πίστεως. Here it is clear that God does not "distribute" various situations in life such as being a Jew, a Greek, a slave or a freeman; he "distributes" faith. This usage suggests the following paraphrase of 0717: "Let each one live his life in accordance with his call from God in Christ and with the faith which God has distributed to him." Note in addition that apart from his own call to become an apostle (R 0101, 1 Cor. 0101), Paul did not refer to other "church offices" with the term κλῆσις. Rather, apostles, prophets, teachers, healers, tongue-speakers, etc. are set (ἔθετο) by God in the congregation (1 Cor. 1228). See Akira Satake, "Apostolat und Gnade bei Paulus," *NTS* 15 (1968), 97-102.

For these reasons I must reject Ernst Käsemann's fascinating attempt to use 1 Cor. 0717 as a basis for equating the meanings of χάρισμα and κλῆσις/καλέω in Paul's theology. See his "Ministry and Community in the New Testament," *Essays on New Testament Themes*, Studies in Biblical Theology No. 41 (London, 1964), pp. 65-69 (trans. W.J. Montague from *Exegetische Versuche und Besinnungen* I, 2nd edn. [Göttingen, 1960], 110-114). There are other weaknesses in Käsemann's argument, e.g., his unconvincing claim that χάρισμα and κλῆσις in R 1129 are synonyms. Also his contention that 1 Cor. 0707 expresses a principle ("each has his own special gift from God") which Paul extended in 0717 assumes falsely that Paul thought marriage was also a *chárisma* and that 0707 and 0717 belong to the same line of argumentation. It is also most unlikely that Paul valued circumcision and uncircumcision (0718-19) as *charísmata*. Indeed, Friedrich Grau (*Der neutestamentliche Begriff Charisma, seine Geschichte und seine Theologie* [diss. printed in typescript, Tübingen, 1946], pp. 163-165) argues that Paul never thought of the "old man" in connection with *charísmata* but rather only of the "new creation." See also Otto Merk, *Handeln aus Glauben: Die Motivierungen der Paulinischen Ethik* (Marburg, 1968), p. 110.

138

on this question. For on the one hand it does not appear to be referring to an issue in the Corinthian congregation,[485] and on the other hand it does appear to refer specifically to the importance of social status. By the examples he used in 0718, Paul seems to indicate that it was important for the Jewish Christian to continue to live as a Jew as well as for the Gentile Christian to remain in his "religious status" as a Gentile. Is it, then, Paul's intention to say that remaining in one's religious status has a special value?[486]

To the contrary, he based his admonitions in 0718 on the following reason: "Circumcision is nothing; uncircumcision is nothing; but keeping the commands of God is everything" (0719). That is, such religious statuses mean nothing in Christ; any change in one's religious status would therefore be completely irrelevant to salvation. Paul's point is not that the changes he mentions are prohibited. Rather, he claimed that the question of religious status is not at all important.[487] What really counts is keeping the commands of God.

In 0721ab Paul argued toward the same conclusion with a second

---

[485] There is no indication that the Corinthians asked Paul anything about the importance of circumcision or about relations between Jewish and Gentile Christians. Nor is there any other evidence from 1 Cor. that the Jewish law was a problem in this congregation. See further Dieter Georgi, "Der Kampf um die reine Lehre im Urchristentum als Auseinandersetzung um das rechte Verständnis der an Israel ergangenen Offenbarung Gottes," Antijudaismus im Neuen Testament?--Exegetische und Systematische Beiträge, eds. W. Eckert, N.P. Levinson and M. Stöhr (Munich, 1967), pp. 83-85. In the absence of the problems Paul addressed in Gal. 0502-06, we must ask why he used circumcision/uncircumcision as examples in this letter to the Corinthians. In the next chapter I argue that it was the threefold thought-pattern which Paul expressed in Gal. 0328 which prompted his choice of examples in 1 Cor. 0717-24. See also above, pp. 129-131.

[486] See, e.g., the claim of E. Neuhäusler ("Ruf Gottes und Stand des Christen: Bermerkungen zu 1 Kor 7," Biblische Zeitschrift, Neue Folge 3 [1959], 48-49): "Gott teilt nicht nur das Maß des Glaubens einem jeden zu, sondern bestimmt auch den Stand, in dem der von ihm Erwählte durch den Ruf betroffen wird, d.h. er ruft den Juden als Juden, und den Sklaven in der Gebundenheit seines Sklaventums."

[487] Thus, the intent of Paul's argument here differs substantially from the treatment of the "circumcision-problem" in Acts 15. This is shown particularly by a very interesting reading of Acts 1502 in the so-called "Western text" in which the verb μένω appears: ἔλεγεν γὰρ ὁ Παῦλος μένειν οὕτως καθὼς ἐπίστευσαν διϊσχυριζόμενος. Eldon J. Epp translates this phrase: "For Paul spoke maintaining firmly that they (Gentile converts) should remain just as when they believed"; and he comments: "Thus, the D-text has sharpened up the issues in the controversy." The Theological Tendency of Codex Bezae Cantabrigiensis in Acts (Cambridge, 1966), pp. 101-102.

example: "Were you a slave when you were called? Don't worry about it."[488]
That is, the legal-social status of the Christian is also irrelevant with
respect to God's call in Christ. Between these two examples, Paul repeated
his conclusion from 0719c ("keeping the commands of God is everything"), but
in a different key: "Let each one continue in that calling with which he was
called" (0720). The claim that 0719c and 0720 express the same idea in "different keys" is supported by Paul's earlier usage of καλέω in 0715.

In 0715 Paul discussed the case of the Christian whose non-Christian
spouse wanted to dissolve their marriage. Although Paul had encouraged the
Corinthians to continue to live in such marriages on the grounds that the
Christian's power of holiness was stronger than the non-Christian's unclean-
ness (0712-14), he did not encourage them to resist the change in social status which would result from such divorces. To the contrary, Paul assured the
Christians that they were not enslaved in such marriages and that God had
called them to peace (0715). Obviously, God's call was in no way transgressed
or rejected by this change in social status.[489] Furthermore, at no point in
ch. 7 did Paul support his preference for celibacy by stating or implying that
the Christian who changed his status by marrying thereby questioned or rejected
God's calling.

On this basis it is clear that for Paul religious and social-legal
statuses are neither hindrances nor advantages with respect to "living

---

[488]In light of the contrasting phrases in 0718 (circumcision/uncircumcision)
we expect Paul in 0721cd to mention the contrast to the phrase "were you a
slave?" namely, "were you a freeman?" But he does not. This "irregularity"
is made all the more striking by the fact that 0722 *is* parallel to 0719 in
that both the state of slavery and the state of freedom are shown not to be
hindrances to a relation (as "slave" or "freedman") to Christ. See the exegesis of 0721cd below, pp. 157-158.

[489]The weakness in Neuhäusler's attempt to define the relationship between
κλῆσις and *Stand* becomes very obvious in his treatment of 0715 ("Ruf Gottes
und Stand des Christen," pp. 45-47). He claims that the purpose of 0715c
("God has called you to peace") was to assure any Corinthian Christian who
was living in a "mixed marriage" that he was free "in der κλῆσις seines
Standes zu bleiben." In order to make this claim, Neuhäusler had to ignore
the function of 0714 and put 0715c in its place. Having thus displaced 0715c,
he finds the basis for Paul's statement in 0715b ("in such a case the brother
or sister is not enslaved") in the pneumatic freedom which Paul proclaimed in
0612 ("All things are lawful for me, but I will not be mastered by anything").
This is a clever suggestion, but it destroys the line of Paul's own argument.
For it is the power of the Christian to sanctify the non-Christian spouse
which Paul urged was the basis for continuing to live in the marriage, and it
is the "call to peace" which Paul used to support his judgment that the
brother or sister is not enslaved.

140

according to God's calling" (0717, 0724). The really important thing is to keep God's commands and to continue in His calling.[490]

God's call had come to the Corinthians without regard to their various religious and social-legal situations. For Paul this fact meant that nothing was to be gained in God's eyes (παρὰ θεῷ) by any change in the religious or social statuses of the ones whom he had called. Within this perspective any attempt by the Corinthians to "improve" their relation to God by making a change in their social or religious status was tantamount to *not* continuing in God's calling. That is, to act as if religious or social status did make a real difference to God was to challenge the adequacy of that which God had already done, namely his distribution of faith to the Corinthians and his calling them through Christ.

What, then, had the Corinthians done to prompt Paul's admonitions in 0717-24? In what way did they *not* continue in God's calling? As has been noted above, there is no evidence that Paul's choice of examples in this pericope was influenced by actual problems in the Corinthian congregation. No particular activity of the Jews or the slaves in the congregation had moved Paul to write 0717-24.[491] It was rather the behavior of the men and women as such which stimulated him to write ch. 7 in this letter; and an important clue to understanding their actions can be found in 0126, in which Paul's only other use of κλῆσις in 1 Cor. appears.

Paul's admonition in 1 Cor. 0126 runs: "For consider your call (Βλέπετε γὰρ τὴν κλῆσιν ὑμῶν), my brothers, not many of you are wise (σοφοὶ)

---

[490] While Paul does not seem to have used any general term for social and religious status, the Stoics, according to A. Bonhöffer, used the word πρόσωπον to refer to position in life, such as rich or poor, slave or master (*Epiktet und das Neue Testament*, Religionsgeschichtliche Versuche und Vorarbeiten 10, [Giessen, 1911], p. 39). Note also that Bonhöffer compared the use of κλῆσις/καλέω in Paul and Epictetus, and he concluded that "es weder bei Epiktet noch im Neuen Testament das bedeutet, was wir heutzutage Beruf nennen. In I Kor. 7,20, wo man diese allgemeine Bedeutung finden will, handelt es sich genau wie in den übrigen Stellen des Neuen Testaments um die göttliche Berufung zum Heil, welche, als überragendes Gut, jede Änderung der äußeren Lebensumstände, unter welchen sie stattfand, überflüssig macht. Bei Epiktet aber ist die κλῆσις entweder eine außerordentliche göttliche Berufung zu einer außerordentlichen Lebensaufgabe, zu einem μαρτύριον, oder aber jeder durch die Umstände (καιρός, ἀνάγκη καλεῖ) sich anzeigende Aufruf zur Erfüllung einer bestimmten sittlichen Pflicht." *Epiktet und das Neue Testament*, p. 208.

[491] This is not to say that there was no "bite" in 0718-19 or 0721-23. Paul is not simply calling on examples which he had previously discussed with the Corinthians and about which there necessarily existed full agreement. Nevertheless, it seems clear that Paul wrote these words with the intention of bringing supportive material to his main argument in ch. 7 regarding male/female relationships. He expected the examples in 0717-24 to support his argument precisely because no tension in the areas of Jew/Greek or slave/free relationships was known to him.

according to human standards (κατὰ σάρκα), not many are powerful (δυνατοί), not many are wellborn (εὐγενεῖς)."[492] With these words Paul urged the Corinthians to remember that most of those whom God had called to become Christians at Corinth were "mere nothings" in the eyes of the world.[493] The actual social status of most of the Corinthians formed the basis for the contrast Paul stressed by his argument in 0118-0208: God has made foolish the wisdom of the world and has called and chosen what is foolish and weak in order to shame the wise and the strong. Therefore no human being can boast before God.

But the Corinthians *had* been "boasting of men" (0321, 0406-07), and their faith was in the wisdom of men rather than in the power of God (0205). Thus, Paul not only sought to clarify God's gracious calling of the Corinthians by reproaching them on the basis of their social background; he also resisted any claim made by these Christians that they had *become* "wise" or "powerful" or "wellborn" in a religious sense as a result of God's call. According to Paul, God had not brought the Corinthians into such an exalted religious status when he called them.[494] Nor did God expect that they would achieve such a new status by their own efforts, as a consequence of having answered his call.

Nevertheless, the Corinthians had been boasting--both about their new, exalted religious status (0408: they were already "filled," "rich" and "kings") and about the new morality which they claimed was appropriate to this status (0501-02: one of their members was "living with his father's wife"). For the Corinthians, God's call had led to a "breakthrough"[495] in their

---

[492]Conzelmann (*1. Korintherbrief*, p. 65) correctly concludes: "Κλῆσις ist hier eher der Akt der Berufung als der Zustand des Berufenseins." So also U. Wilckens, *Weisheit und Torheit* (see above, p. 62 n. 201), p. 41, and K.L. Schmidt, *TDNT* III, 492 n. 1. Even Lietzmann (see above, p. 135 n. 475) translated this verse: "Seht doch eure (eigene) Berufung (zum Christentum) an ..." (*An die Korinther* I-II, p. 10.)

[493]For an intelligent discussion of the "social and intellectual standing" of Christians in the first century, see C.F.D. Moule, *The Birth of the New Testament*, pp. 156-161.

[494]See the recent Harvard dissertation by Birger A. Pearson, "The ΠΝΕΥΜΑΤΙΚΟΣ - ΨΥΧΙΚΟΣ Terminology in 1 Corinthians. A Study in the Theology of the Corinthian Opponents of Paul and Its Relation to Gnosticism," (1969), pp. 111-112. Pearson suggests that "the term εὐγενεῖς in 1 Cor. 1:26f. does not simply refer to aristocratic birth, but to a claim of the Corinthian opponents to εὐγένεια, a technical term whose background is to be found in Hellenistic Judaism." Pearson notes that the terms εὐγένεια and σοφία are linked in the section of Philo's *De Virtutibus* entitled Περὶ εὐγενείας: "Philo begins this section by remarking that natural or bodily εὐγένεια is of no consequence, but what is important is the εὐγένεια which comes to one whose soul has received wisdom." Pearson concludes: "It is this notion of εὐγένεια that P may be polemicizing against in 1 Cor. 1:26f. This would explain why the Jeremianic triad of 'sophos' 'ischyros' 'plousios' becomes in P's application of Jeremiah 9:23f., the 'sophoi,' the 'dunatoi' and the 'eugeneis' (cf. also 1 Sam 2:10-LXX)."

[495]Cf. K. Stendahl, *The Bible and the Role of Women*, pp. 32-33.

understanding of male/female relationships, and this new understanding encouraged behavior which even the pagans rejected (0501). The Corinthians boasted: "All things are lawful for me" (0612), apparently basing their claim on the belief that their exalted religious status made irrelevant (or perhaps praiseworthy) such bodily activities as sexual intercourse with prostitutes (0615-16).

Paul's reply to this religiously motivated behavior was directed against the same self-understanding which he argued against in 0118-0208. In 0126-29 Paul challenged the Corinthians' understanding of God's calling and its effects; in 0617-20 he called in question their understanding of the relation of God's Spirit to their earthly existence: "Don't you know that your body is a temple of the Holy Spirit which is in you? ...So glorify God in your body." It is consistent that those Christians who thought that they had become spiritually "wellborn" when they were called also believed that God's Spirit dwelled not in their bodies but in their minds.[496]

Paul's use of the term σῶμα in his polemical reply to this viewpoint indicates sharply that the Spirit's temple was not the mind or soul alone but was the Christian's entire self--including his physical body.[497] God had not

---

[496] The belief that the soul or mind could be the dwelling place of God was a commonplace in popular Hellenistic philosophy. For some examples, see J. Weiβ, *Der Erste Korintherbrief*, p. 166. Specifically, the immortal νοῦς was often distinguished from the mortal ψυχή. Birger Pearson (see above, n. 494) has shown that the immediate background of the opponents of Paul in Corinth was the adaptation of this view made by Hellenistic Judaism under the influence of Gen. 0207, on account of which the distinction became πνεῦμα-ψυχή. In a striking way, the background for 0612-20 is expressed in the same text by Philo which Pearson cites with reference to 1 Cor. 0126. That is, in Philo, *De Virtutibus* 188 (Cohn-Wendland V, 325, 4-8), the concepts "wisdom," "noble birth" and the "mind as the temple of God" are related to each other:

> "When God on account of his kindness and love for man desired to establish this (sc: τὴν εὐγένειαν ὡς μέγιστον ἀγαθόν) among us also, he found no worthier temple (νεών) on earth than the mind (λογισμοῦ). For as the better part it alone bears an image of the good (ἀγαλματοφορεῖ τἀγαθόν), even though some of those who have tasted--or have only sipped--of wisdom (σοφίας) may disbelieve."

Without having noted the connection with 1 Cor. 0619, Pearson (pp. 111-112) remarks: "This passage provides one more example of the capacity of the higher soul of man (here called λογισμός, a synonym for νοῦς) to receive wisdom. But it also tells us that the one whose soul has received wisdom is the one who is truly εὐγενής." See also Philo's statement that God has two temples: ὁ κόσμος and ἡ λογικὴ ψυχή (*De Somniis* I, 215 = Cohn-Wendland III, 251, 12-15).

[497] See Eduard Schweizer, *ThW* VII, 1062-1063, and Rudolph Bultmann, *Theology of the New Testament* (New York, 1951), I, 194-195 (trans. Kendrick Grobel, *Theologie des Neuen Testaments*, pp. 191-192). An interesting discussion of many of the problems in this pericope is presented by R. Kempthorne, "Incest and the Body of Christ. A Study of I Cor. vi. 12-20," *NTS* 14 (1968), 568-574. His conclusion that the "prostitute" in ch. 6 is the same person as the "stepmother" in ch. 5 is not convincing.

called the Corinthians out of their somatic being. Rather, as God had given
the Corinthians somatic existence (0619) and as he would raise them up as
somatic creatures (0614), so in the present any "body" whom God had called was
an actual "member of Christ" (0615). This relationship of Christ to the
believer is so close that Paul compared it directly to sexual union (0616-17).
Since the Corinthians belonged bodily to Christ (0620), they were not free to
give themselves to prostitutes, i.e., to sexual union under the power of
πορνεία.[498]

For Paul, Christ was the Lord of the body, i.e., of the total person
in his worldly relationships. Thus, he resisted the exalted Corinthians' high
evaluation of "spiritual gifts" (1201) because they thereby devalued the more
important and more somatic gift of ἀγάπη and the "this-worldly" task of
οἰκοδομή--"building up the church" (1412). God was to be glorified in the
body (0620). For this reason, Paul could not agree that to say there was "no
male and female in Christ" meant that sexual activity was excluded from the
lordship of Christ. Sexual freedom was not a conclusion which Paul could draw
from his understanding of the unity of male and female in Christ. Neither
could he agree that this unity meant freedom from sexuality or from temptation.
Therefore, in ch. 7 Paul began his answer to the Corinthians' questions by
stressing the importance of a fully physical marriage.

Paul's line of reasoning in ch. 7, which appears at first to be
rather difficult to follow, becomes much easier to understand when it is seen
that Paul's major problem of communication in these verses was caused by his
interest in recommending celibacy as a better style of life for the Corinthians without at the same time agreeing with the theology behind the celibacy
already being practiced in the congregation.[499] Paul wished that every

---

[498]Erhardt Güttgemanns (_Der Leidende Apostel und Sein Herr: Studien zur
paulinischen Christologie_ [Göttingen, 1966], p. 230) expresses this point well:
"Das σῶμα ist eine auch im Eschaton bleibende ontologische Struktur des Mensch-
seins, die den Menschen und den Kyrios so zueinanderordnet, daß das σῶμα nicht
mehr der πορνεία gehören kann....Am σῶμα hat der Kyrios also das Objekt und den
Ort seiner Herrschaft, so daß sich dort keine andere Macht niederlassen oder
dieser 'Ort' einer anderen Herrschaft untertan werden kann."

[499]It has often been argued that the statement in 0701b, "It is a good thing
not to touch a woman," was quoted by Paul from the letter he had received from
the Corinthians. Origen was the first commentator to make this judgment (see
Claude Jenkins, "Origen on I Corinthians," _JTS_ IX [1907-08], 500, lines 13, 22-
23). John C. Hurd (_The Origin of 1 Corinthians_ [New York, 1965], p. 68) has
prepared a table of modern opinion on this question, indicating that Heinrici,
Lock, Goudge, Robertson and Plummer, Zahn, Parry, D. Smith, Moffatt, Jeremias,
and Morris concluded that Paul was quoting the Corinthians. The words themselves, however, also expressed Paul's own viewpoint, as the remainder of the
chapter indicates. It was not celibacy but rather the reasons for it and the
religious evaluation of it which divided Paul and the Corinthians.
    NB: For a detailed outline of 1 Cor. 7 in the form of an analysis
of Paul's style of argumentation, see below, pp. 166-171.

Christian could live a sexually ascetic life, as he did (0707).[500] In ch. 7
he supports this preference for celibacy with a variety of reasons, the most
important of which was his belief that a married person's interests were
divided between the Lord and the spouse (0732-35). Paul thought that the
unmarried person could give "undivided devotion to the Lord" and live a more
ordered (0735), less anxious (0732), less troubled (0728) and happier (0740)
life.[501]

Paul also used a variety of ways in ch. 7 to make clear his disagreement with the theology of exaltation which had led to the sexual asceticism which the Corinthians were already trying to practice.[502] He began by
reminding the Corinthians that they were still living in the realm of temptation (0702)[503] and that their attempts at sexual asceticism within marriage
were an invitation to Satan.[504] Therefore to those who had not actually

---

[500]For a good discussion of Paul's interest in having other Christians imitate him, see D.M. Stanley, "'Become imitators of me...': The Pauline Conception of Apostolic Tradition," *Biblica* 40 (1959), 859-77.

[501]Note that as in 0612-20, Paul's chief argument is based on the intimate
somatic relationship of the believer to Christ. Paul's statement in 0734
about the "holiness in body and spirit" of the unmarried, devoted Christian
woman would seem to indicate a disparagement of all sexual intercourse, and
not of *porneia* alone. Yet, Paul insisted that it was no sin to marry; and he
even spoke of the "holiness" of the unbelieving spouses of the Corinthian
Christians in 0712-14, where he assured the believers that there was no Christian reason not to live in such marriages.
  Note also that John G. Gager ("Functional Diversity in Paul's Use of
End-Time Language," *JBL* 89 [1970], 331-333) is correct in stressing the secondary importance of eschatological expectation for Paul's pro-celibacy argument.
Paul used the eschatological material in 0729-31 as additional, general support
for his preference for celibacy, which he based on the importance of "undivided
devotion."

[502]For a recent discussion of asceticism in the Corinthian congregation and
the pertinent secondary literature, see the unpublished diss. by David R.
Cartlidge, "Competing Theologies of Asceticism in the Early Church," (Harvard,
1969), pp. 23-58. A very interesting attempt to sketch the background for the
"spiritual marriages" described in 0736-38 is made by David L. Balch, "1 Cor.
7:36-38 and Its Background: Moses as an Ascetic θεῖος ἀνήρ," unpubl. B.D. thesis (Union Theological Seminary: New York, 1969). (The major argument of this
thesis is now available in Balch's article, "Backgrounds of I Cor. VII: Sayings
of the Lord in Q; Moses as an Ascetic ΘΕΙΟΣ ΑΝΗΡ in II Cor. III," *NTS* 18 [1972],
351-364.) See also J.C. Hurd, *The Origin of 1 Cor.*, pp. 158-163, 222-223;
R.H.A. Seboldt, "Spiritual Marriage in the Early Church: A Suggested Interpretation of 1 Cor. 7:36-38," *Concordia Theological Monthly* 30 (1959), 103-119 and
176-189; and D. Doughty, *Heiligkeit und Freiheit, passim.*

[503]See the warning in 1 Cor. 1012. Note also the similar point in R 0817-18,
where Paul contrasted the "sufferings of this present time" with the "glory
that is to be revealed to us."

[504]See 1 Th. 0305 and Gal. 0601. For a discussion of "the present" as the
time of "temptation," see Karl Georg Kuhn, "New Light on Temptation, Sin and
Flesh in the New Testament," in *The Scrolls and the New Testament*, ed. Krister
Stendahl (New York, 1957), pp. 94-113.

received celibacy as a *chárisma* from God (0707) Paul recommended a fully sexual marriage (0702, 0709, 0736) in which the husband has control over the σῶμα of his wife *and* the wife has control over the σῶμα of her husband (0703-04).[505] Because of the natural limits to sexual self-control, even attempts at temporary celibacy agreed upon by the marriage partners for the sake of prayer should be kept brief (0705).[506] Furthermore, celibacy was only one of God's gifts (0707); and it was clear to Paul that those Christians who were "burning with desire" (0709, cf. 0736) had not received it and should not strive after it. For Paul, the Corinthians' own experiences (i.e., their difficulties in remaining celibate) and the present time of temptation (i.e., the period *before* the general resurrection) were decisive objections to their claims to be exalted and to be free from sexuality.[507]

In addition to these attempts to bring the exalted Corinthians "down to earth," Paul made one of his rare references to a word of the Lord in order to support his admonition that married Christians should not separate (0710).[508] Then in 0725 he claimed that he had no word from the Lord regarding virgins. Could these unusual references to the existence and nonexistence of words from the Lord have been stimulated by a claim by the Corinthians that they knew

---

[505]It would be false to conclude that Paul wanted to present his "position on marriage" in ch. 7. D. Doughty (*Heiligkeit und Freiheit*, pp. 135-143) correctly stresses that Paul's entire argumentation in ch. 7 must be understood as a polemic against a false theology of asceticism. Thus one looks in vain for a positive view of marital love and family life here (see G. Bornkamm, *Paulus*, p. 214). Paul says nothing about procreation or child-raising as reasons for marriage.

In view of the specific purpose of his argument, the most striking feature of 0702-05 is Paul's reference to the man and the woman as equals, which he underlined by his use of the adverb ὁμοίως. Throughout ch. 7 Paul took care to address both the woman and the man in each of the situations he discussed (only in 0736-38 did he speak to the man without also addressing the woman). Else Kähler (*Die Frau in den paulinischen Briefen* [Frankfurt, 1960], pp. 85-86) has also emphasized the *gleichwertige Gegenseitigkeit* of man and woman which Paul encouraged in ch. 7. She writes: "Triumphiert in der Porneia die *Einseitigkeit*, so in der Ehe die *Gegenseitigkeit*." Yet Paul did not have a positive case to make for marriage as such. The important factor here is that for Paul the conviction that there was "no male and female in Christ" did not mean that "maleness" and "femaleness" were overcome but rather that each Christian, whether male or female, was to be equally valued and respected.

[506]See also 1 Th. 0403-08, quite probably written from Corinth early in Paul's ministry there.

[507]See also 1 Cor. 0303, where Paul pointed to the Corinthians' jealousy and strife as clear evidence that they were not exalted but were "of the flesh" and were "behaving like ordinary men."

[508]Paul's only other explicit references to sayings of the Lord are 1 Cor. 0914 and 1 Th. 0415-17a (cf. 1 Cor. 1551-52). See also the special traditions on which Paul calls in 1 Cor. 1123-25 and 1503-07.

words of the Lord which supported their view that Christians were called to sexual asceticism?

One such saying is recorded in Lk. 2034-36:

And Jesus said to them (the Sadducees), "The sons of this age marry and are given in marriage; but those who have been judged worthy to attain to that age and to the resurrection from the dead neither marry nor are given in marriage for they can no longer die--they are like angels and are sons of God, being sons of the resurrection."

Note especially the present tense of the verbs in this saying as well as the distinction between two classes of men. Such words could have been very important to the *pneumatikoi* in Corinth who were striving to practice sexual asceticism as a sign of their exaltation.[509] Lk. 1829-30 records another saying in which Jesus speaks of the great benefit received by those who have "left house or *wife* or brothers or parents or children for the sake of the Kingdom of God." Such words could have helped to motivate the separations Paul was trying to prevent in 1 Cor. 0710. But what evidence is there that the Corinthians knew of such sayings?

In a recent article, Quentin Quesnell has shown that Luke has preserved a number of sayings of the Lord which express a clear preference for sexual asceticism.[510] A connection between this sayings-tradition and the congregation in Corinth has been suggested by James M. Robinson on the basis

---

[509] In addition to their sexual asceticism, the Corinthians could boast of their "speaking in tongues" as a sign that they were "like angels" (see 1 Cor. 1402-29 and 1301).

[510] "Made Themselves Eunuchs for the Kingdom of Heaven (Matt. 19:12)," *Catholic Biblical Quarterly* 30 (1968), 335-358. Quesnell argues that the Q material is treated differently by Matt. and Lk. precisely on the question of celibacy and virginity. For example Matt. 1929 (=Lk. 1829) does not mention the "wife" among the things that a man leaves "for the Kingdom of Heaven" (neither does Mk. 1029). Some other examples are Lk. 1426 in comparison with Matt. 1037 and 1929, and the reasons offered in Lk. 1418-20 for not coming to the "great banquet" (including, "I have married a wife") in comparison with the reasons offered in Matt. 2205 for not coming to the "marriage feast." Quesnell (p. 345) also notes that the parallels to the Lukan saying quoted above (2034-36) clearly assume that the resurrection is a future event (Matt. 2230=Mk. 1224).

that these sayings and the Corinthians shared a very similar understanding of Jesus and Wisdom.[511] The probability of this hypothesis that the Corinthians knew and used such a sayings-tradition is increased by David Balch's striking observation that only in "Q" and in 1 Cor. 0738 does the rare verb γαμίζω appear.[512] On this basis, Balch suggests that in 0736-38 Paul took up the negative judgment on those who "marry and are given in marriage (γαμοῦσιν καὶ γαμίσκονται/γαμίζονται)" which is found in Lk. 2034, 1727 (Q) precisely in order to state firmly that the Christian who marries does not sin (οὐχ ἁμαρτάνει).[513] Even though Paul wanted to recommend celibacy (0738b),

---

[511]"Kerygma and History in the New Testament," in *The Bible in Modern Scholarship*, ed. H. Philip Hyatt (London, 1966), pp. 127-131. Robinson (p. 129) concludes: "I Corinthians and Q have in common then the issue of Jesus and wisdom. It is hence possible that the Q material may in part have had such a *Sitz im Leben* as the conflict in Corinth." Heinz-Wolfgang Kuhn ("Der irdische Jesus bei Paulus als traditionsgeschichtliches und theologisches Problem," *ZThK* 67 [1970], 311-316) has developed this hypothesis. Kuhn (p. 315) also suggests that Paul's references to the nonexistence of words from the Lord were meant to oppose the Corinthians' use of such tradition.

[512]"I Cor. 7:36-38 and Its Background: Moses as an Ascetic θεῖος ἀνήρ," pp. 20-22. (See now Balch, *NTS* 18 [1972], 357.) Balch notes that the rare form γαμίζω appears no where else in the NT or the LXX and is found only once in extra-biblical Greek: Apollonius Dyscolus (ii A.D.), *De Syntaxi* 280.11.

[513]In addition, Balch (pp. 42-55; now *NTS* 18, 358-364) seeks to show that this high evaluation of celibacy arose in Hellenistic Judaism among those who honored Moses as a θεῖος ἀνήρ and who sought to imitate him (Philo, *De Vita Mosis* I, 158-162 = Cohn-Wendland IV, 158,5-159,9). In Moses the fruits of virtue had been perfected; it was his honor in wisdom (σοφῷ) to serve the Being Who truly is (*De Vita Mosis* II, 67 = Cohn-Wendland IV, 216, 6-10). Philo then made a striking connection between sexual asceticism and the reception of revelation by Moses:

"First he (Moses) had to be clean, as in soul so also in body, to have no dealings with any passion, purifying himself from all the calls of mortal nature, food and drink and intercourse with women (τῆς πρὸς γυναῖκας ὁμιλίας). This last he had disdained for many a day, almost from the time when, possessed by the spirit (θεοφορεῖσθαι), he entered on his work as a prophet (ἤρξατο προφητεύειν), since he held it fitting to hold himself always in readiness to receive the oracular messages."

(tr. Colson, *De Vita Mosis* II, 68-69 = Cohn-Wendland IV, 216, 13-19). Balch's attempt to link 1 Cor. 7 and 2 Cor. 3 by means of this text and others is very interesting, but it goes beyond the limits of my investigation here.
  In any case, such a background for the combined appearance of sexual asceticism and prophecy in the Corinthian congregation is fully consistent with the Philonic background to 1 Cor. 0126-20 and 0617-20 which is described above, p. 142 n. 496. This hypothesis is strengthened by D. Georgi's judgment that 1 Cor. 1-4 indicates that the Corinthians' pride was based on having received wisdom, which was understood to be revelation. "Der Kampf um die reine Lehre im Urchristentum," p. 87 n. 18.

he insisted in this context that he who marries does well (0738a).[514] Despite
their claims and their boasting, the Corinthians were not exalted, they were
not "like angels" (Lk. 2036); and according to Paul it was dangerous for them
to strive to live as if they were already angels, i.e., as if they had overcome the distinction between male and female. In contrast to the "words of
the Lord" in Q which may well have been used by the Corinthians to support
their claim that their sexual asceticism was an important sign of their exalted
status, Paul made it clear that he had a "command from the Lord" stating that
married Christians should *not* separate. He also made it clear that he had *no*
"command of the Lord" regarding the status of Christian virgins (male or
female).[515]

What, then, have these investigations of texts outside of 1 Cor. 7
contributed to our understanding of the content and manner of Paul's response
to the Corinthians in that chapter?

1.   My discussion of 1 Cor. 0126 suggested that Paul could use the term
κλῆσις to remind the Corinthians that they had not become "wise" or
"powerful" or "wellborn" when God called them to be saints (0102). Their
"calling" had not brought to them experiences of religious exaltation about
which they could boast.

2.   The Corinthians had been boasting, both about their new religious
      status and their new morality (0502). In the above treatment of 1
Cor. 0612-20, it was suggested that Paul's use of σῶμα in this pericope was
meant to be a sharp attack on the basis of that morality, namely the belief

---

[514]The consistency in Paul's seemingly inconsistent uses of καλόν, καλῶς and
κρεῖττον in 1 Cor. 7 becomes evident when it is seen that it was Paul's intention to recommend celibacy as a "better" way of Christian living without at
the same time giving any encouragement to the theology of exaltation which
called for the celibacy which the Corinthians were already trying to practice.
Thus, on the one hand it is "good" to be like Paul and not touch a woman (0701,
0708). Yet in the face of temptation and lack of self-control, it is "better"
to marry than to burn with desire (0709) or to remain separate because of a
falsely understood spirituality (0702-05). On the other hand it is "good"
(i.e., not a sin) when a man actually marries his partner in "spiritual
marriage" (0738a), but it is "better" if he refrains from marriage if he has
the gift of celibacy (0737). In any case, in view of the "present crisis"
Paul said that it is "good" for those who are married to remain in marriage
and those who are single to remain celibate (0726).

[515]Notice that Paul also disagreed with the Corinthians' theology of celibacy when he insisted that widows were free to be married "in the Lord"
(0739); to be sure, he thought that they would be "happier" if they remained
celibate, but he did not think that they would achieve a higher spiritual
status by doing so.
      Notice also that Paul's claim that he possessed "the right to be
accompanied by a wife, as the other apostles and the brothers of the Lord and
Cephas" (0905) may be a polemic indication that the Corinthians had been
calling upon apostolic examples in order to support their confidence in sexual
asceticism as a sign of true Christianity.

that God was only concerned about the believer's νοῦς. Against this exalted, other-worldly view which denied that the physical body had any positive value in God's eyes, Paul argued that the total person (including physical sexuality) is a member of Christ and a temple of the Holy Spirit. God was to be glorified where the Christians existed in the world, namely in their bodies.

3. It was proposed that the Corinthians knew and used such pro-celibacy sayings of the Lord as Lk. 2034-36 (Q) to support their theology of celibacy. This hypothesis has the following consequences:

a. A direct connection between the Corinthians' theology of exaltation (expressed in Lk. in terms of "resurrection") and sexual asceticism is firmly established. These sayings in Q indicate the basis on which the Corinthians could have concluded that God's calling demanded renunciation of sexuality and dissolution of marriage, i.e., the basis for the claim that God's call should result in a change of the Christian's sexual status.

b. Both Paul's rare reference to a command of the Lord in 1 Cor. 0710 and his unique remark in 0725 that he knew of no saying of the Lord about virgins can be explained first of all as pointed attempts to correct the Corinthians' theology.

c. The fact that living as a Christian in sexual asceticism could be described as living "like angels," links this exalted celibacy with another "angelic" activity which was very important to the Corinthians, namely, "speaking in tongues."[516] This connection suggests that Paul's manner of dealing with the "tongue-speakers" in Corinth might illuminate the way in which 0717-24 functions in ch. 7.

Indeed, the similarities in Paul's treatment of celibacy and ecstatic speaking are quite striking. Paul himself spoke in tongues ("I thank God that I speak in tongues more than you all"--1418); he was celibate (0708). Paul recommended speaking in tongues ("Now I want you all to speak in tongues" --1405); he recommended celibacy (0707-08, 0738b). Paul counted speaking in tongues among the chárismata (1210, 1401); he stressed that celibacy was a chárisma (0707). Nevertheless, Paul warned against the dangers of speaking in tongues (1404, 1412, 1419); and he warned against the dangers of sexual

---

[516]See Johannes Behm, TDNT I, 726; note esp. his citation from Wilhelm Bousset (Göttingische Gelehrte Anzeigen [1901], p. 773): "Utterance with tongues is the speech of angels in which the secrets of the heavenly world are revealed." For further developments in the connection between celibacy and speaking in tongues, see P. Suso Frank, ΑΓΓΕΛΙΚΟΣ ΒΙΟΣ: Begriffsanalytische und begriffsgeschichtliche Untersuchung zum "engelgleichen Leben" im frühen Mönchtum, Beiträge zur Geschichte des alten Mönchtums und des Benediktinerordens 26 (Münster, 1964), pp. 178-192.

150

asceticism (0702, 0705, 0709). He relativized the importance of speaking in tongues by insisting that the highest *chárisma* is ἀγάπη ("If I speak in tongues of men or of angels, but have not love..."--1301). Those who were striving after spiritual gifts should seek first to excel in οἰκοδομή ("Since you are eager for manifestations of the Spirit, strive to excel in building up the congregation"--1412). Paul also relativized the importance of celibacy and "spiritual marriages" by insisting that the Corinthians' first task was to "live according to the fact that God had called them" (0717).[517] Those who were striving to prove that they were exalted by means of sexual asceticism should rather "continue in the calling by which they were called" (0720).[518] That is, they should keep "the commandments of God" (0719); they should "continue in the calling in the sight of God" (0724). Furthermore, Paul did not accept speaking in tongues as a sign that the Corinthians were already exalted. Rather, he stressed that ecstatic speaking and prophesying will pass away when the perfect (τέλειον) comes (1308-10); only faith, hope and love will continue.[519] Likewise, only this love is the final criterion for Christian life in the present (1301-03).[520] In the same way, Paul rejected sexual asceticism as a sign that the Corinthians were already exalted. Although he preferred celibacy, he refused to recognize it as a spiritual achievement for which the Corinthians should strive or about which they could boast.[521] The important

---

[517] Paul stressed the importance of this admonition and its parallels (0720, 0724) by stating, "This is what I command in all the congregations" (0717d).

[518] Because Paul made it clear that sexual asceticism was by no means a condition of salvation, David Cartlidge ("Competing Theologies of Asceticism in the Early Church," pp. 50-55) classifies him as a "moderate ascetic."

[519] See H. Conzelmann, *1. Korintherbrief*, pp. 272-273. He explains: "Die drei 'bleibenden' sind so oder so diejenigen Gaben, die nicht in eine pneumatische Emanzipation und Selbsterbauung führen können."

[520] Helmut Koester ("ΓΝΩΜΑΙ ΔΙΑΦΟΡΟΙ. The Origin and Nature of Diversification in the History of Early Christianity," *HTR* 58 [1965], 312) states this point quite lucidly: "*Agape* is the only phenomenon in which the eschatological future is directly present in the church (I Cor. 13:8-13). *Agape* controls the exercise of any other religious qualities and leaves no room for the demonstration of eschatological fulfillment." See also Ulrich Wilckens, "Urchristlicher Kommunismus," *Christentum und Gesellschaft*, eds. W. Lohff and B. Lohse (Göttingen, 1969), pp. 129-44, esp. pp. 137-141.

[521] Contrary to the interpretation of Richard Kugelman (*The Jerome Biblical Commentary*, eds. R.E. Brown, J.A. Fitzmeyer, R.E. Murphy [London, 1968], II, 262, §34), Paul precisely did *not* say that "the virgin already anticipates the life of the resurrection" or that "virginity places the baptized existentially in the future." Such language sounds like the Corinthians! Indeed, according to Paul the present experience of the Corinthians is *not* a desirable anticipation of the future or the Parousia. For at *no* time would it become fitting for men to boast about their spiritual achievements or to act as if *agápe* were not essential. See Doughty, *Heiligkeit und Freiheit*, pp. 151-152.

matter to the Lord was whether or not the Corinthians were living lives which corresponded to his call.

This comparison is instructive; and it strongly reinforces the insights into chap. 7 which have been gained from 0126-29 and 0612-20, namely that God's calling was not a call to religious exaltation but rather to the crucified Christ and that God had not called the Corinthians out of their somatic being but rather into a new life of glorifying him "in the body." In 0717-24 Paul transposed this exhortation to glorify God in the body into a new key by which he was able both to stress the fundamental importance of Christian existence *in the world* and to deny the importance of *any* particular worldly status in which a Christian found himself. He did this by forcefully pointing again to God's call in Christ, to God's dividing of faith--and by emphatically urging the Corinthians to live according to *that* calling, to continue in *that* call.

Since God had called the Corinthians into κοινωνία with his crucified Son (0109),[522] it was this fellowship and not any status in the world which determined their relationship to God.[523] Thus, there was no status that could become either the *content* of God's call or the *confirmation* of that call. "Walking according to the calling" did not include a withdrawal from the world (as at Qumran)[524] nor did it require any changes in worldly status. Attempts to change one's religious status by becoming circumcized or by undoing circumcision (or by renouncing one's sexuality or by dissolving one's marriage) had been made completely irrelevant by God's calling. The person who had been called was no longer defined as a Jew or a Greek, as a male or a female, as a slave or a freeman, but as a saint (0102); and this "holiness in Christ" was not a status but a new way of existing in the world under the grace and the

---

[522]See R 0828-30: "We know that in everything God works for good with those who love him, who are *called* according to his purpose. For those whom he foreknew he also predestined *to be conformed to the image of his Son*, in order that he might be the firstborn among many brethren. And those whom he predestined he also *called*; and those whom he *called* he also justified; and those whom he justified he also glorified." (RSV--my emphasis).

[523]Werner Bieder (*Die Berufung im Neuen Testament*, Abhandlungen zur Theologie des Alten und Neuen Testaments 38 [Zürich, 1961], pp. 67-69) is correct in stressing that the *einmalige Berufung* was meant to determine all later actions of the Christian. He notes that the perfect tenses in 0717 point to the calling's continuing effectiveness. See also Heb. 0915.

[524]D. Wiederkehr, *Die Theologie der Berufung in den Paulusbriefen*, p. 132. For a summary of recent discussion of this point, see Herbert Braun, *Qumran und das Neue Testament* (Tübingen, 1966), I, 192-193.

command of God.[525] Christians who were anxious about their worldly statuses
were taking the world "too seriously" (καταχρώμενοι--0731).

Indeed, it is the call of God (and not "the foreshortened time and
world" alone) which seems to be the basis for Paul's ὡς μή exhortations in
0729-31. For in this second hortatory interruption of chap. 7 (the first is
0717-24), Paul especially emphasized one of his points from 0717-24, namely
that whereas the various earthly activities and relationships in which Christians were involved were not to be rejected, their definitive character for
Christian existence had been negated.[526]

In short, Paul in 0717-24 sought to clarify two points with special
reference to the Corinthians' concern about their exalted religious status and
their attempts to confirm that status by sexual asceticism: 1) Every circumstance of life is radically relativized by God's call. The Christian's self-
definition does not come from his earthly status but from God's call in the
crucified Christ.[527] 2) Existence in the world, in the body, is of decisive
importance because it is precisely in earthly, historical relationships,
rather than in individualistic ecstasy or spiritual achievement, that the
crucified Christ is Lord and God is glorified.[528] This, in light of 1 Cor.
0126-29, 0612-20, 0729-31 and 1201-1440, is the meaning of "walking in

---

[525] Doughty (Heiligkeit und Freiheit, pp. 194-195) rightly observes that for
Paul no worldly situation is in itself either Christian or non-Christian;
therefore, the call of God did not establish the Corinthians in a new status
but rather put them under the task of realizing their Christian calling by
keeping the commands of God wherever they were.

[526] See Wolfgang Schrage, "Die Stellung zur Welt bei Paulus, Epiktet und in
der Apokalyptik. Ein Beitrag zu 1 Kor 7,29-31," ZThK 61 (1964), 151; and O.
Merk, Handeln aus Glauben, pp. 113-115. This interpretation is strengthened
especially by the fourth example: it is not "buying" as such that is called
in question but rather κατέχειν, i.e., the "keeping, the seizing, the possess-
ing." As Schrage (p. 151) says: "Wer kauft, soll nicht so tun, als kaufe er
gar nicht, sondern er soll nicht meinen, er könne über das Gekaufte in alle
Zukunft verfügen." Also, Paul did not criticize in principle either crying
or rejoicing (see R 1215).
   Against A. Bonhöffer (Epiktet und das N.T., p. 173), who said that
in 1 Cor. 0729-31 Paul is advising renunciation of sexual intercourse in
marriage, Herbert Braun ("Die Indifferenz gegenüber der Welt bei Paulus und
bei Epiktet," Gesammelte Studien [Tübingen, 1962], p. 159) correctly interprets 0729b ("let those who have wives live as though they had none") when he
concludes that the men "sollen nicht ihr Herz an die Frau hängen."

[527] See 0722 ("For a slave who has been called is a freedman of the Lord.
Likewise a freeman who has been called is a slave of the Lord."), which is a
striking illustration of the new self-definition given to the Christian by
Christ. This verse anticipates the language in 0729-31.

[528] See above, pp. 22-23. Note again in this context that "walking according to the calling" means "keeping the commands of God"--and Paul made it
quite clear that his argument for celibacy was not based on a command of God.

accordance with the fact that you have been called" (0717) and of "continuing in the calling by which you have been called (0720)." This interpretation of 1 Cor. 0717-24 as a very significant part of Paul's response to the Corinthian *pneumatikoi* has altered sharply the commonly accepted understanding of this passage and has shown that Paul used κλῆσις in 0720 (as in 0126) according to its usual meaning but with a sharply polemical nuance. Furthermore, this interpretation has shown that it was not Paul's intention in 1 Cor. 7 to urge the Christians in Corinth to "stay as you are," as if there were some Christian value in maintaining the status quo as such.[529] At no point did Paul suggest that a change in social position was a challenge to the Christian's call from God.[530] Indeed, Paul said it was better for a person who had not been given the gift of celibacy to marry--a social change. Versus the ascetic theology of the Corinthians, he maintained the freedom of the widow to remarry in the Lord--a social change. Moreover, he said that the believer who was married to a non-believer who no longer wanted the marriage was free to separate from such a marriage (0715)--a social change. Indeed, it is precisely in light of God's call to peace that the believer is not enslaved in such a marriage.[531]

On this basis it becomes clear that neither God's calling nor Paul's opinion was opposed in principle to changes in life's circumstances such as marriage or separation from marriage.[532] Even Paul's treatment of

---

[529]W. Bieder (*Die Berufung im N.T.*, p. 58) is correct, however, in noting that Paul's "theology of calling" does have a "conservative" tendency in that it does not alienate a man from his situation in the world but rather challenges him to be a Christian right where he is. It claims that the Christian's earthly situation is no disadvantage to him in terms of fellowship with God. On the other hand, perhaps the "revolutionary" tendency in Paul's "theology of calling" is his insistence that all who have fellowship with God in Christ should have fellowship with each other (1 Cor. 1127-33), that all were baptized into *one* body--the body of Christ (1213-27).

[530]Paul's words in 0726 ("In view of the present distress, I think it is good for a person to be what he already is.") should not be taken out of their specific context, namely as part of Paul's multifaceted argument in chap. 7 in favor of celibacy.

[531]Although D. Wiederkehr (*Die Theologie der Berufung in den Paulusbriefen*) did not explain why the Corinthians wanted to change their worldly statuses or which statuses they wanted to change, he did correctly conclude (p. 130) that the worldly situation, whatever it happened to be and however it might be changed by various circumstances, is the space and place where the calling was to be obeyed.

[532]Despite his translation of κλῆσις with *Stand*, G. Bornkamm (*Paulus*, p. 214) expresses this conclusion quite vividly: "Leitmotiv und Maßstab der paulinischen Weisung ist allein das Verhältnis der Glaubenden zu dem kommenden Herrn. Wie die Glaubenden konkret ihr Christsein verwirklichen und bewähren sollen, dafür nimmt Paulus dem einzelnen die Entscheidung nicht ab." See also above, pp. 22-23.

circumcision, in his example given in 0718-19, was not based on a prohibition
of this act. Rather, his point was that both this act and its undoing were
worthless in God's eyes. In this context it would be rather strange to suggest that Paul was opposed to that change in social status brought about by
manumission, i.e., the change from slavery to freedman-status. Since there is
no more evidence for "strivings" on the part of "restless slaves" in Corinth
than there is for "trouble" by "Judaizers" there, no special motive can be
found that might have influenced Paul to resist *this* social change.

Of course, Paul did not want any Christian who was in slavery to
think that his manumission would bring him any closer to God or that his
slave-status was a disadvantage before God.[533] Paul made this quite clear in
0721ab: "Were you a slave when you were called? Don't worry about it." Yet,
there is no basis in Paul's argumentation in chap. 7 or in his use of the
example of circumcision/uncircumcision in 0718-19 for concluding that he was
advising Christian slaves to "stay in slavery" in 0721cd. Moreover, in light
of the fact that manumission was an act which *happened* to a person in slavery
(i.e., it was not within his power to refuse it),[534] "becoming free" in 0721c
is not analogous to the decisions to become circumcized or to undo circumcision which are advised against in 0718-19.[535] Rather, 0721d should be viewed
as analogous to 0715, i.e., to the case in which the non-believing spouse of
a Christian wanted to dissolve the marriage. Neither manumission nor the
dissolution of a mixed marriage were events over which the Christian who was
involved had much control. In both cases Paul acknowledged that Christians
were in fact involved in such changes in social status, and then he continued
his argument.

Thus, the foregoing analysis of Paul's theological argumentation in
chap. 7 and related passages has led to conclusions which are in full agreement with the results of the analysis in chapter II of the social and legal
circumstances of persons in slavery in first-century Greece, namely that
there is no reason in this context for Paul to have advised Christians in
slavery to "stay in slavery." And since Paul's argument in chap. 7 is not a

---

[533]Neither did Paul want a Christian's status as a slave to be a disadvantage to him in the congregation. See the comments on the "latecomers" to the
Lord's supper, above, p. 62 n. 201.

[534]See above, pp. 110-111.

[535]Thus, the crucial difference between Paul's first and second example in
0717-24 is the amount of control which the respective actors had over the
actions in question. Whereas it can naturally be assumed that the Jew or
Gentile in 0718 was free to decide whether or not he would undergo the operation which would change his religious status, the person in slavery did not
possess the freedom to choose his legal status.

theological sanctification of the status quo, there was no special need for
Paul to make an "exception" in the case of the manumitted slave by advising
him to "take freedom." Thus, both of the traditional interpretations of
1 Cor. 0721 have been shown to be inappropriate both to the actual legal
situation in the first century and to Paul's theology of calling. What, then,
is the point of Paul's admonition in 0721d?

C. *The Meaning of 0721d: "Live according to God's call."*

In 0717, 0720 and 0724, Paul expressed the same, basic admonition:
"Live according to your calling from God in Christ." By means of his first
example in this pericope (0717-24), Paul argued that religious statuses mean
nothing in Christ. He concluded: "But keeping the commands of God [is what
really counts]" (0719c).[536] This conclusion is a transposition into a special
key of the basic admonition: "Live according to God's call."[537] In 0721,
Paul argued toward the same conclusion by means of a second example in which
he declared that the legal-social status of a Christian is also irrelevant
with respect to God's call in Christ. In view of the above analysis of Paul's
argumentation in chap. 7, does it not also seem likely that a similar admonition should be found at the end of this second example?

What is found, of course, is an incomplete phrase which ends with
the word χρῆσαι--the aorist imperative, second person singular form of the
verb χράομαι. Thus the question becomes: Is there any evidence which suggests that Paul could have used the verb χράομαι to express in yet another
way the admonition which has been shown to be his basic point in this pericope?

Walter Bauer noted that Josephus and some other writers used the
term χράομαι in connection with the words τοῖς νόμοις in order to express the
meaning: "to live in accordance with the laws."[538] A thorough examination
of the various ways in which Josephus used χράομαι indicates that this term
can mean not only "to live in accordance with the laws" but also "to keep the

---

[536]Cf. Gal. 0615: "For neither circumcision counts for anything, nor uncircumcision, but a new creation." See Gottlob Schrenk, *TDNT* II, 551.

[537]See above, pp. 139-140.

[538]*A Greek-English Lexicon*, p. 892 (5th ed., col. 1748). Bauer refers to
this usage by Herodotus, the tragic writers, Josephus (*Contra Apionem* 2,125
and *Antiquitates Judaicae* 16,27), Hermas (*Similitudes* 1,3 and 1,6). He also
cites 1 Tim. 0108: οἴδαμεν δὲ ὅτι καλὸς ὁ νόμος, ἐάν τις αὐτῷ νομίμως χρῆται.

156

laws of God," "to live according to certain customs," and "to follow a mode of life."[539] The word χράομαι appears in the writings of Josephus approximately 530 times. In most cases it bears the meaning "to use" (e.g., "to use advisors," "to use power," "to use words," "to use swords") or "to treat" (e.g., "to treat as a friend," "to treat with brutality"). At least twenty-seven times, however, it bears the meaning "to live according to" (e.g., "to live according to the laws of the Jewish nation" = "...καὶ συναυξῆσαι χρώμενα τοῖς πατρύοις τῶν Ἰουδαίων νόμοις." [Ant. XIV, 116], "to live in peace according to their own laws" = "...τοῖς ἰδίοις νόμοις χρωμένους ζῆν μετ᾽ εἰρήνης κτλ." [Ant. XI, 281]) or "to keep" in the sense of "keeping the laws which God has approved" ("Χρώμενοι τε νόμοις οὓς ἀγαθοὺς ὁ θεὸς παραδίδωσι διατελοῦητε." [Ant. IV, 295] and "'ἀλλὰ σὺ μέν,' εἶπεν, 'ὦ Μωυσῆ, χρῶ νόμοις οἷς αὐτὸς ἐσπούδακας κτλ.'" [Ant. IV, 145]; see also Ant. XIII, 257). Ten times this term is used with ἔθεσι to mean "to follow [Jewish] customs" (e.g., "...οἱ Ἰουδαῖοι τοῖς αὐτῶν ἔθεσι χρῆσθαι κτλ." [Ant. XII, 126]). Three times it is used with διαίτῃ to mean "to follow a way of life" (e.g., "γένος δὲ τοῦτ᾽ ἔστιν διαίτῃ χρώμενον τῇ παρ᾽ Ἕλλησιν ὑπὸ Πυθαγόρου καταδεδειγμένῃ." [Ant. XV, 371]). In these texts the verb χράομαι is clearly used in a way which offers a new possibility for the interpretation of χρῆσαι in 1 Cor. 0721d.[540]

Indeed, on the basis of this well-documented connotation of the verb χράομαι in the first century A.D.[541] two suggestions for the completion of 0721d may be made:

1) μᾶλλον χρῆσαι ταῖς ἐντολαῖς θεοῦ ("By all means, keep the commands of God"). This reading is based directly on the conclusion of the first example in this pericope, 0719c: ἀλλὰ τήρησις ἐντολῶν θεοῦ ("But keeping the commands of God [is what really counts]").

[539] My comprehensive investigation of the use of χράομαι in the writings of Josephus was made possible by Prof. Dr. K.H. Rengstorf, director of the Institutum Judaicum Delitzschianum in Münster and editor of the "Josephus-Konkordanz" (still in preparation). I am especially grateful to Herrn stud. theol. Krieg of the Institutum Judaicum, who accurately prepared for me an index of all the appearances of χράομαι and its compounds which are listed in the manuscript of this concordance.

[540] In his entry on χράομαι, Bauer (see above, n. 538) listed 1 Cor. 0721 immediately after his two references to Josephus. It is probably the case that his judgment that κλῆσις in 0720 = Stand would have prevented him from considering the connotation found in Josephus in connection with 0721d. In any case, it is clear that the interpretations of 0720 and 0721cd have had great influence on each other.

[541] Note that this meaning of χράομαι is found not only in Josephus but also in Hermas and 1 Tim. 0108 (see above, n. 538).

2) μᾶλλον χρῆσαι τῇ κλήσει ("By all means, live according to your calling [in Christ]"). This reading is based on the thrice-repeated admonition which is the theme of 0717-24.[542]

In favor of the first suggestion is the fact that 0719c and 0721d are parallel in that they conclude the two illustrations used by Paul in this section. Both of these phrases are incomplete and require the reader to supply the missing words from the context. While there has been no question about the words needed to complete 0719c because the term ἀλλά clearly introduces a sharp contrast to the predicates of 0719a and 0719b ("...is nothing"),[543] the completion of 0721d has been more difficult because the meaning of μᾶλλον is not clear[544] and because this use of χράομαι without an expressed object has no parallel in Paul's writings.[545] Perhaps Paul relied on the clarity of his vivid expression in 0719c to provide his readers with the conceptual frame which they needed in order to understand his abrupt admonition in 0721d.

On the other hand, the fact that 0719 and 0721 are *not* parallel in structure and content favors the second suggestion (μᾶλλον χρῆσαι τῇ κλήσει). that is, on the basis of the antithetical parallelism (circumcision/uncircumcision) in 0719, the reader would expect the status of the freeman to be taken up in 0721c. In order for 0721 to be parallel to 0719, 0721c would need to read: ἐλεύθερος ἐκλήθης; μή σοι μελέτω.[546] But as it is, Paul appears

---

[542]See above, pp. 134-135.

[543]1 Cor. 0719c is a good example of the grammatical phenomenon known as ellipsis, i.e., of the case in which an idea is not fully expressed grammatically but in which the reader is expected to supply the omission because it is self-evident. Greek writers used this convention in order to make their expression brief and lively. Grammarians have also distinguished a second type of omission known as brachylogy, in which the incompleteness of the phrase appears to be the result of the arbitrariness of the writer rather than of possibilities in the use of the language about which rules can be developed. In this case, the writer believes that his abruptness in expression is clarified by the immediate context. 1 Cor. 0721d can be described as a brachylogy. Note this remark by R. Kühner and B. Gerth (*Ausführliche Grammatik der griechischen Sprache*, 4th ed. [Hannover, 1955], II, 560): "Die Gewandtheit und Schnelligkeit im Denken, die den Griechen in so hohem Grad eigen war, bewirkte, daß die Brachylogie bei ihnen wohl häufiger war als bei irgend einem anderen Volke." See also F. Blass and A. Debrunner, *A Greek Grammar of the New Testament and Other Early Christian Literature*, tr. and rev. Robert W. Funk (Chicago, 1961), p. 253.

[544]That is, does μᾶλλον express a contrast to the action described in 0721c or to the admonition in 0721b—or is it an elative comparative which should be translated "by all means"?

[545]Two elliptical uses of χράομαι are known to me from Epictetus. II,21,20: τοῖς οὐχ ὡς δεῖ χρωμένοις (τοῖς θεωρήμασιν) and II,23,16: Τί ἐστι τὸ χρώμενον;

[546]In this context such a phrase would be translated: "Were you a freeman when you were called? Don't think your social status is important."

suddenly to leave his illustration in 0721ab to address directly in 0721cd those Christians in Corinth who were in slavery.[547] Remembering that some of these Christians might be manumitted at any time, Paul spoke a special word to them in 0721cd in order to urge them "to live according to" their calling in Christ in their new social status as freedmen.[548] In this case, as in 0715c, after referring to a possible change in the social status of the Corinthian Christians, Paul emphasized the call of God as the enduring and determining factor in the Christian's life. The brief and forceful repetition of Paul's basic admonition in 0720, "Let each one continue in the calling by which he was called," would have provided Paul's readers with the conceptual frame they needed in order to grasp his abrupt exhortation in 0721d.

Although this second suggestion for completing 0721d seems to me to be the preferable one, it is difficult to exclude one reading in complete favor of the other. Since, indeed, 0719c is a special way of expressing the basic point made in 0720, the actual content of 0721d would be the same in either case.

---

[547]The fact that the "expected" parallelism of slave/freeman *is* found in 0722 ("For a slave who has been called is the Lord's freedman. Likewise, a freeman who has been called is Christ's slave.") emphasizes all the more Paul's departure from this parallelism in 0721c. Paul's use of the strongly adversative particle ἀλλά at the beginning of 0721c is further support for the suggestion that Paul interrupted his train of thought to speak directly to the slaves in the Corinthian congregation. See above, p. 113 n. 429. See also ·Kühner-Gerth, *Ausführliche Grammatik* II, 282; Blass-Debrunner-Funk, *A Greek Grammar of the N.T.*, p. 232, §448; and J.D. Denniston, *The Greek Particles* (Oxford, 1959), pp. 9-11.

[548]At first glance, the aorist tense of χρῆσαι in 0721d may seem to pose an objection to this interpretation. Following the present tense of περιπατείτω in 1717 and μενέτω in 7020, the present imperative form χρῶ would seem to be required in 0721d. (Note the present imperative form of χράομαι used by Josephus in *Ant*. IV, 145 [quoted above]; a present imperative is used in Hermas, *Sim*. 1,4: Ἡ τοῖς νόμοις μου χρῶ ἤ ἐκχώρει ἐκ τῆς χώρας μου. = "Either live according to my law or get out of my country.") In the context of the "use slavery"/"take freedom" debate, those favoring "take freedom" have usually stressed this aorist tense in favor of the translation: "seize" or "grasp" [the possibility of freedom]. Those who have favored "use your slavery" have minimized or ignored the force of this aorist. The rather wide variety of nuances which could be expressed by the aorist imperative is discussed in detail by Blass-Debrunner-Funk, *A Greek Grammar of the N.T.*, pp. 173-174, §337. Here the distinction between present and aorist imperatives is made as follows: "In general precepts (also to an individual) concerning attitudes and conduct there is a preference for the present, in commands related to conduct in specific cases (much less frequent in the NT) for the aorist." In 0721d, then, we are apparently dealing with such a command related to conduct in the specific case in which a Christian slave was manumitted. On this basis, 0721 could be paraphrased: "But if, indeed, you are able to be manumitted, act (in your new status of freedman) according to your call in Christ." Note also that this use of the aorist imperative supports my proposal that 0721cd is an "interruption" in Paul's argument directed specifically to those slaves in Corinth whose manumission might soon occur.

In short, my detailed account of the actual options open to the members of the Corinthian congregation who were in slavery, my analysis of Paul's critical response in chap. 7 and related passages to the theology and ethics of the Corinthian *pneumatikoí*, and this discussion of the meaning of χράομαι in 0721d lead me to conclude that in 1 Cor. 0721 Paul said: "Were you a slave when you were called? Don't worry about it. But if, indeed, your owner should manumit you, by all means (now as a freedman) live according to God's call."[549]

---

[549]See below, chap. V, for additional exegetical comments which clarify this translation. Note that Prof. Glen Bowersock of Harvard's Classics Dept. has suggested to me an alternative completion of 0721d which would express an admonition which would have made good sense to a person who was manumitted and which would be more satisfactory with respect to Bowersock's sense of Greek style, namely: μᾶλλον χρῆσαι τῷ ἐλευθέρῳ γενέσθαι. This phrase would be translated: "By all means, use your becoming free" (as the new situation in which you walk according to God's call). This use of such an articular infinitive *is* more elegant than either of the suggestions made above. (The articular infinitive in the dative appears only once in the N.T., used by Paul in 2 Cor. 0213 to denote cause. See Blass-Debrunner-Funk, *A Greek Grammar of the N.T.*, p. 207 §401.) The chief disadvantage of this suggestion is the fact that an additional phrase (such as the one supplied above: "as the new situation in which you walk according to God's call") is still needed in order to prevent a continuing misunderstanding of the force and intent of the aorist imperative.

CHAPTER IV

THE STRUCTURE OF 1 CORINTHIANS 7

The above discussion has shown that 1 Cor. 0717-24 played a significant role in Paul's response to the theology and ethics of the Corinthians. But the question may be asked: Does this pericope really belong in 1 Cor. 7?[550] It introduces two topics, namely circumcision and slavery, which seem to be out of place in the middle of Paul's discussion of male and female relationships in chap. 7.[551] Furthermore, when reading chap. 7, it is quite easy to go directly from 0716 to 0725.[552]

In this chapter, I seek to demonstrate the appropriateness of 0717-24 in 1 Cor. 7 on the basis of the form of the entire passage, the connection between male/female, Jew/Greek and slave/free in Paul's thinking, and the consistency in Paul's style of argumentation throughout chap. 7.

A. *The "A-B-A" Form of 1 Cor. 7.*

J.J. Collins has recently stressed again the importance of the "A-B-A" or "A-B-B-A" (chiastic) pattern in Paul's letters.[553] He points to a number of examples in 1 and 2 Cor. and Romans which clearly demonstrate that Paul frequently interrupted his main line of thought in order to

---

[550] For example, Karl Clemen (*Die Einheitlichkeit der paulinischen Briefe* [1894], p. 35) wanted to place 0717-24 in a period of Paul's literary activity prior to his writing of 1 Cor. He based his judgment chiefly on the contradiction he found between the emphasis placed on "remaining" in this pericope and the specific cases of change which are discussed in chap. 7. J. Weiß (*Der Erste Korintherbrief*, p. 191) noted that Straatman and Baljon also wanted to remove 0717-22 from chap. 7. Weiß was almost persuaded by Clemen's arguments.

[551] Note that Origen created unity and coherence in 1 Cor. 7 by allegorically interpreting circumcision and manumission as ways of referring to the act of separating oneself from one's wife. See Claude Jenkins, "Origen on I Corinthians," *JTS* IX (1907-08), 506-507.

[552] A further difficulty is the apparent abruptness of the phrase εἰ μή which introduces 0717.

[553] "Chiasmus, the 'ABA' Pattern and the Text of Paul," *Studiorum Paulinorum Congressus Internationalis Catholicus* (Rome, 1963), II, 575-583. See p. 577 for a brief history of scholarship. See also N.W. Lund, *Chiasmus in the New Testament* (U. of N. Carolina Press, 1942) for the history of earlier scholarship. Lund (p. 35) states that J.A. Bengel (*Gnomon novi testamenti*, Tübingen, 1742) was the first to grasp the significance of chiastic forms in the writings of the N.T. and to apply this analysis to exegesis.

162

introduce an illustration or a clarification of a general principle or a
defense of his apostleship.[554]

Perhaps the clearest example in 1 Cor. is found in chapters 12-14.
Chapter 13 functions as "B" (in terms of a clarification of a general princi-
ple--ἀγάπη) between chapters 12 and 14 (which both deal with "spiritual gifts").
It is this pattern which clarifies the form of 1 Cor. 7, where 0717-24 functions as "B" (in terms of a clarification of a general principle--κλῆσις)
between 0701-16 and 0725-40.[555] In both cases, Paul introduced a theological
generalization in order to relativize the importance of certain spiritual
gifts.[556]

Thus, the fact that Paul changed the subject in 0717-24 is fully in
accord with his manner of arguing in other parts of 1 Cor. as well as in his
other letters.[557] But why did Paul change the subject to circumcision and
uncircumcision and to slaves and freemen? What connection do these topics
have to Paul's argument in 1 Cor. 7 or to the situation in the Corinthian
congregation?

B. The Thought-Pattern of 1 Cor. 7 and Gal. 0328.

As has been shown above, there is no evidence that Paul's choice of
examples in 0717-24 was influenced by actual problems in the Corinthian congregation. No particular activity of the Jews or the slaves in the congregation had moved Paul to write 0717-24. None of the problems or tensions in the
congregation had been caused by Christian slaves as slaves. Nor is there any
evidence that the pneumatic enthusiasm in the congregation had affected the

---

[554]Rom. 9 (A) 10 (B) 11 (A); Rom. 1216-21 (A) 1301-07 (B) 1308-13 (A); Rom.
1401-12 (A) 1413-23 (B) 1501-13 (A); 1 Cor. 0801-13 (A) 0901-1013 (B) 1014-
1101 (A). For a chiastic analysis of smaller units, see J. Jeremias, "Chiasmus
in den Paulusbriefen," ZNW 49 (1958), 145-156 (now in Abba, Studien zur neutestamentlichen Theologie und Zeitgeschichte [Göttingen, 1966], pp. 276-290).

[555]Lund (Chiasmus in the N.T., pp. 151-163) tried (unconvincingly) to find
an "A-A1-A2-B-B-A2-A1-A" pattern in 1 Cor. 7. He was right, however, in explaining the unity of chap. 7 by referring to 0717-24 as "B-B" (counting
"circumcision" and "slavery" as separate units) in a chiastic-type structure.

[556]See above, pp. 149-151. In comparison with εἰ μή in 0717, notice that
the term ἔτι in 1231 (which introduces ch. 13) also appears to be abrupt
(P[46] and D* read ει τι). Following Paul's use of the phrase ἐν τοῖς τοιούτοις
("in cases such as these") in 0715, perhaps the best translation of εἰ μή at
the beginning of 0717 is: "In any case..." (= εἰ δὲ μή). See Blass-Debrunner-
Funk, A Greek Grammar of the N.T., p. 191, §376 and p. 233, §448. See also
H. Conzelmann, 1. Korintherbrief, p. 150, who rightly rejects Günther Harder's
novel proposal that εἰ μή introduces a conditional sentence which limits the
second ὡς clause in 0717. (ThLZ 79 [1954], 367-369).

[557]See also J.C. Hurd, The Origin of 1 Cor., p. 178, who follows J. Weiß
in identifying an "A-B-A" pattern in 1 Cor. 0725-40; 0729-35 = "B." See the
analysis of 1 Cor. 7 below, pp. 166-171.

behavior or attitudes of the Christian slaves with respect to their slave-status. Likewise, Paul gives us no evidence of specific Jew-Gentile tensions in the congregation.[558] There were, to be sure, many slaves and many Jews in the Christian congregation at Corinth, but no direct connection between their behavior and Paul's admonitions in 0717-24 can be found.

Since 1 Cor. 0701 indicates that Paul began answering questions from the Corinthian congregation at that point in his letter, it might be supposed that those Christians had asked him something about how Christian slaves were to regard their social status or Christian Gentiles their uncircumcision.[559] But the formula which Paul used to refer to the Corinthians' questions is conspicuously absent from 0717-24.[560] Thus, there is no evidence that Paul's mention of slavery in 0721-23 was prompted by a question from Corinth.[561]

In the light of these conclusions that neither the Corinthians' actions nor their questions encouraged Paul to mention the contrasting pairs, i.e., circumcision/uncircumcision and slave/freeman, in 0717-24, I propose a reason for Paul's choice of these examples which tightly links 0717-24 to the rest of the chapter: These examples came to Paul's mind because they were two parts in a three-part thought-pattern which he also expressed in Gal.

---

[558]Note, e.g., that Paul did not criticize the disunity at the Lord's table (ch. 11) in these terms (see above, p. 62 n. 201 and p. 138 n. 485).

[559]For example, W.L. Westermann (*Slave Systems*, p. 157) claimed that Paul had been asked directly by the Corinthians "whether manumission must be granted to, or sought for, slaves who had embraced the faith."

[560]This formula, περὶ δέ, occurs six times in the last ten chapters of 1 Cor., as follows:

1) "Concerning the matters about which you wrote" - 0701
2) "Concerning the virgins" - 0725
3) "Concerning food offered to idols" - 0801
4) "Concerning spiritual gifts" - 1201
5) "Concerning the contribution for the saints" - 1601
6) "Concerning our brother Apollos" - 1612

C.E. Faw ("On the Writing of First Thessalonians," *JBL* 71 [1952], 221) has checked the entire N.T. evidence and concludes that the Pauline usage of this phrase "is confined to the answering of specific questions or problems brought up in letters from the churches to which he is writing."

[561]Doughty (*Heiligkeit und Freiheit*, p. 67) also concludes that in 0717-24 Paul was not taking up new themes which had been suggested to him by the Corinthians. Moreover, he is correct (p. 80) in his judgment that 0717-24 was not meant by Paul to be a free-floating excursus on circumcision and slavery.

0328: "There is neither Jew nor Greek, there is neither slave nor free, there is no male and female; for you are all one in Christ Jesus."[562]

In 1 Cor. 7, Paul answered questions about marriage, virginity and celibacy on the basis of *his* understanding of the meaning of "no male and female in Christ."[563] It was, therefore, quite natural for him to illustrate his argument with the other two examples which for him expressed the irrelevance of any particular earthly position in which a Christian might find himself, an irrelevancy which had been created by God's call in Christ.[564]

Indeed, Paul may have selected these particular contrasting pairs to illustrate his "theology of calling" and theology of baptism in order to oppose the Jewish prayers and Greek proverbs in which such differences in earthly position were held to be quite important. In his *TDNT* article on γυνή, Albrecht Oepke observes:

> Characteristic of the traditional position and estimation of woman is a saying current in different forms among the Persians, Greeks and Jews in which man gives thanks that he is not an unbeliever or uncivilised, that he is not a woman and that he is not a slave.[565]

---

[562]To my knowledge no one has offered a convincing reason, beyond that of Paul's putative interest in using comprehensive examples, for Paul's referring to circumcision and slavery in the midst of his discussion of male and female relationships. David Cartlidge ("Competing Theologies of Asceticism in the Early Church," p. 57 n. 1) has seen that all the elements of Gal. 0328 can be found in 1 Cor. (Jew/Greek--1213, slave/free--0721-23, and male/female--0501-0740) without noticing that all three of these dichotomies appear within ch. 7 itself.

[563]See above, chap. 3, especially pp. 143-148.

[564]See above, pp. 138-140. See also pp. 129-130 for my argument that Gal. 0328, when viewed in the context of Paul's specific concern about Jew/Greek problems in Galatia, clearly contains a threefold thought-pattern which was a part of Paul's vocabulary prior to his composition of Galatians.

[565]*TDNT*, I, 777. Among the Jews, this prayer is traced back to Rabbi Judah ben El'ai (pupil of Akiba, c. A.D. 150) in *Tosefta Berakoth* 7,18 (see also *Jer. Ber.* 13b). According to R. Judah, a man is bound to say the following three blessings daily: "Blessed art thou...who hast not made me a heathen (גוי), ...who hast not made me a woman (אשה), and...who hast not made me a brutish man (בור)." In the *Babylonian Talmud, Menakoth* 43b, R. Aḥa bar Jacob (c. A.D. 330) is said to have changed the third blessing to "...who hast not made me a slave (עבד)." See P. Billerbeck, *Kommentar zum N.T.*, III, 611.

Among the Greeks, Thales is said to have given thanks to Fortune that he was not born a brute, a woman or a barbarian (Diogenes Laertius I, 33). See also Plutarch, *Life of C. Marius*, 46.

Note also that this prayer appears in the morning service of the modern Jewish prayer-book (Singer, 6th ed.). Both men and women say: "Blessed art thou, O Lord, our God, King of the universe, who hast not made me a heathen....who hast not made me a bondman." The men say: "Blessed art thou...who hast not made me a woman." Then the women say: "Blessed art thou ...who hast made me according to thy will."

H. Schlier reports that Oepke thinks that Paul was influenced to expand his
often used dichotomy, Jew/Greek, in conscious opposition to such a prayer of
thanksgiving.[566] Although the first prayer in this form which is known to us
is attributed to a rabbi from the middle of the second century A.D., the conservative nature of liturgical tradition suggests that it may well have been
in use a century earlier.[567]

In any case, it is clear from Gal. 0328 (see also 1 Cor. 1213 and
Col. 0311) that these three contrasting pairs formed a "thought-pattern" which
Paul used in a powerful way to describe a very significant result of Christian
baptism. It also seems clear that for Paul there was a close connection between God's call and baptism and that this connection is expressed in his
choice of examples to illustrate his "theology of calling" in 1 Cor. 0717-24.[568]
So, "circumcision" and "slavery" are not "out of place" in 1 Cor. 7. Indeed,
they are important indications of the context in which Paul considered the
questions from the Corinthians about male and female relationships, namely
the irrelevance in Christ of any particular earthly status *and* the decisive
importance of walking according to God's call *in the world*.

---

[566] *Der Brief an die Galater*, Meyers Kommentar VII, (Göttingen, 1965), p.
174. Apparently Schlier has this opinion from Oepke privately, for it is not
expressed in the *TDNT* nor is any other reference given. Schlier notes that
Zahn and Bousset held the same opinion about the background of Gal. 0328; but
he offers no opinion of his own. Madeleine Boucher ("Some Unexplored Parallels
to 1 Cor. 11,11-12 and Gal. 3,28: the NT on the Role of Women," *CBQ* 31 [1969],
50-58) also concludes that Gal. 0328 was formulated in conscious reply to such
a prayer.

[567] David Kaufmann ("Das Alter der drei Benedictionen von Israel, vom Freien
und vom Mann," *Monatsschrift für Geschichte und Wissenschaft des Judentums* 37
[1893], 14-18) took Gal. 0328 to be important evidence for the age of this
threefold prayer. He (p. 15) judged 0328 to be "ein offenbarer Hinweis auf
die allbekannte Stelle im jüdischen Gebete, die...Nationalität, Stand und
Geschlecht so scharf betont." He suggested that the version of the prayer
given by R. Aḥa bar Jacob (including the "slave" phrase; see above n. 565)
was earlier than that attributed to R. Judah. Kaufmann (p. 15) stressed that
in any case R. Judah was not the creator but the transmitter of this prayer.
See Joseph Heinemann, *Prayer in the Period of the Tanna'im and the Amora'im:
Its Nature and Its Pattern* (Jerusalem, 1964), pp. ii-iii, for comments on the
pre-third century history of the *barakha* liturgical formulas. (Note that
Saul Lieberman's remarks on *Berakoth* 7,18 in *The Tosefta according to Codex
Vienna* [New York, 1955] shed no light on this problem.)

[568] See R. Bultmann, *Theology of the New Testament* I, pp. 311-313. Note that
in Hermas, κλῆσις can be a direct designation of baptism: Mand. 4,3-6, Sim.
8,11,1, and 9,14,5. See Bultmann, II, 160-161.

C. *The Style of Paul's Argumentation in 1 Cor. 7.*

A further indication that 0717-24 "belongs" in 1 Cor. 7 is the consistency in Paul's style of argumentation throughout the chapter. The following analysis indicates that Paul's manner of stating general principles, giving reasons and explications, making exceptions and using parallel expressions
continues into and through 0717-24 without varying significantly. Notice the
frequency with which Paul makes exceptions to his "general principles."

SUMMARY OF THE ANALYSIS OF CHAPTER 7

(Reference to written questions received from the Corinthians. 0701a. Topic
of the Questions: Male and Female Relationships.)

1. The Cases of Unmarried and Married Christians Who are Practicing
   Celibacy. 0701a-07

2. The Case of the Christian Who Has Not Been Married (ἄγαμος) and the
   Widow. 0708-09

3. The Case of the Christian Married to a Believer. 0710-11

4. The Case of the Christian Married to a Non-Believer Who Wants the
   Marriage to Continue. 0712-14

5. The Case of the Christian Married to a Non-Believer Who Wants to End
   the Marriage. 0715-16

6. A Theological Generalization with Examples from Jew/Gentile and Slave/
   Free Circumstances. 0717-24

7. The Case of the Virgins (παρθένοι). 0725-28
   (Reference to the Corinthians' question and to Paul's authority to
   give an answer. 0725)

8. A Second Theological Generalization with Examples from a Variety of
   Circumstances. 0729-31

9. A Second Consideration of the Case of the Unmarried (ἄγαμοι). 0732-35

10. The Case of the Christian Trying to Remain Celibate in "Spiritual
    Marriage." 0736-38

11. A Second Consideration of the Case of the Christian Widow. 0739-40

Guide to the Analysis: Statements in parentheses describe the form of the
text or make brief exegetical comments. Statements in quotation marks
represent the text itself. The terms used to analyze Paul's argument are
italicized. Each term refers to the first term above it which is closer
to the left margin. E.g., in SECTION 1, the *1st Explication* refers to the
General Exception (not to the *Reason*), and in SECTION 2, the *Reason* refers
to the *Exception* (not to the *General Principle*).

ANALYSIS OF CHAPTER 7

(Reference to written questions received from the Corinthians. 0701a)

SECTION 1. The Cases of Unmarried and Married Christians Who are Practicing Celibacy. 0701b-07

A General Principle: (held both by the "weak" Corinthians and by Paul): "Yes, it *is* good for a man to have nothing to do with women." 0701b

    A General Exception: "But let each man have his own wife and each woman her own husband." (male/female parallelism) 0702bc

        Reason: "because there is so much immorality,"(we are still living in "the time of temptation") 0702a

            1st Explication: "Husband and wife must give each other conjugal rights." (male/female parallelism) 0703

                Reason: "A Christian rules his/her spouse's body, but not his/her own." (male/female parallelism) 0704

            2nd Explication: "Do not deny each other sexual contact." 0705a

                Exception: "except by mutual agreement for devotion to prayer." 0705b

            3rd Explication: "Even having separated by mutual agreement, afterwards come together again." 0705c

                Reason: "Otherwise, Satan may tempt you through lack of self-control." 0705d

    Comment on General Exception: "I recommend a fully physical marriage, not as a command but as a concession." 0706

Supporting Expression of Preference: "I wish that every Christian could follow the principle of celibacy as I do." 0707a

    Reason for Exception: "I recommend this exception, i.e., full marriage, because the ability to remain celibate is a gift from God which is not given to every Christian." 0707bc

SECTION 2. The Case of the Christian Who Has Not Been Married (ἄγαμος) and the Widow. 0708-09

A General Principle: "It is a good thing if they stay as I am myself, i.e., unmarried." 0708

    Exception: "But if they cannot live a celibate life, they should marry." 0709a

        Reason: "For it is better to marry than to be burning with passion." (Such desire in itself is a sign that the necessary "gift" has not been given.) 0709b

SECTION 3. The Case of the Christian Married to a Believer. 0710-11

A General Principle: "A wife must not separate herself from her husband."
0710b

   Reason: "This is a command of the Lord." 0710a

   Exception: "But if indeed the wife does leave her husband, she has two
   options: 1) Remain unmarried 2) be reconciled to her husband."
   0711ab

Restatement of this Principle: "The husband must not divorce his wife." 0711c

SECTION 4. The Case of the Christian Married to a Non-Believer Who Wants the
         Marriage to Continue. 0712-14

A General Principle: A Christian whose non-believing spouse wants the relationship to continue should not break up the marriage." (male/female
parallelism) 0712-13

   Reason: "For the non-believing spouse is 'made holy' through the believing partner." (male/female parallelism) 0714ab

      Supporting Comment: "Otherwise your children would be 'unclean', but
      as it is they are 'holy'." 0714cd

(Exception to the Principle of Staying in the Marriage: see the next Case)

SECTION 5. The Case of the Christian Married to a Non-Believer Who Wants to
         End the Marriage. 0715-16

Exception to the Principle of Remaining in the Marriage: "If, on the other
hand, the unbelieving partner wants a separation, let him/her have it."
0715a

   Explication: "In such cases the Christian is not 'enslaved'." 0715b

   Reason: "God has called you into peace." 0715c

   Supporting Comment: "The Christian marriage partner has no assurance
   that he will be able to save his/her spouse." (male/female parallelism) 0716

SECTION 6. A Theological Generalization with Examples. 0717-24

A General Principle: "In any case, let each one live his life in accord with
the fact that the Lord has distributed [faith] to him and that God has
called him." 0717abc

   Supporting Comment: "That is what I teach in all our congregations."
   0717d

   Explication: (Jew/Greek parallelism)
     1) "Was a man already circumcized when he was called? He should not
       try to change his condition with an operation." 0718ab
     2) "Was a man uncircumcized when he was called? He should not
       become circumcized." 0718cd

Reasons: (antithetically stated)
1) "Neither circumcision nor uncircumcision makes any difference."
   0719a
2) "But, on the other hand, keeping the commands of God is what
   matters." 0719b

Abbreviated Restatement of the Principle: "Each person should continue in
that calling into which he was called." 0720

Explication: "Were you a slave when you were called? Don't worry about
it." 0721ab

Exception and *Explication:* "But if, indeed, you become manumitted,
by all means (as a freedman) live according to [God's calling.]"
0721cd

Reasons: (slave/free parallelism)
1) "For a slave who has been called in the Lord is the Lord's freedman." 0722a
2) "Likewise, a freeman who has been called is Christ's slave."
   0722b

Explication of 2nd Reason: "You were bought with a price: do not
become slaves of men."ᐟ 0723

Restatement of the General Principle: "Each one should continue to live in
accord with his calling [in Christ]--in the sight of God." 0724

SECTION 7. The Case of the Virgins (παρθένοι). 0725-28

(Reference to the Corinthians' question and to Paul's authority to give an
answer. 0725)

A General Recommendation: "It is good, I think, for a person to be what he
already is." 0726b

Reason: "Because of the present distress." 0726a

Explication: (married/unmarried parallelism)
1) "Are you bound to a wife? Do not seek to become free." 0727ab
2) "Are you free from a wife? Do not seek to become married."
   0727cd

Exception: (male/female parallelism)
1) "But if indeed you do marry, you do not sin." 0728a
2) "And if the virgin should marry, she does not sin." 0728b

Restatement of the Reason: "Those who marry will have afflictions in the
flesh, and I would spare you that." 0728cd

SECTION 8. A Second Theological Generalization with Examples. 0729-31

(A general principle is not stated. It could have been: "A Christian is not
to be determined by his worldly circumstances but by his relation to Christ.")

Reason: "The appointed time has become short." 0729a

1st Explication: "Those having wives should live as if they had no
wives." 0729b

2nd Explication: "Those who mourn should live as if they were not mourning." 0730a

3rd Explication: "Those who rejoice should live as if they were not rejoicing." 0730b

4th Explication: "Those who buy goods should live as if they did not possess them." 0730c

5th Explication: "Those who make use of the world should live as if they were not taking it too seriously." 0731a

Restatement of the Reason: "For the form of this world is passing away." 0731b

SECTION 9.   A Second Consideration of the Case of the Unmarried (ἀγάμοι). 0731b

(Again, the general principle is not stated. It could have been: "It is better for you to stay as you are, i.e., unmarried.")

1st Reason: "I want you to be free from anxiety." 0732a

   1st Explication: (the man: unmarried/married)
   1) "The unmarried man is concerned for the affairs of the Lord--how to please the Lord." 0732b
   2) "But the married man is concerned for the affairs of the world--how to please his wife." 0733

      Supporting Comment: "His interests are divided." 0734a

   2nd Explication: (the woman: unmarried/married)
   1) "The unmarried woman (ἄγαμος) and the virgin (πάρθενος) are concerned about the things of the Lord--in order that they should be holy both in body and in spirit." 0734b
   2) "But the married woman is concerned about the things of the world--how to please her husband." 0734c

2nd Reason: "I say this for your own benefit--not to lay restraint on you." 0735a

   1st Explication: "I say this to promote good order." 0735b

   2nd Explication: "And to secure your undivided attention to the Lord." 0735c

SECTION 10.   The Case of the Christian Trying to Remain Celibate in "Spiritual Marriage." 0736-38

Exception: (made in this case *before* the statement of the general principle) "Let him do what he wants: let them marry--he is not sinning." 0736de

   1st Condition: "If anyone thinks that he is not behaving properly toward his virgin." 0736a

   2nd Condition: "If his passions are strong." 0736b

   3rd Condition: "If it 'has to be'." 0736c

The Preferred, General Principle: "A Christian does well when he keeps his virgin partner as she is." 0737d

   Condition: "Whoever is firmly established in his heart." 0737a

      1st Explication: "I.e., whoever is under no compulsion and has power over his will." 0737b

      2nd Explication: "I.e., whoever has determined in his heart to preserve his partner in her virginity." 0737c

Restatement of Exception in Relation to the Principle: "He who marries his virgin does well. But he who does not marry her does better." 0738

SECTION 11. A Second Consideration of the Case of the Christian Widow. 0739-40

The General Principle: (repeating 0710b) "A wife is bound to her husband as long as he lives." 0739a

   Exception and *Explication:* "If he should die, however, she is free to marry anyone she chooses from within the Lord's fellowship." 0739bc

      Limiting Expression of Preference: (restating 0708) "I think she is happier if she remains a widow." 0740a

         Authority for Preference: "And I also think that I have the Spirit of God." 0740b

   This method of analyzing 1 Cor. 7 reveals the importance of "exceptions" in Paul's style of argumentation in this chapter.[569] Already in 0702 he introduced a significant exception to his own clear preference for celibacy. Apart from 0707a, the rest of section 1 (0701-07) is an argument in support of the "exception." In sections 2, 3, 10 and 11, "general principles" which affirm either the stability of marriage or the value of celibacy are followed by "exceptions." Section 4 which affirms the viability of mixed marriages is followed by a section which clarifies the "exception" to that advice. Section 7 contains both a "general recommendation" and the "exception" to it. Of those sections which deal directly with male and female relationships, only section 9, which does not mention a "general principle," lacks an "exception."

   Sections 6 and 8 are theological generalizations, and there are no exceptions to the principles laid down there. But the complex use of "supporting comments," "explications," "reasons" and various parallelisms which characterizes the other sections of this chapter is also the outstanding feature of these sections. Thus, in addition to Paul's frequent use of "A-B-A"

---

[569]The clarity which this kind of analysis brings to the flow of Paul's argument in this chapter suggests that other difficult Pauline texts might become easier to understand if similarly analyzed.

structures and the special "thought-pattern" expressed also in Gal. 0328, Paul's style of argumentation demonstrates that 0717-24 is an integral part of 1 Cor. 7.[570]

The quickness to mention "exceptions" which is characteristic of Paul's style in this chapter is found also in 0721cd, which abruptly introduces the contrast to the social status mentioned in 0721ab. These words do not express an "exception" to a "general principle" nor do they really express an "exception" to the "explication" of the preceding "general principle." Rather, in 0721cd Paul took account of a possible change in social status in much the same manner as he did in section 5 (0715) and in section 11 (0739bc). Notice that in all three of these verses, a reference to a change in social status is followed by an "explication" which stresses the Christian's unchanging relationship to Christ. In 0715c, God's call is brought in as the determining factor in the case; and in 0739c the "Lord's fellowship" is also the decisive factor. These allusions to the absolute priority of the Christian's relationship to God in Christ support my interpretation of 0721d, namely that the Christian in slavery who becomes manumitted by his owner should continue to live according to God's call.

This analysis of 1 Cor. 7 serves not only to demonstrate the consistency of Paul's style of argumentation throughout 0701-40 but also to present my solutions to many of the exegetical problems in this chapter. It is not within the scope of this book to justify all these judgments with detailed exegesis. But in the following chapter I seek to clarify the exegesis of 0721-24 in light of the context for understanding this verse which is provided by the foregoing analysis of the social-legal situation of slaves in Corinth and the theological-ethical situation in the Christian congregation there.

---

[570]Of these three, the most important argument is based on the "thought-pattern." Because this thought-pattern is closely linked with the basis from which Paul responded to the theology of the Corinthians, it seemed more persuasive to introduce this evidence after my analysis of the theological-ethical situation in Corinth had been presented in chapter III above.

CHAPTER V

EXEGETICAL COMMENTS AND CONCLUSIONS

As was indicated above in chapter I, no thoroughly convincing
interpretation of 1 Cor. 0721 has ever been made on the basis of an analysis
of its grammar and syntax alone. For this reason interpretations of other
parts of 1 Cor. 7 and presuppositions about slavery in the first century A.D.
have always played decisive roles in the explication of this verse. The particular value of my approach to 1 Cor. 0721 may be found in my intensive
investigation of the actual legal and social situations of those persons who
were in slavery in first-century Corinth and in my attempt to understand
1 Cor. 7 as an important part of Paul's response to the *pneumatikoí* in the
Corinthian congregation. Each of these analyses has led to the striking conclusion that *both* of the traditional, conflicting interpretations of 1 Cor.
0721 ("use slavery"/"take freedom") are inappropriate to the actual situation
in Corinth and in the Christian congregation there.

When Paul asked, δοῦλος ἐκλήθης; the term δοῦλος referred to a very
complex and diversified legal and social status which differs in many very
significant ways from the slavery practiced in modern times. For this reason,
the first step toward a better exegesis of 1 Cor. 0721 must be a better
understanding of slavery in first-century Greece. When Paul wrote 1 Corinthians, about one-third of the population in Corinth was in slavery and
another third had been in slavery and had been manumitted. It is clear that
Paul was familiar with this social-legal institution and the Greek and Roman
laws which regulated its practice in Corinth. Indeed, some of the first
people whom he baptized into Christ at Corinth were in slavery at the time.

The second step toward a better exegesis is a more precise understanding of Paul's use of κλῆσις and καλέω in 1 Cor. 0717-24 and 0126. God
had called persons from a wide variety of social backgrounds to become saints
in Christ at Corinth (0102). In 0717-24, Paul repeatedly stressed the fact
that God's call had made irrelevant every particular social and religious
status. At the same time, he exhorted the Corinthians to live their lives in
accord with God's call in whatever status they found themselves, to keep the
commands of God in the midst of their various relationships, whatever they
were. Paul's emphasis on "walking" and "continuing" in God's calling was
part of his polemic against the belief of many of the Corinthians that Christian existence was demonstrated by individual ecstasy and spiritual achievements such as celibacy, speaking in tongues and the possession of wisdom.

173

Paul's line of reasoning throughout 1 Cor. 7 becomes much easier to understand when it is seen that he wanted to recommend celibacy as a better style of life for the Corinthians without at the same time giving any support to the theology of exaltation (and its "break-through" in male and female relationships) which was the reason for the celibacy already being attempted in the congregation. Even Paul's choice of examples in 0717-24 ("uncircumcision"/"circumcision" and "slave"/"free") was determined by the link between these dichotomies and "male"/"female" in a thought-pattern which represented *Paul's* understanding of the "break-through" in Christ (see Gal. 0328) rather than by any unrest caused by Jews or slaves in the congregation or by any questions about circumcision or slavery in the letter from the Corinthians which he began to answer in 0701. Although it is clear that Paul did not agree with the effect which the Corinthians' exalted self-understanding had on male and female relationships in the congregation, his description of the Corinthians in no way indicates that relationships between Christian slaves and their owners were at all disturbed by their pneumatic Christianity.

Thus, when Paul wrote the phrase μή σοι μελέτω, his advice was not prompted particularly by the slaves in the Corinthian congregation but rather by his concern for any Christian who might have been concerned about his social, legal or religious status. To be sure, not everyone who was in slavery worried about his status. Paul knew that many of the slaves in Corinth enjoyed more favorable living conditions than many free laborers. He had encountered no color or race line separating freemen from slaves in the first century. He knew that most persons in slavery were treated well; they had been born in the house of their owner and they had been trained to perform important domestic, industrial, business, or public tasks.

Owning and using men and women as slaves were such normal parts of daily life in the Mediterranean world of the first-century A.D. that no one except the Essenes asked if the institution should exist or not. Paul apparently regarded slavery as a normal part of society in a world that was "passing away" (0731).[571]

---

[571]Nowhere in Paul's writings can we find an attempt either to justify or to call in question the institution of slavery as such. Indeed, no New Testament writing gives any teaching or judgment regarding the origin of slavery. Justin Martyr (*Dialogue with Trypho* 134) is the first Christian writer to mention how slavery began (and his concern is Jew/Christian relations, not slavery as such). Thus W.L. Westermann (*Slave Systems*, pp. 157,161) was wrong when he claimed that "Paul was under the compulsion of finding an explanation for the employment of slave labor in a world formed and controlled by an all-merciful Deity....The slave system...was to Paul the result of the offense of Adam, a punishment for the original sin." Westermann apparently confused Paul with Augustine (*De Civitate Dei* 19,15). Paul was under no compulsion to explain the origin of slavery; he never connected this institution with the orders of creation or the will of God. The fact that Paul did not give slavery such a theological sanction became important to those Christians who later fought against this institution.

As far as we know, there were no anti-slavery tracts in the first century which Paul might have read. Indeed, none of the authors who had been in slavery ever attacked the status in which they had once lived. A number of the authors whom Paul might have read believed that the most important matter in life was "inner-freedom," which could be enjoyed irrespective of one's legal or social status. Thus, Paul's words to the Christians who were in slavery ("Don't worry about it") were by no means unique in the first century. But the context in which Paul gave this advice determined its special meaning: Since you have been called by God, your legal status no longer determines your existence. Stop being concerned about it.[572] For you are already a "freedman in Christ" (0722).

Paul did not want any Christian who was in slavery to think that his manumission would bring him any closer to God or that his slave-status was any disadvantage in his relation to God. He knew that most of those persons who were in slavery were looking forward to their manumission, and he wanted to make it plain that this event in their lives should not any longer be an occasion for special concern--either in anticipation of legal freedom (and perhaps Roman citizenship) or in dread of loss of security. Yet, Paul knew of no unrest or revolutionary impulses among the slaves at Corinth. Both the social situation there and the evidence from 1 Corinthians lead me to the conclusion that 1 Cor. 0721ab was not stimulated by "restless" Christian slaves but rather was written to illustrate Paul's "theology of calling."

The aspect of first-century slavery perhaps least understood by interpreters of 1 Cor. 0721 is the relation of the slave to his manumission. Contrary to modern assumptions, manumission was a very common occurrence in the first century A.D., and the owner who manumitted a slave did so to serve his own advantage. That is, manumission was an important key to the success of the slave-system in the first century in that it was used as a means for increasing the efficiency and contentment of those yet in slavery. Slaves who did their work well could reasonably hope to be set free as a reward. Paul's words in 0721c, ἀλλ' εἰ καὶ δύνασαι ἐλεύθερος γενέσθαι, are indefinite enough to refer to any of the manumission-procedures used at Corinth during the first century.[573] That is, in 0721c Paul simply referred to the possibility that a Christian in slavery might become a freedman; he said nothing about the "how" or "why" of this manumission.

---

[572]This translation of 0721b emphasizes the force of the present imperative with μή.

[573]Thus, H. Greeven (Das Hauptproblem der Sozialethik in der neueren Stoa und im Urchristentum, p. 51) was correct in opposing the presupposition of J. Weiß (Der erste Korintherbrief, p. 188) that Paul referred only to self-purchase in this verse. See above, pp. 17, 112.

Although the unusual phrase ἀλλ' εἰ καί has caused a variety of comment and disagreement, it is the phrase δύνασαι ἐλεύθερος γενέσθαι which has been one of the sources of greatest confusion in interpreting 1 Cor. 0721. For at first glance it appears as if Paul was referring to a situation over which the person in slavery had a large amount of control; the term δύνασαι seems to suggest that the slave could decide to accept or reject manumission. Indeed, both of the traditional interpretations of 0721 have been based on the assumption that the slave was free to say yes or no to a friendly or disinterested offer of manumission by his owner. On this basis, 0721d has been quite naturally interpreted as advice to accept or reject such an offer. But such a friendly or disinterested offer of manumission rarely, if ever, occurred. Manumission was not an act which was "accepted" or "refused" by the slave. It happened to him. And while some slaves were undoubtedly glad that it did, others would have preferred to remain in slavery.

To be sure, the person in slavery could encourage his owner to manumit him by doing good work as well as by offering him a sum of money in the hope of buying himself out of slavery. It seems most unlikely, however, that Paul had any interest in opposing hard work by Christians in slavery.[574] And in light of the meaning of κλῆσις in 0720 and the rhythm of "exceptions" in the flow of Paul's argument in 1 Cor. 7, there is no reason to suppose that Paul objected to the manumission of a Christian in slavery even if his or her initiative played a role in it.[575]

In view of the fact that manumission was the result of a decision by the slave's owner, perhaps Paul's use of δύναμαι in 0721c may be explained by his concentration on the slave in this verse. That is, the owner of the slave had no role to play in Paul's presentation of his examples in 0717-24. Therefore, he spoke of manumission solely from the point of view of the person in slavery.[576] Note also that this use of δύναμαι is reminiscent of

---

[574]Note Paul's admonition to the Christians at Thessalonica that they should work with their hands and be dependent on no one (1 Th. 0411-12). See also 2 Th. 0310: "We gave you this command: If anyone will not work, let him not eat."

[575]Note also that there is no evidence from 1 Corinthians or any other Pauline writing that he thought there was any special value in remaining a slave in the "last days." Indeed, is there any reason to think that it would have been more difficult for a slave to endure the "travail" of this period as a freedman? Or (to speak in the terms of 1 Cor. 7) could the slave have served the Lord more single-mindedly as a slave? The reverse would seem to be the case. In any case, a slave's legal status was a matter determined by his owner.

[576]If Paul had wanted to refer to the same event from the perspective of the owner of a slave, he might have written: ἀλλ' εἰ καὶ ὁ δεσπότης ἀπελευθερώσει σε, ...

Agrippa's words to Festus in Acts 2632: "This man could have been set free (ἀπολελύσθαι ἐδύνατο) if he had not appealed to Caesar." Although Paul is the subject of ἐδύνατο, it was not Paul but Festus who could have set Paul free.[577] It is unusual for δύναμαι to be used in this manner in the present tense, but all other evidence points to the conclusion that in 0721c Paul was referring to any situation in which a Christian slave became a freedman. In the context of the options open to slaves in the first century and of Paul's argument in 1 Cor. 7, 0721c should be translated: "But if, indeed, you become manumitted..."

In addition to being based on false assumptions about first-century manumission-practices or on an unwarranted assumption that 0721c referred only to an act of "self-purchase," all attempts to make 0721d read "use slavery" have flattened out the force of ἀλλά at the beginning of 0721c. That is, 0721c has been read as an extension of 0721b, as if Paul had meant to say: "Were you a slave when you were called? Don't worry about it. And even if you are able to become free..."[578] On this basis, 0721d has been interpreted as an admonition to the slave that he prove that he was not worried about his legal status by "staying in slavery."[579]

The correct reading of 0721c, however, allows the particle ἀλλά to carry its full adversative force.[580] It signals an interruption in Paul's train of thought, and the content of 0721c shows that Paul did indeed break into the parallelism of this section in order to give some special advice to the Christian slaves in Corinth. On the basis of the antithetical parallelism in 0719, the reader would expect the status of the freeman to be taken up in 0721c. To be sure, this anticipated parallelism is taken up in 0722, and the term γάρ at the beginning of 0722 introduces a reason to support 0721b: "Don't worry about being in slavery...for the slave is a freedman of the Lord." Rather than providing a counterpart to 0719b or an antecedent to 0722b ("the freeman is a slave of Christ") in 0721cd, Paul gave special advice to those Corinthians whose legal-social status could be changed at any time by their owners.

All the exegetes who have completed 0721d with the phrase "use slavery" not only have minimized the force of ἀλλά at the beginning of 0721c but

---

[577]See Blass-Debrunner-Funk, *A Greek Grammar of the N.T.*, p. 181, §358,1. On the law in this case, see A.N. Sherwin-White, *Roman Society and Roman Law in the New Testament*, p. 65.

[578]J. Weiß (*Der erste Korintherbrief*, p. 188), e.g., wrote that ἀλλά in this case was "das steigernde 'ja'." See above, p. 113 n. 429.

[579]So, e.g., H. Schlier, *TDNT* II, 501.

[580]See Bauer, *A Greek-English Lexicon*, pp. 37-38. See also Kühner-Gerth, *Ausführliche Grammatik* II, 282-283, and J.D. Denniston, *The Greek Particles*, pp. 3-11. Notice the use of ἀλλά in 0707, 0710, 0719 and 0735.

also have insisted that the terms εἰ καί in 0721c be combined and translated
"even if."[581] It is true that Paul did use these terms with the sense "even
if" or "although" in 2 Cor. 0416, 0708a, 0708c and 1211. But note also that
in 1 Cor. 0407, 0711-12 and 0727-28 as well as in 2 Cor. 0402-03, 0708b-09
and 1105-06 καί is used emphatically in the protasis of a conditional sentence
and thus is grammatically separate from εἰ.[582] In the three examples cited
from 1 Cor. as well as in 2 Cor. 0708b, an adversative δέ follows the εἰ.
Notice that there are no examples of εἰ καί meaning "although" or "even if"
in 1 Cor., but that in 1 Cor. 7 an emphatic καί appears both before (ἐὰν δὲ
καί--0711) and after (ἐὰν δὲ καί--0728) the usage of εἰ καί in 0721c. These
usages suggest that on grammatical grounds alone εἰ and καί in 0721c should
be translated "if, indeed."[583] In view of the social and legal context, this
is the translation which is required.

The results of this grammatical analysis of 0721c seem to exclude
the "use slavery" reading and to support the "take freedom" interpretation of
0721d. Actually, these results say nothing about 0721d as such. They indicate
only that in 0721c Paul was talking about the possibility that a Christian
slave might be set free by his owner. The condition which 0721c describes is
the act of manumission. If manumission occurred, the Christian slave was exhorted to do something. At this point the traditional interpretations of
1 Cor. 0721 show themselves to be either impossible or useless. For the
freedman could not "use slavery," and exhorting a freedman to "take freedom"
would have had no point. Thus, the way is clear for a new proposal.

In view of the threefold repetition in 0717-24 of the basic admonition, "Live according to God's call," I have proposed that in 0721d Paul exhorted any Christian slave who might be manumitted "to live (as a freedman)

---

[581]Note that in the ninth-century, interlinear Greek/Latin MS. called Codex
Boernerianus (G) the καί is dropped from 0721c. Hermann Josef Frede (*Altlateinische Paulus-Handschriften* [Freiburg, 1964], p. 51) traces the basis of
this text back to "Archetype Z," which is from the middle of the 4th century
in Italy. Frede notes that Codex G gives evidence of comprehensive editorial
work paired with careful text-critical understanding. G. Zuntz (*The Text of
the Epistles*, The British Academy, 1953) did not comment on 1 Cor. 0721.
Apparently the καί was dropped in favor of the "take freedom" interpretation
of 0721d.

[582]For a good discussion of all these texts see Margaret E. Thrall, *Greek
Particles in the New Testament: Linguistic and Exegetical Studies* (Leiden,
1962), pp. 79-81.

[583]Thrall (p. 81) concludes that "it is probable that this verse [0721]
contains a third example of the idiom. This would mean that Paul is advising
Christian slaves to take advantage of the opportunity of emancipation." So
also C.F.D. Moule, *An Idiom-Book of New Testament Greek*, p. 167. Denniston
(*The Greek Particles*, p. 303) also notes this way of using εἰ καί. See Blass-
Debrunner-Funk, *A Greek Grammar*, p. 189, §372, for "εἰ with the indicative of
reality."

according to God's calling." A thorough investigation of the various ways in
which Josephus used χράομαι has shown that this term can mean "to live according to," "to keep [the laws of God]" and "to follow [a way of life]."[584] Thus,
in view of the conclusion to the first example given by Paul in 0717-24,
namely "but keeping the commands of God [is what really counts]," 0721d could
be completed: "By all means, keep the commands of God."[585] Also, in view of
the thrice-repeated admonition in 0717-24, it could be completed: "By all
means, live according to [your calling in Christ]." There are a few reasons
for preferring the latter reading. In either case the actual content of 0721d
is essentially the same. For in 0719c Paul expressed in another key the basic
point he made in 0720 (0717, 0724).

In accord with his quickness in his style of arguing in 1 Cor. 7 to
mention "exceptions," Paul broke into the illustrations of his "theology of
calling" in 0717-24 in order to take account of a possible change in the
social-legal status of Christian slaves at Corinth. As in his discussion of
the change in the social status of the Christian whose mixed marriage dis-
solved (0715) and the widow who married (0739bc), so in 0721cd Paul stressed
the Christian's relation to Christ as the enduring and determining factor in
his life. Not manumission but living in accord with God's call in Christ
(i.e., keeping God's commands) was the significant matter.

Paul continued this emphasis on the enduring and determining relationship of the Christian to his Lord in 1 Cor. 0722. Because of the call of
God the slave had become a freedman of the Lord (ἀπελεύθερος κυρίου) and the
freeman had become a slave of Christ (δοῦλος Χριστοῦ). This is the only use
of the term ἀπελεύθερος in Paul's writings, and the parallelism in 0722
strongly suggests that Paul meant it to refer to the close relationship which
existed between the Christian in slavery and the Lord.[586] The relationships

---

[584] In connection with 1 Cor. 0721d, C.H. Dodd ("Notes from Papyri," *JTS* XXVI
(1924), 77-78) drew attention to an absolute use of χράομαι in the *Oxyrhynchus
Papyri* XVI (1865), 4ff. Unfortunately, it does not illuminate the problem in
0721d. Furthermore, as Dodd said, "the late date [6th or 7th century A.D.]
detracts somewhat from the value of the comparison." Dodd thought this comparison supported the "take freedom" interpretation.

[585] J.H. Moulton (*A Grammar of N.T. Greek* II, 165) judged that μᾶλλον in Mt.
0626 and in 1 Cor. 0721 was used as an elative comparative: "By all means..."

[586] Paul's readiness to use such a potentially loaded phrase as "the slave
who has been called in the Lord is a freedman of the Lord" is a further indication that he knew of no dissatisfaction among the slaves in the Corinthian
congregation which had been exacerbated by the spiritual exaltation there.

between freedmen and their former owners which are prescribed by Greek and Roman law verify this suggestion.[587]

According to both Greek and Roman law, the manumitted slave continued to live in a legal and personal relation to his former owner, which often involved many obligations. Under Greek law these obligations were specified in a *paramoné*-contract which usually was written with a time limit. Roman legislation demanded that the freedman give his patron *obsequium, operae, officium* and *bona* throughout his life. The patron also had obligations to help his former slaves. In this context, the choice of the term ἀπελεύθερος to describe the relationship of the Christian slave to his Lord is quite interesting. For it indicates that the slave's legal status was no longer the primary determining factor in his life (he was a "*freedman* of the Lord") at the same time that it strongly emphasizes the personal relationship between the slave and Christ (he was a "freedman *of the Lord*").[588] Since this relationship was understood to be a permanent one, it seems likely that Paul had the Roman concept of "freedman" in mind when writing 0722.[589]

In the same way, the Christian freeman was not to view his legal freedom as the primary determining factor in his life. For God's call had changed him into "a slave of Christ."[590] His social status granted him neither superior access to divine things nor superior rank in the congregation (see 1 Cor. 1127-34). As in the case of the Christian in slavery, the Christian freeman had been called by God without regard for his social status. "In the Lord," his social-legal status was irrelevant. Indeed, the really important matter was that he was "in the Lord."

---

[587]As my excursus on "Sacral Manumission" (above, pp. 121-125) has shown, neither in 1 Cor. 0722-23 nor in his doctrine of redemption in general did Paul use language which had anything significant in common with the practice of manumission followed by the priests of Apollo at Delphi.

[588]H. Conzelmann (*1. Korintherbrief*, p. 153) has missed the double-edged force of this term because he did not consider the Roman legal context. Consequently, he strained to find an incongruity in the parallelism in 0722a and 0722b, and he falsely concluded: "ἀπελεύθερος ist er nicht im Verhältnis zum Herrn, sondern zu seinem einstigen Sklavenstand."

[589]Francis Lyall ("Roman Law in the Writings of Paul--The Slave and the Freedman," *NTS* 17 [1970], 78) takes the relationship described in 1 Cor. 0722 as a sign that Paul was influenced by Roman rather than by Greek law. Lyall (p. 77) supports my conclusions very nicely when he writes regarding 0721-22: "The texts are quite clear, making a fascinating contrast between the position of the slave and the freedman yet showing that the two men are fundamentally in the same position in relation to Christ."

[590]Only in 1 Cor. 0722 did Paul refer to a large number of Christians as "slaves of Christ." See Gerhard Sass, "Zur Bedeutung von δοῦλος bei Paulus," *ZNW* 40 (1941), 24-32. Cf. David Daube, *The New Testament and Rabbinic Judaism* (London, 1956), pp. 278-284.

In 0723 Paul extended this emphasis on the enduring and determining relationship of the Christian to his Lord. At first glance, the verse reads easily as direct address to the Christian freeman who is first mentioned in this pericope in the previous sentence: τιμῆς ἠγοράσθητε· μὴ γίνεσθε δοῦλοι ἀνθρώπων. This statement and exhortation have a number of peculiar features:

1) On the basis of the parallelism between 0718/0721, between 0719/0722 and between 0720/0724, 0723 is not expected. That is, according to the pattern which can be discerned in 0717-24, 0723 is an intrusion.

2) Although the phrase "You were bought with a price" fits very well with the designation of the Christian freeman as a "slave of God" (0722b), this language could be used outside the immediate context of slavery, as in 1 Cor. 0620 where it supports Paul's stress on the Lordship of Christ over the total existence of the Christian.

3) In both 0723a and 0620a the action of redemption is described quite vaguely.[591] It is not said who purchased the Christian, from whom he had been purchased, nor what the purchase-price was.[592] What is clear, however, is that the Christian's existence was changed because he had been bought with a price, with the result that he should neither join himself to a prostitute (0615-20) nor should he become a slave of men (0723b).

4) In light of the well-known Greek practice of time-limited self-sale into slavery,[593] it is easy to conclude that in 0723 Paul was saying straightforwardly: "Your total somatic existence belongs to God. Therefore do not sell yourselves into slavery." The pertinence of such an admonition is suggested by the specific case, reported in 1 Clement 5502, of self-sale into slavery by Christians who wanted to gain money to ransom others.

5) The vagueness of this verse, however, is increased by the verb used in 0723b. It is not a term expressing the idea "to sell" but rather the ambiguous word "to become." This general way of speaking seems to refer to any of the ways by which the Christian might become enslaved to anyone else than

---

[591]See Kurt Niederwimmer, *Der Begriff der Freiheit im Neuen Testament* (Berlin, 1966), pp. 175-176, for a good summary of the various procedures for manumission and redemption which have been proposed as background for 1 Cor. 0723a. Note, however, that it has now been shown that Paul in no way relied on the practice of sacral manumission at Delphi in expressing his doctrine of redemption or in his formulation of 1 Cor. 0722-23 (see above, pp. 121-125).

[592]See Werner Elert, "Redemptio ab hostibus," *ThLZ* 72 (1947), 265-270, esp. p. 266 n. 1. See also Friedrich Büchsel, *TDNT* I, 125.

[593]Time-limited self-sale into slavery was also practiced by Romans and Jews in the first century A.D. See above, pp. 46-47.

Christ. From this perspective, the verse could be read as an expression in yet another key (see 0719c) of the basic exhortation in 0717-24. That is, to become slaves of men would be to regard social or religious status as more decisive than the calling from God in Christ.

Thus, there are good reasons for finding physical and spiritual slavery in 0723. It may be that Paul intended to use language that would cover both kinds of slavery, since in his anthropology the spiritual and the physical are very closely related (σῶμα).[594] In any case, it should be noted that the exhortation in 0723b was not motivated by an interest in preventing the Corinthians from changing their social or legal status but rather by the fact that they belonged to Christ, body and soul.

In 0724 Paul recapitulated his basic point in this pericope: "Each one should continue to live according to his calling [in Christ]--in God's sight." The phrase "in God's sight (παρὰ θεῷ)" is not just a rhetorical flourish at the end of this section. Rather it stresses the point that the Corinthians would be judged by God not by men.[595] Neither social or religious status nor spiritual achievement or wisdom were significant criteria for Christian existence, despite what men might think. No social change could improve a Christian's relationship to God. No spiritual achievement could remove the Christian from the demand to keep the commands of God, which are epitomized in agápe. Since God had called the Corinthians into koinonía with his crucified Son, it was this fellowship and not any status in the world which determined their relationship to God.

When viewed in its context as a significant part of Paul's response to the pneumatikoí in Corinth who were claiming that sexual asceticism was one of the signs of their exalted state, 1 Cor. 7 does not indicate that Paul had any interest in preventing changes in the social positions of the Christians in Corinth. Marriages, divorces and manumissions were all normal events in the social fabric which belonged to a world that was "passing away." Paul's primary concern was that the Christian live according to his calling from God wherever he happened to find himself, that he keep the commands of God in the midst of his various relationships, whatever they might be.

---

[594] See C.K. Barrett, *First Epistle to the Corinthians*, pp. 171-172. See also D. Doughty, *Heiligkeit und Freiheit*, pp. 76-79; D. Daube, *The New Testament and Rabbinic Judaism*, p. 278; and W. Bieder, *Die Berufung im Neuen Testament*, p. 60.

[595] See 1 Cor. 0404c-05: "My judge is the Lord. So pass no premature judgment; wait until the Lord comes. For he will bring to light what darkness hides, and disclose men's inward motives; then will be the time for each to receive from God such praise as he deserves." (*NEB*)

Thus, 1 Cor. 7 is not the place where Paul developed his "theology of marriage." Nor did he intend to "discuss" the topic of slavery in 0721-23. In 0721ab Paul introduced the case of the Christian slave as a second example in order to illustrate his "theology of calling" in 0717-24. In 0721c he interrupted his argument long enough to take account of a possible change in the legal and social status of those Corinthian Christians who were in slavery, namely, manumission. In 0721d he made a special application of his basic exhortation in 0717-24, namely: "By all means (as a freedman) live according to God's calling."

In view of this background, 1 Cor. 0717-24 should be translated as follows:

In any case, let each one live his life in accord with the fact that the Lord has distributed [faith] to him and that God has called him. That is what I teach in all our congregations.

Was a man already circumcized when he was called? He should not try to change his condition with an operation. Was a man uncircumcized when he was called? He should not become circumcized. Neither circumcision nor uncircumcision makes any difference. But keeping the commands of God is what really counts. Each person should continue in that calling into which he was called.

Were you a slave when you were called? Don't worry about it. But if, indeed, you become manumitted, by all means [as a freedman] live according to [God's calling.] For a slave who has been called in the Lord is the Lord's freedman. Likewise, a freeman who has been called [in the Lord] is Christ's slave. You were bought with a price: do not become slaves of men. Each one should continue to live in accord with his calling [in Christ]--in the sight of God.

BIBLIOGRAPHY

(List of Works Cited)

Alford, Henry. *The Greek Testament.* Vol. II. Boston, 1883.

Allard, P. *Les esclaves chrétiens, depuis les premiers temps de l'Église.* Paris, 1876 (6th edn., 1914).

Allo, E.-B. *Première épître aux Corinthiens.* 2nd edn. Paris, 1956.

Alt, Albrecht. *Kleine Schriften zur Geschichte des Volkes Israel.* Munich, 1953.

Balch, David L. "Backgrounds of I Cor. VII: Sayings of the Lord in Q; Moses as an Ascetic ΘΕΙΟΣ ΑΝΗΡ in II Cor. III," *NTS* 18 (1972), 351-364.

_____. "I Cor. 7:36-38 and Its Background: Moses as an Ascetic θεῖος ἀνήρ," B.D. thesis. Union Theological Seminary, New York, 1969.

Balsdon, J.P.V.D. *Life and Leisure in Ancient Rome.* Toronto, 1969.

Bang, M. "Die Herkunft der römischen Sklaven," *Mitteilungen des kaiserlichen deutschen archaeologischen Instituts, Römische Abteilung* 27 (1912), 189-221.

Baron, Salo. *A Social and Religious History of the Jews.* 2nd edn. New York, 1952.

Barrett, C.K. *A Commentary on the First Epistle to the Corinthians.* Black's N.T. Commentaries. London, 1968.

Barrow, R.H. "Freedmen," *Oxford Classical Dictionary* (Oxford, 1949), p. 371.

_____. *Slavery in the Roman Empire.* London, 1928 (reprinted by Barnes and Noble, New York, 1968).

Bauer, Walter. *A Greek-English Lexicon of the New Testament and other Early Christian Literature.* (Trans. W.F. Arndt and F.W. Gingrich from 4th German edn., 1952) Chicago, 1957.

_____. "Review of Kiefl, *Die Theorien des modernen Sozialismus,*" *ThLZ* 41 (1916), cols. 511-512.

_____. *Wörterbuch zu den Schriften des Neuen Testaments und der übrigen urchristlichen Literatur.* 5. Auflage. Berlin, 1963.

Bavinck, H. "Chr. beginselen en maatsch. verhoudingen," *Chr. en Maatsch* I (1908), 35-36.

Behm, Johannes. "*glossa,*" *TDNT* I, 719-726.

Bellen, Heinz. "Μᾶλλον χρῆσαι: Verzicht auf Freilassung als asketische Leistung?" *Jahrbuch für Antike und Christentum* 6 (1963), 177-180.

Bengel, Johann Albrecht. *Gnomon novi testamenti.* Tübingen, 1742 (reprinted by J.F. Steinkopf, Stuttgart, 1970).

Bengston, Hermann. *Grundriss der Römischen Geschichte mit Quellenkunde (Bd. I: Republik und Kaiserzeit bis 284 N. Chr.)*. Munich, 1967.

Berger, Adolf. *Encyclopedic Dictionary of Roman Law*. Transactions of the American Philosophical Society. New Series, Vol. 43, Part 2. Philadelphia, 1953.

Bieder, Werner. *Die Berufung im Neuen Testament*. Abhandlungen zur Theologie des Alten und Neuen Testaments 38. Zürich, 1961.

Bihlmeyer, Karl, ed. *Die Apostolischen Väter*. 1. Teil, 2. Auflage. Tübingen, 1956.

Bischoff, A. "Exegetische Randbemerkungen," *ZNW* IX (1908), 166-172.

Blass, F., and Debrunner, A. *A Greek Grammar of the New Testament and Other Early Christian Literature*. (Trans. and rev. Robert W. Funk) Chicago, 1961.

Bloch, M. *Die Freilassungsbedingungen der delphischen Freilassungsinschriften*. Diss., Strassburg, 1914.

Bömer, Franz, *Untersuchungen über die Religion der Sklaven in Griechenland und Rom*. 4 Bde. Akademie der Wissenschaften und der Literatur: Abhandlungen der Geistes- und Sozialwissenschaftlichen Klasse. Mainz, 1957-1963.

Bohatec, Josef. "Inhalt und Reihenfolge der 'Schlagworte der Erlösungsreligion' in 1 Kor. 1,26-31," *Theologische Zeitschrift* 4 (1948), 252-271.

Bonhöffer, Adolf. *Epiktet und das Neue Testament*. Religionsgeschichtliche Versuche und Vorarbeiten 10. Giessen, 1911 (reprinted by A. Töpelmann, Berlin, 1964).

Bornkamm, Günther. *Das Ende des Gesetzes: Paulusstudien*. Gesammelte Aufsätze, Bd. I, 3. Auflage. Munich, 1961.

_____. *Paulus*. Stuttgart, 1969.

_____. *Studien zu Antike und Urchristentum*. Gesammelte Aufsätze, Bd. II. Munich, 1959.

Boucher, Madeleine. "Some Unexplored Parallels to 1 Cor. 11,11-12 and Gal. 3,28: the New Testament on the Role of Women," *CBQ* 31 (1969), 50-58.

Bourguet, E., Colin, G., Daux, G., Salač, A. and Valmin, N., eds. *Fouilles de Delphes III: Epigraphie*. Paris, 1929-1939.

Bowersock, Glen W. *Augustus and the Greek World*. Oxford, 1965.

Braun, Herbert. *Qumran und das Neue Testament*. 2 Bde. Tübingen, 1966.

_____. *Gesammelte Studien zum Neuen Testament und seiner Umwelt*. Tübingen, 1962.

Broneer, Oscar. "Corinth: Center of St. Paul's Missionary Work in Greece," *Biblical Archaeologist* 14 (1951), 77-96.

Brugnoli, Giorgio. *C. Suetoni Tranquilli, Praeter Caesarum Libros Reliquiae: De Grammaticis et Rhetoribus*. Editio Altera, Bibliotheca Scriptorum Graecorum et Romanorum Teubneriana, 1963.

Brunt, P.A. "Review of Westermann, *Slave Systems*," *JRS* 48 (1958) 165-168.

Buckland, W.W. *The Roman Law of Slavery: The Condition of the Slave in Private Law from Augustus to Justinian.* Cambridge, 1908.

Bultmann, Rudolph. *Theology of the New Testament.* 2 vols. (Trans. Kendrick Grobel), New York, 1951, 1955.

Cadbury, H.J. "Erastus of Corinth," *JBL* 50 (1931), 42-58.

Calderini, Aristide. *La manomissione e la condizione dei liberti in Grecia.* Milan, 1908.

Cameron, A. "Inscriptions relating to sacral manumission and confession," *HThR* 32 (1939), 143-179.

von Campenhausen, Hans Frhr. *Die Begründung kirchlicher Entscheidungen beim Apostel Paulus (Zur Grundlegung des Kirchenrechts).* Sitzungsberichte der Heidelberger Akademie der Wissenschaften: Philosophisch-historische Klasse. Heidelberg, 1957.

Carcopino, Jérôme. *Daily Life in Ancient Rome.* (Trans. E.O. Lorimer) New Haven, 1941.

Cartlidge, David R. "Competing Theologies of Asceticism in the Early Church," unpublished Th.D. diss. Harvard University, 1969.

Cassian, Bishop. "The Revision of the Russian Translation of the N.T.," *The Bible Translator* 5 (1954), 27-31.

Ciccotti, Ettore. *Il tramonto della schiavitù nel mondo antico.* Turin, 1899. (*Der Untergang der Sklaverei im Altertum.* Trans. Oda Olberg. Berlin, 1910.)

Clemen, Karl. *Die Einheitlichkeit der paulinischen Briefe an der Hand der bisher mit Bezug auf sie aufgestellten Interpolations- und Compilationshypothesen.* Berlin, 1894.

Cohen, Boaz. *Jewish and Roman Law: A Comparative Study.* 2 vols. New York, 1966.

Cohn, Leopoldus and Wendland, Paulus, eds. *Philonis Alexandrini. Opera Quae Supersunt.* 7 vols. Berlin, 1896-1930 (reprinted by Walter de Gruyter, Berlin, 1962).

Cohoon, J.W., ed. and tr. *Dio Chrysostom.* Loeb edn. Vol. 2. Cambridge, Mass., 1939.

Coleman-Norton, P.R. "The Apostle Paul and the Roman Law of Slavery," *Studies in Roman Economic and Social History in Honor of Allan Chester Johnson.* ed. P.R. Coleman-Norton. (Princeton, 1951), pp. 166-177.

Colin, G., ed. *Bulletin de correspondance hellénique* XXII. Paris, 1898.

Collins, John J. "Chiasmus, the 'ABA' Pattern and the Text of Paul," *Studiorum Paulinorum Congressus Internationalis Catholicus*, 2 vols. (1961, 1963), 575-583.

Collitz-Baunack-Bechtel, eds. *Sammlung der griechischen Dialektinschriften.* Göttingen, 1884-1915.

Colson, F.H., ed. and tr. *Philo*. Loeb edn. 10 Vols. Cambridge, Mass., 1962.

Conybeare, F.C., ed. and tr. *Philostratus. The Life of Apollonius of Tyana*. Loeb edn. Cambridge, Mass., 1950.

Conzelmann, Hans. "Korinth und die Mädchen der Aphrodite (Zur Religions-geschichte der Stadt Korinth)," *Nachrichten der Akademie der Wissenschaften in Göttingen*, Philologisch-Historische Klasse (1967), 247-261.

_____. *Der erste Brief an die Korinther*. Meyers Kommentar V. Göttingen, 1969.

Cook, S.A., Adcock, F.E., and Charlesworth, M.P., eds. *Cambridge Ancient History*. Vol. 10. Cambridge, 1952.

Crook, John. *Law and Life of Rome*. Ithaca, New York, 1967.

Cross, Frank. *The Ancient Library of Qumran*. 2nd edn. New York, 1961.

Cumont, Franz. *The Mysteries of Mithra*. (Trans. T.J. McCormack from 2nd French edn.) New York, 1956.

_____. *The Oriental Religions in Roman Paganism*. (English trans. 1911) New York, 1956.

Dareste, R., Hausoullier, B., and Reinach, Th. eds. *Recueil des inscriptions juridiques greques*. Vol. 2. Paris, 1898.

Daube, David. "Concessions to Sinfulness in Jewish Law," *Journal of Jewish Studies* X (1959), 1-13.

_____. "Slave Catching," *Juridical Review* 64 (1952), 12-28.

_____. *Studies in Biblical Law*. Cambridge, 1947.

_____. *The New Testament and Rabbinic Judaism*. London, 1956.

Daux, G. "Delphes au IIème et Ier siècle," *Bibliothèque des écoles fran-çaises d'Athènes et de Rome* CXL (Paris, 1936), 46-209.

Davis, David B. *The Problem of Slavery in the Western World*. Ithaca, 1966.

Deissmann, A. *Light from the Ancient East*. (Trans. L.R.M. Strachan from 4th German edn., 1922) New York, 1927 (reprinted by Baker Book House, Grand Rapids, 1965).

Denniston, J.D. *The Greek Particles*. Oxford, 1959.

Denniston, J.D. et al., eds. *The Oxford Classical Dictionary*. Oxford, 1949.

Dill, S. *Roman Society from Nero to Marcus Aurelius*. London, 1904 (reprinted by Meridian Books, New York, 1964).

Dinkler, E. "Zum Problem der Ethik bei Paulus: Rechtsnahme und Rechts-verzicht (1 Kor 6,1-11)," *ZThK* 49 (1952), 167-200.

Dittenberger, W., ed. *Sylloge Inscriptionum Graecarum*. 3rd edn. Leipzig, 1915-1924.

von Dobschütz, Ernst. *Die Urchristlichen Gemeinden: Sittengeschichtliche Bilder*. Leipzig, 1902.

Dodd, C.H. "Notes from Papyri," *JTS* 26 (1924), 77-78.

Dölger, F.J. *Antike und Christentum*. Vol. I. Münster, 1929.

Doughty, Darrell. "Elaboration over Understanding," *Interpretation* 23 (1969), 475-476.

_____. *Heiligkeit u. Freiheit, eine exegetische Untersuchung der Anwendung des paulinischen Freiheitsgedankens in I Kor 7*. Diss. Göttingen, 1965.

Duff, A.M. *Freedmen in the Early Roman Empire*. 2nd edn. with Addenda. Cambridge, 1958.

Edwards, Thomas Charles. *A Commentary on the First Epistle to the Corinthians*. New York, 1886.

Ehrhardt, Arnold A.T. *Politische Metaphysik von Solon bis Augustin. (Bd. 2: Die Christliche Revolution)*. Tübingen, 1959.

Elert, Werner. "Redemptio ab hostibus," *ThLZ* 72 (1947), 265-270.

Epp, Eldon Jay. *The Theological Tendency of Codex Bezae Cantabrigiensis in Acts*. Cambridge, 1966.

Epstein, I., ed. *The Babylonian Talmud*. London, 1936-1952.

Faw, C.E. "On the Writing of First Thessalonians," *JBL* 71 (1952), 217-232.

Finley, M.I. "Between Slavery and Freedom," *Comparative Studies in Society and History* 6 (1964), 233-249.

_____. "Slavery," *International Encyclopedia of the Social Sciences*. Ed. D.L. Sills. (New York, 1968), Vol. 14, 307-313.

_____, ed. *Slavery in Classical Antiquity*. 2nd edn. New York, 1968.

Forbes, C.A. "The Education and Training of Slaves in Antiquity," *Transactions of the American Philological Association* 86 (1955), 321-360.

Foucart, Paul. *Mémoire sur l'affranchisement des esclaves par forme de vente à une divinité*. Paris, 1867.

Fowler, H.N., ed. *Corinth*. 16 vols. American School of Classical Studies at Athens, 1929ff.

Frank, P. Suso. 'ΑΓΓΕΛΙΚΟΣ ΒΙΟΣ: *Begriffsanalytische und begriffsgeschichtliche Untersuchung zum "engelgleichen Leben" im frühen Mönchtum* (Beiträge zur Geschichte des alten Mönchtums und des Benediktinerordens 26). Münster, 1964.

Frede, Hermann Josef. *Altlateinische Paulus-Handschriften*. Aus der Geschichte der lateinischen Bibel 4. Freiburg, 1964.

Friedlaender, Ludwig. *Petronius: Cena Trimalchionis*. Leipzig, 1906 (reprinted Amsterdam, 1960).

Gagé, J.-G. "Graeco-Roman Society and Culture, 31 B.C.-A.D. 235," *The Crucible of Christianity*. Ed. Arnold Toynbee. (London, 1969), 161-170.

_____. *Les classes sociales dans l'empire romain*. Paris, 1964.

Gager, John G. "Functional Diversity in Paul's Use of End-Time Language," *JBL* 89 (1970), 331-333.

Georgi, Dieter. "Der Kampf um die reine Lehre im Urchristentum als Ausein-andersetzung um das rechte Verständnis der an Israel ergangenen Offenbarung Gottes," *Antijudaismus im Neuen Testament? Exegetische und systematische Beiträge*. Eds. W. Eckert, N.P. Levinson, und M. Stöhr. (Munich, 1967), pp. 82-94.

_____. *Die Gegner des Paulus im 2. Korintherbrief (Studien zur Religiösen Propaganda in der Spätantike)*. Wissenschaftliche Monographien zum Alten und Neuen Testament 11. Neukirchen-Vluyn, 1964.

_____. *Die Geschichte der Kollekte des Paulus für Jerusalem*. Theologische Forschung: Wissenschaftliche Beiträge zur Kirchlich-Evangelischen Lehre 38. Hamburg, 1965.

Godet, Frederick. *Commentary on St. Paul's First Epistle to the Corinthians*. (Trans. A. Cusin) Edinburgh, 1886.

Goodenough, Erwin R. "Paul and Onesimus," *HThR* 22 (1929), 181-183.

Goodspeed, Edgar J. "Gaius Titius Justus," *JBL* 69 (1950), 382-383.

_____. "Paul and Slavery," *JBR* 11 (1943), 169-170.

_____. *Problems of New Testament Translation*. Chicago, 1945.

_____. *The Meaning of Ephesians*. Chicago, 1933.

Gordon, Mary L. "The Nationality of Slaves under the Early Roman Empire," *JRS* 14 (1924), 93-111 (= Finley, *Slavery in Classical Antiquity*, pp. 171-189).

Görlich, E.J. "Sklaveco en las Antikva Proksima Oriento," *Biblia Revuo* 1 (1964), 46-51.

Grau, Friedrich. *Der neutestamentliche Begriff Charisma, seine Geschichte und seine Theologie*. Diss. Tübingen, 1946.

Greeven, Heinrich, *Das Hauptproblem der Sozialethik in der neueren Stoa und im Urchristentum*. Gütersloh, 1935.

_____. "Evangelium und Gesellschaft in Urchristlicher Zeit," *Festschrift zur Eröffnung der Universität Bochum*. Eds. H. Wenke and J.H. Knoll. (1965), pp. 105-121.

Grosheide, F.W. *Commentary on the First Epistle to the Corinthians*. The New International Commentary on the New Testament. Grand Rapids, 1953.

_____. "Exegetica: 1 Kor. 7,21," *Geref Theol. Tijdschr.* 24 (1924), 298-302.

Gülzow, Henneke. *Christentum und Sklaverei in den ersten drei Jahrhunderten*. Bonn, 1969.

_____. "Kallist von Rom: ein Beitrag zur Soziologie der römischen Gemeinde," *ZNW* 58 (1967), 102-121.

Güttgemanns, Erhardt. *Der leidende Apostel und sein Herr (Studien zur paulinischen Christologie)*. Göttingen, 1966.

Hands, A.R. *Charities and Social Aid in Greece and Rome.* London, 1968.

Harder, Günther. "Miszelle zu 1 Kor 7,17," *ThLZ* 79 (1954), 367-372.

Harnack, Adolf. *The Mission and Expansion of Christianity in the First Three Centuries.* (Trans. J. Moffatt from 3rd German edn., 1915) New York, 1962.

Hatch, Edwin, and Redpath, Henry A. *A Concordance to the Septuagint and other Greek Versions of the Old Testament.* 3 vols. Oxford, 1897.

Hauck, F. *Die Stellung des Urchristentums zu Arbeit und Geld.* Gütersloh, 1921.

Hausrath, A. *Neutestamentliche Zeitgeschichte. 2. Theil: Die Zeit der Apostel.* Heidelberg, 1875.

Heinemann, Joseph. *Prayer in the Period of the Tanna'im and the Amora'im: Its Nature and Its Patterns.* Jerusalem, 1964.

Herford, R.T. *The Ethics of the Talmud: Sayings of the Fathers.* New York, 1962.

Héring, Jean. *The First Epistle of Saint Paul to the Corinthians.* (Trans. A.W. Heathcote and P.J. Allcock from 2nd French edn.) London, 1962.

Hitzig, H.F. "Zum griechisch-attischen Rechte," *Zeitschrift der Savigny-Stiftung für Rechtsgeschichte (Romanistische Abtheilung)* 18 (1897), 167-171.

Hodge, Charles. *An Exposition of the First Epistle to the Corinthians.* New York, 1857.

Holl, Karl. *Gesammelte Aufsätze zur Kirchengeschichte.* 3 Bde. Tübingen, 1928.

Hunzinger, Claus-Hunno, "Paulus und die politische Macht," *Christentum und Gesellschaft.* Eds. W. Lohff und B. Lohse. (Göttingen, 1969), 117-128.

Hurd, John Coolidge, Jr. *The Origin of 1 Corinthians.* New York, 1965.

Jang, Liem Khiem. *Der Philemonbrief im Zusammenhang mit dem theologischen Denken des Apostels Paulus.* Diss. Bonn, 1964.

Jenkins, Claude. "Origen on I Corinthians," *JTS* IX (1908), 499-508.

Jeremias, Joachim. *Abba: Studien zur neutestamentlichen Theologie und Zeitgeschichte.* Göttingen, 1966.

_____. *Jerusalem in the Time of Jesus (An Investigation into Economic and Social Conditions during the New Testament Period).* (Trans. F.H. and C.H. Cave from 3rd German edn., 1962; with author's revisions to 1967) Philadelphia, 1969.

Jolowicz, H.F. *Historical Introduction to the Study of Roman Law.* Cambridge, 1952.

Jones, A.H.M. *The Greek City from Alexander to Justinian.* Oxford, 1940.

_____. "The Greeks under the Roman Empire," *Dumbarton Oaks Papers* 17 (1963), 1-19.

192

Jones, A.H.M. "Slavery in the Ancient World," *The Economic History Review*. 2nd ser., 9 (1956), 185-199 (= Finley, *Slavery in Classical Antiquity*, pp. 1-15).

Judge, E.A. *The Social Pattern of Christian Groups in the First Century*. London, 1960.

Juncker, A. *Die Ethik des Apostels Paulus*. Halle, 1919.

Kähler, Else. *Die Frau in den paulinischen Briefen*. Frankfurt, 1960.

Käsemann, Ernst. *Essays on New Testament Themes*. Studies in Biblical Theology 41. (Trans. W.J. Montague) London, 1964.

_____. *Exegetische Versuche und Besinnungen*. Göttingen, 1960 (Bd. I, 2. Auflage), 1965 (Bd. II, 2. Auflage).

_____. *New Testament Questions of Today*. (Trans. W.J. Montague) London, 1969.

Kaufmann, David. "Das Alter der drei Benedictionen von Israel, vom Freien und vom Mann," *Monatsschrift für Geschichte und Wissenschaft des Judentums* 37 (1893), 14-18.

Kehnscherper, G. *Die Stellung der Bibel und der alten christlichen Kirche zur Sklaverei*. Halle, 1957.

Kempthorne, R. "Incest and the Body of Christ: A Study of 1 Cor. vi. 12-20," *NTS* 14 (1968), 568-574.

Kiefl, F.X. "Erklärung," *Theologische Revue* XVI (1917), col. 469.

_____. *Die Theorien des modernen Sozialismus über den Ursprung des Christentums*. *Zugleich ein Kommentar zu 1 Kor 7,21*. Munich, 1915.

Klaffenbach, G. *Griechische Epigraphik*. Studien zur Altertumswissenschaft 6. 2. Auflage. Göttingen, 1966.

Klauser, Th., et al. *Reallexikon für Antike und Christentum*. Stuttgart, 1941ff.

Knopf, Rudolf. *Das nachapostolische Zeitalter: Geschichte der christlichen Gemeinden von Beginn der Flavierdynastie bis zum Ende Hadrians*. Tübingen, 1905.

Koester, Helmut, "ΓΝΩΜΑΙ ΔΙΑΦΟΡΟΙ. The Origin and Nature of Diversification in the History of Early Christianity," *HThR* 58 (1965), 279-318.

_____. "Häretiker im Urchristentum," *Die Religion in Geschichte und Gegenwart*, 3. Auflage, Bd. III, 17-21.

Koopmans, Jochem Jan. *De Servitute Antiqua et Religione Christiana: Capita Selecta*. Diss. Groningen, 1920.

Koržensky, J.N. "The Attitude of the Slave with Reference to His Manumission in Roman Comedy," *Vestnik Drevnij Istorii* 61 (1957), 149-158.

Krauss, Samuel. *Talmudische Archaeologie*. 3 Bde. Leipzig, 1910-1912 (reprinted by Georg Olms, Hildesheim, 1966).

Kreissig, H. "Zur sozialen Zusammensetzung der frühchristlichen Gemeinden im ersten Jahrhundert u.Z.," *Eirene: Studia Graeca et Latina.* Československá Akademie Věd VI (1967), 91-100.

Kühner, R. und Gerth, B. *Ausführliche Grammatik der griechischen Sprache.* 2 Bde. 4. Auflage. Hannover, 1955.

Kugelmann, Richard. "The First Letter to the Corinthians," *The Jerome Biblical Commentary.* Eds. R.E. Brown, J.A. Fitzmeyer, and R.E. Murphy. (London, 1968), pp. 254-275.

Kuhn, Heinz-Wolfgang. "Der irdische Jesus bei Paulus als traditionsgeschichtliches und theologisches Problem," *ZThK* 67 (1970), 311-316.

Kuhn, Karl Georg. *Konkordanz zu den Qumrantexten.* Göttingen, 1960.

_____. "Nachträge zur 'Konkordanz zu den Qumrantexten'," *Revue de Qumran* 14 (1963), 163-234.

Laeuchli, Samuel. "Urban Mithraism," *Biblical Archaeologist* 31 (1968), 73-99.

Lake, Kirsopp, ed. and tr. *The Apostolic Fathers.* 2 vols. Loeb edn. Cambridge, Mass., 1912-1913.

Lambertz, M. *Die griechischen Sklavennamen.* 2 Bde. Vienna, 1907-1908.

Lampe, G.W.H. *A Patristic Greek Lexicon.* Oxford, 1968.

Lappas, Josef. *Paulus und die Sklavenfrage.* Diss. Vienna, 1954.

Latte, Kurt. *Heiliges Recht: Untersuchungen zur Geschichte der sakralen Rechtsformen in Griechenland.* Tübingen, 1920 (reprinted 1964).

_____. *Kleine Schriften.* Eds. Gigon, Buchwald, and Kunkel. 1968.

Lauffer, Siegfried. "Die Sklaverei in der griech.-röm. Welt," *Gymnasium* 68 (1961), 370-395.

Lea, Henry C. *Studies in Church History.* Philadelphia, 1883.

Leipoldt, Johannes. *Der soziale Gedanke in der altchristlichen Kirche.* Leipzig, 1952.

_____. *Von den Mysterien zur Kirche: Gesammelte Aufsätze.* Leipzig, 1961.

Lewis, C.T. and Short, Charles. *A Latin Dictionary.* Oxford, 1879.

Liddell, H.D., Scott, R., and Jones, H.S. *A Greek-English Lexicon.* Oxford, 1940.

Lieberman, Saul. *The Tosefta according to Codex Vienna.* New York, 1955.

Lietzmann, H. und Kümmel, W.G. *An die Korinther I.-II.* Handbuch zum Neuen Testament 9. 4. Auflage. Tübingen, 1949.

Lohmeyer, Ernst. *Soziale Fragen im Urchristentum.* Leipzig, 1921.

Lund, N.W. *Chiasmus in the New Testament.* Chapel Hill, 1942.

Lyall, Francis. "Roman Law in the Writings of Paul--Adoption," *JBL* 88 (1969), 458-466.

194

Lyall, Francis. "Roman Law in the Writings of Paul--The Slave and the Freedman," *NTS* 17 (1970), 73-79.

MacMullen, Ramsay. *Enemies of the Roman Order: Treason, Unrest, and Alienation in the Empire.* Cambridge, Mass., 1966.

Marquardt, F. *Das Privatleben der Römer.* 2nd edn. Leipzig, 1886.

Matthews, Shailer. "The Social Teaching of Paul: V. The Social Content of Apostolic Christianity in General," *Biblical World* 19 (1902), 433-442.

Mendelsohn, Isaac. *Slavery in the Ancient Near East: A Comparative Study of Slavery in Babylonia, Assyria, Syria, and Palestine; From the Middle of the Third Millenium to the End of the First Millenium.* Oxford, 1949.

Merk, Otto. *Handeln aus Glauben: Die Motivierungen der Paulinischen Ethik.* Marburger Theologische Studien. Marburg, 1968.

Meyer, Eduard. *Kleine Schriften I.* Halle, 1910.

Migne, J.P., ed. *Patrologiae Cursus Completus. Series Patrum Graecorum.* Paris, 1857-1866. *Series Patrum Latinorum.* Paris, 1844-1866.

Mitteis, Ludwig M. *Reichsrecht und Volksrecht in den östlichen Provinzen des römischen Kaiserreiches.* Leipzig, 1891.

Mitteis, L. und Wilcken, U. *Grundzüge und Chrestomathie der Papyruskunde.* Leipzig, 1912.

Moffatt, James. *The First Epistle of Paul to the Corinthians.* Moffatt N.T. Commentary. London, 1938.

Moir, Ian A. "A Proposed 'Grid' System for Recording Biblical References," *NTS* 13 (1967), 292-293.

Mommsen, Theodor. *De collegiis et sodaliciis Romanorum.* Diss. Kiel, 1843.

_____. *The Provinces of the Roman Empire from Caesar to Diocletian.* 2 vols. (Trans. W.P. Dickson) London, 1886.

Moore, George Foote. *Judaism in the First Centuries of the Christian Era: the Age of the Tannaim.* Cambridge, Mass., 1962.

Morgenstern, J. "Jubilee, Year of," *The Interpreter's Dictionary of the Bible.* Ed. G.A. Buttrick. (New York, 1962) Vol. 2, 1001-1002.

Morrow, G.R. *Plato's Law of Slavery in its Relation to Greek Law.* Urbana, 1939.

Moule, C.F.D. *An Idiom-Book of New Testament Greek.* Cambridge, 1960.

_____. *The Birth of the New Testament.* London, 1966.

Moulton, J.H., Howard, W.F., and Turner, Nigel. *A Grammar of New Testament Greek.* 3 vols. Edinburgh, 1908-1963.

Moulton, J.H. and Milligan, G. *The Vocabulary of the Greek Testament.* London, 1930.

Nestle, Dieter. *Eleutheria: Teil I, Die Griechen.* Tübingen, 1967.

Nestle, Eberhard, Nestle, Erwin, and Aland, Kurt, eds. *Novum Testamentum Graece*. 25th edn. Stuttgart, 1963.

Neuhäusler, E. "Ruf Gottes und Stand des Christen: Bemerkungen zu 1 Kor 7," *Biblische Zeitschrift* N.F. 3 (1959), 43-60.

Niederwimmer, Kurt. *Der Begriff der Freiheit im Neuen Testament*. Berlin, 1966.

Niese, Benedictus, ed. *Flavii Iosephi Opera*. 7 Bde. Berlin, 1895 (reprinted Berlin, 1955).

Nilsson, M.P. *Geschichte der Griechischen Religion*. (Bd. I, 3. Auflage; Bd. II, 2. Auflage) Handbuch der Altertumswissenschaft 5:2. Munich, 1961-1967.

North, Robert. *Sociology of the Biblical Jubilee*. Analecta Biblica 4. Rome, 1954.

Oldfather, W.A., ed. and tr. *Epictetus*. Loeb edn. 2 vols. Cambridge, Mass., 1925.

Overbeck, Franz. *Studien zur Geschichte der alten Kirche*. Chemnitz, 1875.

Pauly, A., Wissowa, G., and Kroll, W., eds. *Paulys Real-Encyclopädie der klassischen Altertumswissenschaft*. *Neue Bearbeitung*. Stuttgart, 1893ff.

Pearson, Birger. "Did the Gnostics Curse Jesus?" *JBL* 86 (1967), 301-305.

_____. "The ΠΝΕΥΜΑΤΙΚΟΣ-ΨΥΧΙΚΟΣ Terminology in 1 Corinthians. A Study in the Theology of the Corinthian Opponents of Paul and its Relation to Gnosticism," unpublished Ph.D. diss. Harvard University, 1969.

Pfleiderer, O. *Die Entstehung des Christentums*. Munich, 1905.

Preisigke, F. *Wörterbuch der griechischen Papyrusurkunden*. Berlin, 1925-1931.

Preuschen, E. "Und ließe meinen Leib brennen: 1 Kor, 13,3," *ZNW* 16 (1915), 127-138.

Pringsheim, Fritz. "Ausbreitung und Einfluss des Griechischen Rechtes," *Sitzungsberichte der Heidelberger Akademie der Wissenschaften*. Philosophisch-historische Klasse (Heidelberg, 1952), 5-19.

_____. *The Greek Law of Sale*. Weimar, 1950.

Quesnell, Quentin. "Made Themselves Eunuchs for the Kingdom of Heaven (Matt. 19:12)," *CBQ* 30 (1968), 335-358.

Rädle, Herbert. "Selbsthilfeorganisationen der Sklaven und Freigelassenen in Delphi," *Gymnasium* 77 (1970), 1-5.

_____. *Untersuchungen zum griechischen Freilassungswesen*. Diss. Munich, 1969.

Reicke, Bo. *Diakonie, Festfreude und Zelos in Verbindung mit der altchristlichen Agapenfeier*. Wiesbaden, 1951.

Rengstorf, K.H. "*doulos*," *Theological Dictionary of the New Testament* (Grand Rapids, Michigan, 1964) Vol. II, 261-280. (*Theologisches Wörterbuch zum Neuen Testament* [Stuttgart, 1935], Bd. II, 264-283.)

Richter, Will. "Seneca und die Sklaven," *Gymnasium* 65 (1958), 196-218.

de Robertis, Francesco. *Il fenomeno associativo nel mondo romano*. Rome, 1955.

Robertson, A. and Plummer, A. *A Critical Exegetical Commentary on the First Epistle of St. Paul to the Corinthians*. International Critical Commentary. 2nd edn. Edinburgh, 1914.

Robinson, James M. "Kerygma and History in the New Testament," *The Bible in Modern Scholarship*. Ed. J. Philip Hyatt. (London, 1966), 114-150.

Ross, Sir David, tr. *The Nicomachean Ethics of Aristotle*. London, 1925.

Rostovtzeff, M. *Social and Economic History of the Roman Empire*. 2 vols. (2nd edn. rev. by P.M. Fraser, 1957) Oxford, 1926.

Rupprecht, A.A. "A Study of Slavery in the Late Roman Republic from the Works of Cicero," unpublished diss. U. of Penn., 1960.

Russell, Kenneth C. *Slavery as Reality and Metaphor in Pauline Letters*. Diss. Pontifical University, Rome, 1968.

Saß, G. "Zur Bedeutung von δοῦλος bei Paulus," *ZNW* 40 (1941), 24-32.

Satake, Akira. "Apostolat und Gnade bei Paulus," *NTS* 15 (1968), 97-102.

Schenk, Wolfgang. "Der 1 Korintherbrief als Briefsammlung," *ZNW* 60 (1969), 219-243.

Schenkl, H. *Epicteti dissertationes ab Arriano digestae ad fidem codicis Bodleiani recensuit*. 2nd edn. Leipzig, 1916.

Schlatter, Adolf. *Paulus der Bote Jesu. Eine Deutung seiner Briefe an die Korinther*. 2. Auflage. Stuttgart, 1956.

Schlier, Heinrich. *Der Brief an die Galater*. 4. Auflage. Meyers Kommentar VII. Göttingen, 1965.

_____. "*eleutheros*," *TDNT* II, 487-502.

Schmidt, K.L. "*klēsis*," *TDNT* III, 491-493.

Schmithals, Walter. *Die Gnosis in Korinth*. 3. Auflage. Göttingen, 1969.

Schrage, Wolfgang. *Die konkreten Einzelgebote in der paulinischen Paränese*. Gütersloh, 1961.

_____. "Die Stellung zur Welt bei Paulus, Epiktet und in der Apokalyptik. Ein Beitrag zu 1 Kor. 7,29-31," *ZThK* 61 (1964), 125-154.

Schweitzer, Albert. *The Mysticism of Paul the Apostle*. 2nd edn. (Trans. W. Montgomery) New York, 1968.

Schweizer, Eduard. *Neotestamentica*. Stuttgart, 1963.

_____. "*sōma*," *ThW* VII, 1024-1091.

Scroggs, Robin. "The Exaltation of the Spirit by Some Early Christians," *JBL* 84 (1965), 366-370.

Seboldt, Roland H.A., "Spiritual Marriage in the Early Church: A Suggested Interpretation of 1 Cor. 7:36-38," *Concordia Theological Monthly* 30 (1959), 103-119 and 176-189.

Seuffert, Lothar. "Der Loskauf von Sklaven mit ihrem Geld," *Festschrift für die Juristische Fakultät Giessen zum Universitäts-Jubiläum*. Ed. Reinhard Frank. (1907), 1-20.

Sevenster, J.N. *Paul and Seneca*. Supplement to Novum Testamentum IV. Leiden, 1961.

Sherwin-White, Adrian Nicholas. *Roman Society and Roman Law in the New Testament*. Oxford, 1963.

Sokolowski, F. "The Real Meaning of Sacral Manumission," *HThR* 47 (1954), 173-181.

von Soden, H. "Sakrament und Ethik bei Paulus," *Marburg. Theol. Stud.* 1 (1931), 1-40 (also *Das Paulusbild in der neueren deutschen Forschung*, 1964, pp. 338-379).

Štaerman, E.M. *Die Blütezeit der Sklavenwirtschaft in der Römischen Republik*. Übersetzungen ausländischer Arbeiten zur antiken Sklaverei 2. (Trans. Maria Bräuer-Pospelova) Wiesbaden, 1969.

Stamm, J.J. and Andrew, M.E. *The Ten Commandments in Recent Research*. Studies in Biblical Theology. 2nd ser., no. 3. London, 1967.

Stanley, Arthur Penrhyn. *The Epistle of St. Paul to the Corinthians*. London, 1855.

Stanley, D.M. "'Become imitators of me...': The Pauline Conception of Apostolic Tradition," *Biblica* 40 (1959), 858-877.

Steinmann, Alphons. "Antwort," *Theologische Revue* XVI (1917), col. 470.

_____. *Paulus und die Sklaven zu Korinth: 1 Kor. 7,21 aufs neue untersucht*. Braunsberg, 1911.

_____. *Sklavenlos und alte Kirche: Eine historisch-exegetische Studie über die soziale Frage im Urchristentum*. 4. Auflage. M.-Gladbach, 1922.

_____. "Zur Geschichte der Auslegung von 1 Kor. 7,21," *Theologische Revue* XVI (1917), cols. 340-348.

Stendahl, Krister. *The Bible and the Role of Women: A Case Study in Hermeneutics*. Philadelphia, 1966.

_____, ed. *The Scrolls and the New Testament*. New York, 1957.

Stevenson, G.H. *Roman Provincial Administration till the Age of the Antonines*. Oxford, 1939.

Strack, H.L. und Billerbeck, P. *Kommentar zum Neuen Testament aus Talmud und Midrasch*. 6 Bde. Munich, 1922-1928.

Strugnell, John. "Flavius Josephus and the Essenes: *Antiquities* XVIII. 18-22," *JBL* 77 (1958), 106-115.

Taubenschlag, R. *The Law of Graeco-Roman Egypt in the Light of the Papyri (332 B.C.-A.D. 640)*. 2nd edn. Warsaw, 1955.

Taylor, Greer M. "The Function of ΠΙΣΤΙΣ ΧΡΙΣΤΟΥ in Galatians," *JBL* 85 (1966), 58-75.

198

Thrall, Margaret E. *Greek Particles in the New Testament: Linguistic and Exegetical Studies*. Leiden, 1962.

Tod, M.N. "Epigraphical Notes on Freedmen's Professions," *Epigraphica* 12 (1950), 3-25.

Treggiari, Susan. *Roman Freedmen during the Late Republic*. Oxford, 1969.

Urbach, E.E. "The Laws regarding Slavery as a Source for Social History of the Period of the Second Temple, the Mishnah and Talmud," *Papers of the Institute of Jewish Studies, London*. (Trans. R.J. Loewe from Hebrew in *Zion* 25 [1960], 141-189) Jerusalem, 1964.

de Vaux, Roland. *Ancient Israel. Vol. 1: Social Institutions*. (Trans. J. McHugh from the first French edn.) New York, 1965.

de Visscher, F. "De l'acquisition du droit de cité romaine par l'affranchissement," *Studia et documenta historiae et iuris* 12 (1946), 69-85.

Vittinghoff, Friedrich. *Römische Kolonisation und Bürgerrechtspolitik unter Caesar und Augustus*. Abhandlungen der Geistes- und Sozialwissenschaftlichen Klasse 14. Mainz, 1951.

_____. "Die Sklavenfrage in der Forschung der Sowjetunion," *Gymnasium* 69 (1962), 279-286.

Vogt, Joseph. "Die antike Sklaverei als Forschungsproblem--von Humboldt bis heute," *Gymnasium* 69 (1962), 264-278.

_____. *Sklaverei und Humanität: Studien zur antiken Sklaverei und ihrer Forschung*. (Historia-Einzelschriften Heft 8) Wiesbaden, 1965.

_____. *Von der Gleichwertigkeit der Geschlechter in der bürgerlichen Gesellschaft der Griechen*. Akademie der Wissenschaften und der Literatur: Abhandlungen der Geistes- und Sozialwissenschaftlichen Klasse 2. Mainz, 1960.

_____. "Wege zur Menschlichkeit in der antiken Sklaverei," (Tübinger Rektoratsrede, 9 May 1958) Tübingen, 1958 (= Finley, *Slavery in Classical Antiquity*, pp. 33-52).

Volkmann, Hans. "Die römische Provinzialverwaltung der Kaiserzeit im Spiegel des Kolonialismus," *Gymnasium* 68 (1961), 395-409.

Wallon, Henri. *Histoire de l'esclavage dans l'antiquité*. 3rd edn. Paris, 1879.

Watson, Alan. *The Law of Persons in the Later Roman Republic*. Oxford, 1967.

Weber, Max. *Gesammelte Aufsätze zur Religionssoziologie*. Tübingen, 1920.

_____. *The Sociology of Religion*. (Trans. Ephraim Fischoff from 4th German edn.) Boston, 1963.

Weiß, Johannes. *Der erste Korintherbrief*. Meyers Kommentar V. 9. Auflage. Göttingen, 1910.

Welles, C. Bradford. "Manumission and Adoption," *Melanges Fernand De Visscher II (Revue Internationale des Droits de L'Antiquité* 3) (1949), 507-520.

Westermann, W.L. "Between Slavery and Freedom," *American Historical Review* 50 (1945), 213-227.

_____. "The freedmen and the slaves of God," *Proceedings of the American Philosophical Society* 92 (1948), 55-64.

_____. "Sklaverei," *Real-Encyclopädie der klassischen Altertumswissenschaft.* Eds. A. Pauly and G. Wissowa. 1894ff. Supplementband VI, 894-1068.

_____. "Slavery and the Elements of Freedom in Ancient Greece," *Bulletin of the Polish Institute of Arts and Sciences in America* 1 (1943), 332-347.

_____. *The Slave Systems of Greek and Roman Antiquity.* Philadelphia, 1955.

_____. "Two Studies in Athenian Manumission," *Journal of Near Eastern Studies* 5 (1946), 92-104.

Whiston, William. *The Life and Works of Flavius Josephus.* Philadelphia, n.d.

Whittaker, Molly, ed. *Die apostolischen Väter I: Der Hirt des Hermas.* Berlin, 1956.

Wibbing, Siegfried. *Die Tugend- und Lasterkataloge im Neuen Testament.* Beihefte zur Zeitschrift für Neutestamentliche Wissenschaft 25. Berlin, 1959.

Wiederkehr, Dietrich. *Die Theologie der Berufung in den Paulusbriefen.* Studia Friburgensia: Neue Folge 36. Freiburg, 1963.

Wilckens, Ulrich. "Urchristlicher Kommunismus," *Christentum und Gesellschaft.* Eds. W. Lohff und B. Lohse. (Göttingen, 1969), 129-144.

_____. *Weisheit und Torheit: Eine exegetisch-religionsgeschichtliche Untersuchung zu 1 Kor. 1 und 2.* Beiträge zur historischen Theologie 26. Tübingen, 1959.

Wilson, Jack H. "The Corinthians Who Say There Is No Resurrection of the Dead," *ZNW* 59 (1968), 90-107.

Windisch, Hans. "Review of A. Steinmann's *Paulus und die Sklaven zu Korinth*," *Deutsche Literaturzeitung*, 1912, cols. 1172-1173.

Zahn, Th. *Sklaverei und Christentum in der alten Welt.* Erlangen, 1879. (also in *Skizzen aus dem Leben der alten Kirche*, 3. Auflage. [Leipzig, 1908], pp. 116-159.)

Zeitlin, S. "Slavery during the Second Commonwealth and the Tannaitic Period," *JQR* 53 (1962/1963), 185-218.

Zuckermandel, M.S., ed. *Tosephta.* Pasewalk, 1880.

de Zulueta, F., ed. *The Institutes of Gaius.* Oxford, 1969 (Vol. 1), 1963 (Vol. 2).

Zuntz, G. *The Text of the Epistles.* The British Academy, 1953.

* * * * * * * *